The Massively Parallel Processor

MIT Press Series in Scientific Computation
Dennis B. Gannon, editor

The Massively Parallel Processor, edited by J. L. Potter, 1985

Parallel MIMD Computation: The HEP Supercomputer and Its Applications,
edited by J. S. Kowalik, 1985

Synchronization of Parallel Programs, by F. André, D. Herman,
and J.-P. Verjus, 1985

The Massively Parallel Processor

edited by
Jerry L. Potter

The MIT Press
Cambridge, Massachusetts
London, England

PUBLISHER'S NOTE

This format is intended to reduce the cost of publishing certain works in book form and to shorten the gap between editorial preparation and final publication. Detailed editing and composition have been avoided by photographing the text of this book directly from the editor's prepared copy.

Library of Congress Cataloging in Publication Data

Main entry under title:
The Massively parallel processor.

(MIT Press series in scientific computation)
Bibliography: p.
Includes index.
1. Parallel processing (Electronic computers)—Addresses, essays, lectures. I. Potter, Jerry L. II. Series
QA76.5.M24375 1985   001.64′4   85–237
ISBN 0–262–16100–1

To my wife and children

Contents

Part III   Software

Series Foreword

It is often the case that the periods of rapid evolution in the physical sciences occur when there is a timely confluence of technological advances and improved experimental technique. Many physicists, computer scientists, and mathematicians have said that such a period of rapid change is now underway. We are currently undergoing a radical transformation in the way we view the boundaries of experimental science. It has become increasingly clear that the use of large-scale computation and mathematical modeling is now one of the most important tools in the scientific and engineering laboratory. We have passed the point of viewing the computer as a device for tabulating and correlating experimental data; we now regard it as a primary vehicle for testing theories for which no practical experimental apparatus can be built. NASA scientists speak of "numerical" wind tunnels, and physicists experiment with the large-scale structure of the universe.

The major technological change accompanying this new view of experimental science is a blossoming of new approaches to computer architecture and algorithm design. By exploiting the natural parallelism in scientific applications, new computer designs show the promise of major advances in processing power. When coupled with the current biennial doubling of memory capacity, supercomputers are on their way to becoming the laboratories of much of modern science.

In this series we hope to focus on the effect these changes are having on the design of mathematical and scientific software. In particular we plan to highlight many major new trends in the design of numerical algorithms and the associated programming and software tools that are being driven by the new advances in computer architecture. Of course, the relation between algorithm design and computer architecture is symbiotic. New views on the structure of physical processes demand new computational models, which then drive the design of new machines. We can expect progress in this area for many years, as our understanding of the emerging science of concurrent computation deepens.

One of the few new machines that can claim to invoke the power of massive parallelism is the MPP, designed by Goodyear Aerospace for NASA. Like many such pioneering projects, more than just hardware must be designed. In particular, the MPP has been the focus of a wide variety of research in algorithm as well as operating systems and programming language design. In this volume Jerry Potter has put together contributions from many of the principal individuals involved in bringing this machine into productive use. The book has been organized to give the reader a thorough understanding of the machine and its applications.

Dennis B. Gannon

Acknowledgments

I would like to express my thanks to all the organizations and individuals involved in generating the material for this book. In particular, the National Aeronautics and Space Administration, Goodyear Aerospace Corporation, and the Computer Sciences Corporation have been most helpful and cooperative in this endeavor. I would also like to thank the authors whose works are included herein and Jim Fischer of NASA for providing the information contained in the bibliography.

Introduction

With 16,834 processing units, the Massively Parallel Processor (MPP) represents the first step toward the large-scale parallelism needed in the computers of to-morrow. Although the MPP was built specifically for image-processing tasks, it is sufficiently general to be used for many applications. The intent of this book is to provide the reader with a comprehensive reference on the MPP with special emphasis on software and applications. The applications articles were selected to represent the broad spectrum of applicability of the MPP and do not necessarily represent NASA's past or present plans for using the MPP. A description of the MPP's architecture is included for completeness.

The book is divided into three parts: Applications, Hardware, and Software. It is not necessary to read the parts in order, and most chapters contain sufficient background information for independent reading.

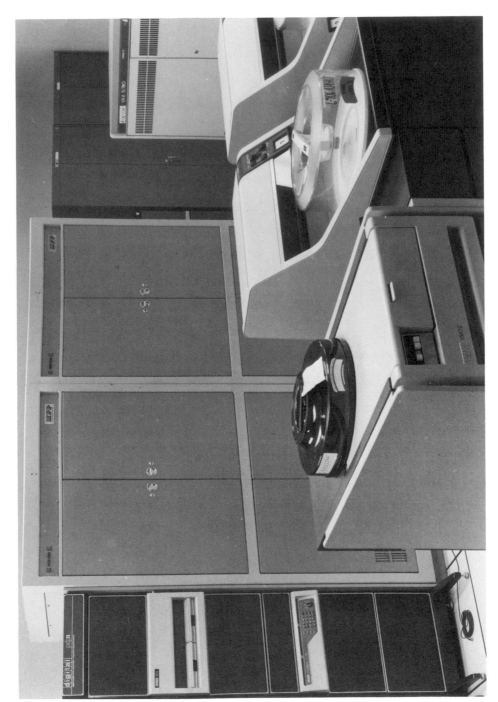

The Massively Parallel Processor

HISTORY OF THE MPP

David H. Schaefer
Department of Electrical and Computer Engineering
George Mason University
Fairfax, Virginia 22030

A FATEFUL MEETING

On the afternoon of January 18, 1977 a small group of apprehensive research engineers had a meeting with Dr. Robert Cooper, at that time Head of the Goddard Space Flight Center, now head of the Defense Department's Advanced Research Projects Agency. As spokesman, I outlined a plan to build a very high speed computer to process image data. The information volume produced by earth scanners and synthetic aperature radar instruments was cited as an example of the voluminous data that would be sent earthward by future spacecraft. Computers capable of processing data at rates as high as 10^{10} operations per second would be needed reasonably soon to handle this flood of information. Computers at that time could only perform 10^8 operations per second, and it was doubtful that serial processors could ever achieve the processing rates that ultimately would be required.

We pointed out that with existing (1977) technology, parallelism could provide the answer. We had designed a computer with 16,384 processing elements operating in parallel. It had the potential of performing six billion eight bit additions per second, and one billion eight bit multiplications per second [1]. This performance was not the 10^{10} operations per second desired, but was certainly a big step in that direction. Dr. Cooper asked what we needed to fabricate such a computer. We replied that if our manpower was doubled and our budget increased five-fold, we would be in good shape. Within the week we had the promise of both.

WHAT HAD TRANSPIRED BEFORE

The Goddard effort to produce ultra high speed image processing systems began in 1970. In that year my section had been asked by NASA headquarters to investigate methods of "processing bit streams between 10^{10} and 10^{12} bits per second." The aim was to develop technology that would allow the construction of hardware capable of reducing data on board spacecraft. We believed that equipment to process data at such high rates would have to utilize very large amounts of parallelism. At that time the only types of processing devices with any large amount of parallelism were coherent optical image processing systems. The Fourier transform of an image on a transparency could be "calculated" instantaneously and in a fully parallel manner by simply placing the transparency in front of a lens in the path of the laser beam. Preliminary designs of a coherent optical landmark tracking system were produced that took advantage of this parallelism [2]. However the lack of fast input devices and the difficulty of performing elementary arithmetic functions led us to the conclusion that this route was not the correct technique for our high speed processors. Still the majesty of the massive parallelism in coherent optical systems had to be retained.

How to keep the parallel concepts, but have a digital design? Our answer - replace the lens that performed parallel operations in a coherent system with components that produce thousands of logical results simultaneously. Light would be the medium for information transfer. Arrays of photo-sensors on these logical components would detect the input, and arrays of light emitters would send the resulting output image on its way through bundles of optical fibers. This was the Tse computer design [3].

"Dave - It really should look like this"

In 1976, Lai-wo Fung, a National Science Foundation Fellow, joined us on a two-year assignment. Conventional silicon components had made such rapid strides that a "Tse computer" could now be built using conventional microcircuit packages. He designed a "Massively Parallel Processing Computer", the design presented to Dr. Cooper.

THE MPP PROJECT

The meeting with Dr. Cooper had taken place in January 1977. The ways of government being what they are, the "Request for Proposals" was not issued until January 1978. As a part of the proposal preparation we had constructed an 8 X 8 version of our design and had run benchmark programs on it. The Request for Proposals consisted only of operational specifications. An appendix describing our design was attached, suggesting one possible method of meeting the specifications. Four contractors responded to the solicitation. Three offered to build the MPP in exactly the form outlined in the proposal appendix. Only Goodyear Aerospace had the fortitude to present an improved version, based on our suggestions, but with superior processing element architecture [4]. Goodyear's machine could perform 1.8 billion eight bit multiplications per second rather than the specified 1.1 billion. They also proposed increasing the amount of memory for each processing element from our suggested 256 bits to 1024 bits.

Goodyear won the contract as a result of these improvements and, interestingly enough, was the low bidder. A study phase of the contract ran from November 1978 to August 1979. One significant change resulting from this study was that eight processing elements were to be packed onto one CMOS chip instead of the originally proposed six per chip. The fabrication contract was awarded in December 1979.

A major trauma took place when the microcircuit manufacturer was unable to produce a processing element chip that would meet specifications. The chip, utilizing CMOS silicon-on-sapphire technology, could not operate at the required 10 megahertz clock rate. However, delays in the program had provided time for HCMOS technology to develop and come to the rescue. In May 1982 prototype HCMOS microcircuits were successfully fabricated by a new semiconductor manufacturer, Solid State Scientific Corporation, and final delivery of chips to Goodyear took place in February 1983.

The MPP was delivered to Goddard on May 2, 1983. Six years had elapsed since the presentation to Dr. Cooper. The total developmental cost of the machine was $6.7 million compared to the 1977 estimate of $3.4 million. The high inflation rates of the late 70's and the addition of the staging memory in 1980 played major roles in this cost growth.

WHERE FROM HERE?

The MPP has opened a new chapter in computing, the pathfinder for future computers that will use massive amounts of parallelism. These highly intelligent computers will eventually have millions of processing elements that will be linked in pyramid, hypercube, and other highly interconnected topologies. Such machines will utilize multidimensional control structures while performing many tera-operations per second. The MPP project motto, "16,384 processors make short work" will be old-fashioned only because of the small numeral.

ACKNOWLEDGMENTS

My thanks to James Fischer, James Strong and Kenneth Wallgren of NASA, all of whom have been very involved with the MPP, and kind enough to help in the preparation of these MPP recollections. The drawing is by James Strong. My thanks to Roland Van Allen whose encouragement and interest in the pre MPP era provided the base needed for the project.

REFERENCES

[1] L.W. Fung "MPPC: A Massively Parallel Processing Computer". In High Speed Computer and Algorithm Organization. D.J. Ruth (Ed.), Academic Press, New York, 1977.

[2] Husain-Abidi, A.S. "Design Concepts for an On-Board Coherent Optical Image Processor." Proceedings of the Conference on Parallel Image Processing for Earth Observation Systems, Goddard Space Flight Center, March, 1972, pp. 141-157.

[3] D.H. Schaefer and J.P. Strong "Tse Computers". Proceeding of the IEEE, January, 1977, pp. 129-138.

[4] K. E. Batcher "Design of a Massively Parallel Processor" IEEE Transactions on Computers, September, 1980, pp. 836-840.

PART I

APPLICATIONS

INVERSION OF POSITIVE DEFINITE MATRICES ON THE MPP

Richard A. White
Computer Sciences Corporation
Silver Spring, MD 20910

Summary -- This report presents a procedure for simultaneously inverting a number of positive-definite matrices on the Massively Parallel Processor (MPP) by assigning each matrix to a separate square subarray of processing elements (PEs). Minor restructuring of a standard Gaussian-elimination algorithm enables all PEs to be active during most of the arithmetic operations. Two additional algorithms increase the utility of the matrix-inversion routine: an efficient matrix-multiplication procedure which can be incorporated into an iterative-correction algorithm to increase the accuracy of inverse-matrix components without resorting to extended-precision arithmetic; and a data-reformatting procedure to facilitate extraction of results to the MPP Main Control Unit (MCU) via the Corner Point Module.

I. INTRODUCTION

Complicated mathematical procedures can be carried out efficiently on the MPP if the data and processing steps can be structured such that most of the MPP PEs are active most of the time. In many cases, achieving this goal will require at least some reworking of the standard algorithms for serial-processing computers.

For matrix inversion, the most straightforward method is Gaussian elimination. Using this method, entries off the principal diagonal of the matrix are eliminated by iteration of three steps: dividing each entry in the current pivot row of the partially diagonalized matrix and of the partially formed inverse by the pivot value; multiplying each new pivot-row value by each element of the pivot column to form product matrices; and then subtracting the nonpivot rows of the product matrices from the corresponding rows of the partially diagonalized matrix and its partially formed inverse.

If the data are structured so that each of the d^2 entries in a d by d matrix is assigned to the corresponding element of a d by d subarray of PEs, then each of the three arithmetic calculations can be carried out for all matrix elements at once. Hence the d iterations of the diagonalization procedure can be carried out in roughly 3d arithmetic steps. Several matrices of the same size can be inverted concurrently, in the same number of arithmetic steps as needed for a single matrix, by assigning each matrix to a different subarray of PEs.

For a typical matrix, the Gaussian-elimination procedure may be complicated by two problems: the matrix may be ill conditioned, so that extended-precision arithmetic is needed; and even for a well-conditioned matrix, the absolute value of the diagonal entry in a pivot column may be significantly smaller than other entries in the column. In the latter case, preservation of numerical accuracy may require interchanging rows so that a larger value can be used as the pivot.

Standard matrix-inversion routines for serial processors can support both of these cases with minimal modification. To increase precision, standard-precision floating-point instructions are simply replaced by their extended-precision counterparts. Row interchanges can be accomplished by means of pointers, without actually moving data, so that pivoting increases total processing time only slightly.

For the MPP, on the other hand, extended precision arithmetic is complicated by the maximum 32-bit length of the shift registers and the quadratic dependence of multiply and divide times on operand length.

Furthermore, row interchange using pointers is probably not feasible at all, so that actual exchanges of data rows become necessary. In addition, each of the several matrices being inverted concurrently will normally require a different pattern of row interchanges, so that during part of the processing the PEs for only one matrix at a time will be active. The MPP Main Control Unit (MCU) will also have to maintain a separate table of row interchanges for each matrix, and use them to unscramble the rows of the final inverted matrices. Very roughly, the time needed to invert m matrices concurrently may become equivalent to $(3+m)d$ arithmetic operations, rather than the $3d$ needed without row interchange.

Although algorithms more sophisticated than Gaussian elimination are available, they tend to be more complicated, and hence finding an alternative algorithm which can be efficiently implemented on the MPP may be difficult.

Accordingly, instead of trying to develop a single MPP matrix-inversion routine which can handle all cases, it makes sense to start with a basic Gaussian-elimination routine for cases which do not require either extended precision or pivot row interchanges. More complex routines can then be developed to handle the more general cases.

This basic routine is, in fact, normally adequate for an important class of matrices: positive definite ones, such as those defining the covariance of multivariate normal distributions. For those matrices, interchanges of pivot rows are not necessary. In addition, the condition number, which gives the maximum ratio of the relative error in any element of the inverse to the relative error in any element in the original matrix, is not greater than the ratio between the largest and smallest eigenvalues of the matrix. For many problems, this ratio, and therefore the maximum loss of numerical precision during the inversion process, can be estimated rather exactly. Specifically, the elements of a positive-definite matrix may be regarded as the coefficients of a quadratic form, with which is associated a family of hyper-ellipsoidal surfaces whose semiaxes are proportional to the square roots of the eigenvalues.

The presentation of the basic Gaussian-elimination algorithm for the MPP begins with a summary of the relevant mathematical formulae, including an optional iterative correction technique to improve final accuracy. The following section describes an allocation of temporary data storage which uses a minimum number of Array Unit (ARU) memory planes. This section is followed by an enumeration of the individual steps, corresponding to low level MPP subroutines, that are required to perform the inversion on the MPP. Several related procedures are then discussed, including algorithms for matrix multiplication and a technique for efficiently extracting data values via the MPP Corner-Point Module. Finally, rough estimates of ARU processing times are presented.

II.   MATHEMATICAL FORMULATION

A.   REPRESENTATION OF INVERSE

The basic problem in matrix inversion is to find, for an arbitrary d by d matrix A, an inverse A^{-1} which satisfies

$$AA^{-1} = I \tag{1}$$

where I is the identity matrix. A^{-1} may be thought of as being composed of d column vectors, v_j, j = 1, 2, ..., d, such that

$$Av_j = I_j, \quad j = 1, 2, ..., d \tag{2}$$

where I_j is the j-th column of I. Each equation of (2) separately may be solved using Gaussian elimination. Since the elimination steps are independent of the right-hand side of equation (2), all columns of A^{-1} may be determined in parallel. Gaussian elimination also yields the determinant of the matrix as a byproduct; it is simply the product of all the pivot values.

B.   OPTIONAL ITERATIVE CORRECTION PROCEDURES

The standard MPP floating-point arithmetic uses a 24-bit representation for the fractional part of the number, corresponding to roughly seven decimal digits. If the ratio between largest and smallest eigenvalues of the matrix to be inverted is large (geometrically, if the d-dimensional ellipsoids associated with the positive-definite form are highly elongated along some axes relative to others), then the accuracy of the inverted matrix will be significantly reduced.

If the resultant accuracy is inadequate for the particular application, two options can be considered. First, the entire computation may be done in extended-precision arithmetic. The standard MPP support software includes an extended-precision format providing 30 bits (roughly 9 decimal digits) of precision, so that some increase beyond standard single-precision floating-point arithmetic would be available without much extra effort. If further increases in precision are needed, however, the maximum 32-bit length of the MPP shift registers would lead to much more complicated arithmetic subroutines.

The second option is to apply corrections to the initial results of the Gaussian elimination. The most straightforward approach is to use an iterative correction procedure. This procedure could also be used in combination with extended-precision arithmetic. This procedure starts by recognizing that the inverse matrix A^i obtained by Gaussian elimination may differ somewhat from the true inverse A^{-1}; the relationship may be written

$$A^i = A^{-1} + D \tag{3}$$

where D is the difference matrix. Then by computing

$$AA^i = I + AD \qquad (4)$$

the maximum relative error in A^i can be estimated from the largest absolute value of any entry in AD.

If this error is unacceptably large, a new estimate A^{ii} can be calculated by computing

$$A^i AA^i = A^i + D + DAD \qquad (5)$$

and then dropping the term in D^2 and substituting for D from equation (3). Solving the resulting equation for A^{-1} gives

$$A^{ii} = 2A^i - A^i AA^i \qquad (6)$$

The error in this new estimate is given by

$$A^{ii} = A^{-1} - DAD \qquad (7)$$

or, alternatively,

$$AA^{ii} = I - (AD)^2 \qquad (8)$$

Since the maximum absolute value of an entry in $(AD)^2$ is at most d times the maximum absolute value of any entry in AD (for the worst case that all entries in AD are equal), repeated iterations of equation (6) will always converge if the largest entry in AD is less than 1/d.

III. DATA STRUCTURES AND TEMPORARY STORAGE REQUIREMENTS

The Gaussian elimination can be thought of as starting with two matrices; namely, A, which is normally not diagonal, and I, which is. As the off-diagonal entries in A are eliminated from one column at a time, the corresponding columns of the I array will acquire nonzero entries off the diagonal. Similarly, the transformed I begins to acquire entries above the diagonal only as the corresponding above-diagonal entries in A are eliminated. After any given step in the elimination process, the only locations which have nonzero values in both matrices are along the principal diagonal. This means that the two matrices can be stored in a single d by d array if one set of diagonal values is stored in a second array.

The MPP routine for inverting positive-definite matrices (and other matrices for which pivot-row interchanges are not needed) uses a single d by d array to store all values which are subject to modification by subsequent steps in the diagonalization process. This array, which will be referred to as the "transformation array," initially contains a copy of the matrix to be inverted. Upon completion of Gaussian elimination, the array contains the matrix inverse.

If determinants are to be computed, the value at each diagonal position in matrix A is saved in a second array, referred to as the "pivot array," as soon as it has been used as a pivot, since the pivot value will not be further modified by subsequent diagonalization steps. The pivot value is in fact copied into all columns of the pivot row, which simplifies the subsequent determinant calculation. The diagonal elements of I in columns which have not yet been processed are not stored, since they are always 1.

In addition to the two sets of memory planes needed for these two arrays, two sets of planes are needed as temporary storage for the values of the pivot row, which are copied vertically to all rows, and of the pivot column, which are copied horizontally to all columns before being used as multipliers. These arrays will be referred to as the "row array" and "multiplier array," respectively.

Two sets of d mask planes each are also needed. These are used by various steps of the algorithm to facilitate copying a row or column into adjacent rows or columns and to select specific columns and rows. The j-th plane in the first set contains zeros in the first j-1 columns and ones in the remaining columns; in the second set, the j-th plane contains zeros in the first j-1 rows and ones elsewhere.

Finally, 2b planes are needed to hold matrix row and column numbers, where b is the number of bits needed to write the number d-1, and two additional planes are used as temporary masks.

Accordingly, total temporary storage requirements (exclusive of memory used by mathematical functions) are $96 + 2(d + b + 1)$ memory planes if standard single-precision arithmetic is used and determinants are to be computed. If determinants are not wanted, 32 fewer planes are needed. To support the standard MPP extended-precision format--consisting of 29 bits of magnitude, 10 for the exponent, and 1 for the sign--24 or 16 additional planes would be needed depending on whether determinants are computed or not.

IV. PROCESSING STEPS

The specific low-level procedures needed to carry out the inversion can be divided into four major steps:

1. Diagonalization of the matrix

2. Computation of the determinant

3. Optional iterative correction

4. Extraction of results

The component low-level procedures for each of these main steps are listed in the following subsections.

A. DIAGONALIZATION OF THE MATRIX

Pivot points are always on the principal diagonal. Steps 2 through 12, below, are repeated for each pivot point in turn, starting at the upper-left corner of the matrix. For the final pivot point, however, steps 9 through 12 are skipped.

1. Generate masks for copying rows and columns.

2. Copy the current pivot row from the transformation array into the row array.

3. Copy the current pivot column of the tranformation array into all columns of the multiplier array.

4. If the determinant is to be computed, copy the row containing the current pivot value from the multiplier array to the pivot array.

5. Replace the pivot column in the row array by a column of ones.

6. Replace the pivot column in the transformation array by a column of zeros.

7. Divide the row array by the multiplier array (only the pivot row contains meaningful results).

8. Copy the pivot row from the row array into the transformation array.

9. Copy the pivot row of the row array into all other rows of the row array.

10. Multiply the row array by the multiplier array, putting the result into the row array.

11. Replace the pivot row in the row array by zeros.

12. Subtract the row array from the transformation array.

This procedure leaves the inverse matrix in the transformation array.

B. COMPUTATION OF THE DETERMINANT

The diagonalization process leaves the full set of pivot values in each column of the pivot array. Hence the determinant can be computed by simply multiplying all the values in one column, using a series of binary steps to first form products of pairs, then of fours, and so on.

For large arrays, however, the determinant may overflow the exponent range for floating-point values. Hence it might be necessary to carry the product formation through only the first few binary steps, and output a set of partial products. Alternatively, problems of overflow can be avoided by taking the logarithms of the pivot values and summing them, again in binary steps. In some applications (for example, in maximum likelihood

classification algorithms), the logarithm is in fact more convenient for subsequent processing.

C.   OPTIONAL ITERATIVE CORRECTION

If iterative correction is desired, the seven steps below
can be repeated until either the maximum number of iterations is
reached or each matrix has met one of three criteria: the re-
sidual error in the approximate inverse, estimated from the
largest value of an element of the error matrix computed by
steps 2 and 3, is less than a specified threshold; the convergence tests in step 4 indicate that steps 6 and 7 will give a
sufficiently close approximation; or it has been determined that
the approximation to the inverse is so bad that the iterative
procedure will never converge.

1.   Left multiply each approximate inverse matrix by the
corresponding original matrix.

2.   Subtract each product matrix from the identity matrix.

3.   Take the absolute value of each element of the difference matrices.

4.   Determine whether convergence has been achieved and
whether additional iterations will be needed.

5.   If convergence has not yet been achieved for all
matrices, left multiply each product matrix by the approximate inverse.

6.   Subtract this product from 2 times the approximate inverse.

7. Use the result as a new approximate inverse for all matrices except any for which convergence has been found to be impossible.

D. EXTRACTION OF RESULTS

The results of the matrix inversion will be a large number of floating-point values, each stored in the memory associated with a different MPP processing element. If the results are to be returned directly to the host computer or stored in a disk file, they can be extracted using the MPP S-register I/O facility. If, instead, the results are needed by the MCU, for example to serve as constants in subsequent MPP computations, it may be more desirable to extract them via the Corner-Point Module.

Extracting 16 different floating-point values one bit at a time through the 16 corner-point elements is a messy procedure, since the MCU must pick out the individual bits for each of the 16 values from the 16-bit strings returned to the PE Control Unit (PECU) Common Register by the Corner-Point Module. An alternative approach to data extraction via the corner-point elements is proposed below.

V.   RELATED PROCEDURES

A. SUBARRAY DATA TRANSFER ROUTINES

In addition to standard MPP support-library functions for arithmetic steps and moving data between memory planes on the same PE, the matrix-inversion procedure invokes more specialized ARU subroutines for transferring data between matrix rows and/or columns. The required subarray-oriented capabilities include copying one row or column in each matrix into one or more adjacent rows or columns, respectively, and generating masks to select specific subarray rows and columns. If iterative correction is used, then matrix multiplication requires additional support for skewing and rotating matrix rows or columns. Some of these subroutines are currently being implemented as part of a support library for subarray manipulations, which also includes a matrix transposition routine.

B. MATRIX MULTIPLICATION

Several pairs of d by d matrices may be efficiently multiplied simultaneously using the MPP by assigning each pair of matrices to its own d by d subarray of PEs, using one set of memory planes to contain the elements of the multiplier matrices, and a second set of planes for the multiplicand elements. The computation requires d multiplications and d-1 additions.

In addition to the arithmetic steps, however, considerable moving of data between PEs is required to ensure that, at each multiplication step, each of the d^2 PEs per matrix pair contains elements from the multiplier and multiplicand which are in fact to be multiplied together, and that the same elements have not already been multiplied in an earlier step. The d products which are added together to form each element of the product matrix must also be brought together and their sum finally stored at the correct PE.

Several alternative ways of structuring the matrices and carrying out the inter-PE data transfers can be devised. Two of these alternatives are discussed below. To simplify the discussion, the multiplier, multiplicand, and product matrices will be denoted by A, B, and C, respectively, so that the multiplication can be written in the matrix form C = AB.

ALGORITHM 1. The most obvious approach is to first transpose matrix A to form A^T. The first row of the product matrix C is then formed by copying the first column of A^T into all columns of a temporary array, multiplying this temporary array point-by-point by the elements of B, and then summing the columns of products. Similarly, computation of the j-th row of C begins by copying the j-th column of A^T into all columns of the temporary array.

Unfortunately, the summation step as described above does not make efficient use of the MPP. Using a pairwise summation strategy, first every even-numbered row (for example) will be copied to the row above, and added to it, with only half the PEs actually being used for summation. Then every other row of these two-sums will be moved up two rows, and pairs of two-sums added to form four-sums, with only one-fourth of the PEs actually performing arithmetic. The overall summation will require $\log_2 d$ such steps per row of matrix C. For the complete multiplication, therefore, $d \log_2 d$ addition steps will be needed, rather than the $d-1$ steps desired.

To avoid the extra summation steps, the procedure can be modified as follows. After the multiplications involving the first column of A^T, the even-numbered rows of products are copied to the rows above, but not added. Then the second column of A^T is used for multiplication, and odd-numbered rows of these products are copied into the rows below. Then, the first addition is performed, using all PEs, to form two-sums for both the first and second rows of C, and alternate pairs of rows of two-sums are copied into the pairs of rows above. This process is repeated to form two-sums for the next two rows of C, and then a further addition is performed to form four-sums. Similar steps combine four-sums into eight-sums, and this process continues until all summations are complete.

This procedure requires using an extra $\log_2 d$ sets of bit planes for temporary storage of the partial sums. In addition, only if d is a power of 2 does this procedure need only d-1 addition steps. Otherwise, the number of additions is equal to one less than the next higher power of 2, and the control logic becomes more complex.

The approximate MPP cycles needed for moving data between row and columns, assuming each value contains n bits, is as follows:

Transposition of A	$4(d+\log_2 d+1)n + 6\log_2 d$
Copying Columns of A^T	$(5d-2)n + (5/4)d^2 + (9/2)d$

Adding Product Rows $(8d-8)n + (11/2)d + d^2/16$
Totals
  Symmetric matrices $(13d-10)n + 10d + (21/16)d^2$
  Nonsymmetric $(17d+41\log_2 d-6)n + 6\log_2 d$
$$+ 10d + (21/16)d^2$$

If the matrix A is symmetric, the transposition step is not needed.

ALGORITHM 2. The need for accumulating partial sums and making d a power of 2 can be avoided by an alternative algorithm which preskews both A and B, in the horizontal and vertical directions, respectively. After each multiplication step, each row of A is rotated left, and each column of B is rotated upwards. This procedure causes each element-by-element product to be formed at the particular PE at which the corresponding element of C will be located, so the products can be added to the running totals after each multiplication step.

The preskewing procedure consists of leaving the first row of A intact, rotating the second row one position to the left, and, in general, rotating the j-th row j-1 positions to the left. Similarly, B is preskewed by rotating the j-th column j-1 positions upwards. The actual skewing procedure is similar to that used for array transposition, i.e., the bit-planes containing the binary number of places that each element is to be shifted serve as masks for successive shifts of 1, 2, 4, 8, and so on, positions. Since each matrix is not coextensive with the whole MPP array, a true rotation is not possible. Instead, only those elements which would not be rotated beyond the edge of the matrix are actually moved leftwards or upwards. The remaining elements are moved in the opposite direction.

The estimated data-transfer cycles for this algorithm are approximately as follows:

Preskewing $4(d^+1)n + 8\log_2 d^$

Rotation $8(d-1)n + 6d + 2d^2$

Total $(4d^+8d-4)n + 8\log_2 d^ + 6d - 2d^2$

where $d^$ denotes the smallest power of 2 which is not less than d.

For floating-point arithmetic and small (d=4), symmetric matrices, this algorithm takes at most 100 more ARU cycles (about 1 percent of the total matrix-multiplication time) for data transfers than does Algorithm 1; for larger values of d or nonsymmetric matrices, Algorithm 2 is faster.

Over a fairly wide range of matrix sizes, the data-transfer overhead adds about 50 percent to the time needed for the multiplications and additions.

C.   EXTRACTION OF ARRAY VALUES VIA CORNER-POINT MODULE

Procedures such as matrix inversion and matrix multiplication leave their results scattered over a large number of PEs. When a large number of PEs contain useful results and the data are to be transferred directly to the host computer or copied to a disk file, the most efficient way to extract the data from the MPP is via standard S-register I/O and the staging buffer. On the other hand, when the data are going to be used by the MCU in subsequent calculations, then it may be faster or more convenient to transfer them directly from the ARU to the MCU.

This direct transfer can be done in two ways. By generating a mask containing a 1 only for the PE containing a desired data value, the value may be placed one bit at a time into the Common Register by executing a series of Read Sum-Or instructions. Alternatively, 16 bits of data at a time may be loaded using the Read Corner Elements instruction.

Using the Sum-Or network has the advantage that successive bits of a single value can be placed, properly ordered, directly into the Common Register. The need for repeated execution of an instruction which takes more than one ARU cycle, however, makes this a very slow way to extract multiple data value.

Although the Read Corner Elements instruction extracts 16 bits per execution, it has another disadvantage: each of the 16 bits comes from a different PE, so considerable reformatting of data is needed to reconstruct a single value. Such reformatting is very slow on the serial MCU processor. Accordingly, the data should be preprocessed in the ARU so that the results placed in the Common Register by the Corner-Point Module will be 16 contiguous bits of a single data value. An algorithm for this preprocessing is outlined below. Since this algorithm involves breaking apart each group of 16 contiguous bits at a PE, it has been named "hexadecimation."

The MPP Array Unit is divided into 16 32-by-32 subarrays, with the PE at the southeast corner of each subarray able to place one bit into the Common Register. In the following discussion, each subarray will be designated by an index i between 0 and 15, which represents the relative bit position in the Common Register into which its corner-point value is placed by the Corner-Point Module. The data values to be extracted will be considered to occupy 16 contiguous memory planes (which might represent the upper or lower half of 32-bit floating-point values); the relative addresses of these memory planes will be designated by an index j between 0 and 15.

The procedure for reformatting the data consists of five main steps, as follows:

1. Load memory planes 0 through 15 into shift-register planes 0 through 15, respectively.

2. Rotate the shift registers in each subarray i by i bits.

3. Route the contents of the shift-register planes east/west and north/south in multiples of 32 rows or columns so that the data that were initially in shift-register plane j of subarray i end up in plane j of subarray (i+j) mod 16.

4. Rotate the shift registers in each subarray i by i+1 bits.

5. Copy the contents of shift-register planes 0 through 15 into relative memory planes 15 through 0, respectively.

This procedure causes all 16 bits of the data values which were originally in subarray i to be located in relative memory plane i. The 16 bits originally at the southeast corner of sub-array i end up at the corner-point PEs of plane i. Other values are so positioned that consecutive values that were originally at adjacent PEs of the same subarray can be read out by loading the corner points into the Common Register, routing the ARU memory plane one PE, loading the new corner point contents into the Common Register, and so on.

The data reformatting procedure requires approximately 750 ARU instruction cycles for 16-bit data, or 1500 cycles for standard floating point. Once the first 16-bit value in a block has been brought to the corner point PEs, each subsequent set of 16 bits may be routed and loaded into the Common Register in two ARU instruction cycles. The MCU, however, will be slower. In addition to issuing a separate PECU call for each 16-bit value, the MCU must store each value into local memory, update and test loop counters, and initialize registers for each block of data transfers. For large blocks, average MCU time per 16-bit value is expected to be at most 500 nanoseconds, corresponding to a data transfer rate of 4 megabytes per second.

VI. TIMING ESTIMATES

As indicated in the Introduction, the procedure outlined in Section IV requires approximately 3d arithmetic steps to invert a set of d by d positive definite matrices if no iterative cor-rection is required. In addition to these floating-point arith-metic operations, data transfer functions require a significant number of ARU cycles. A few cycles are also needed for generating masks.

For standard single-precision floating-point arithmetic, the total ARU time is estimated to be 270d microseconds. If extended-precision floating-point arithmetic (30 significant bits) is needed, the estimated time increases to about 370d microseconds. In either case, the actual arithmetic functions represent approximately 80 percent of the execution time.

Computation of the determinants adds about (10d + 70 $\log_2$d) microseconds if a full product is developed; if instead the natural logarithm is computed, the time is approximately (580 + 10d + 35 $\log_2$d) microseconds.

Each full iteration of the optional iterative correction procedure will add about 260d microseconds of ARU time for standard floating point or 370d microseconds for extended precision; roughly one-third of these times represent data transfers rather than arithmetic. The tests for convergence will involve heavy use of the MCU, which will not fully overlap with ARU usage; these tests are expected to add at most 100 microseconds per iteration unless convergence fails for some matrices, in which case additional reporting and bookkeeping overheads may be incurred.

Extending the matrix-inversion routine to support pivot-row interchanges for matrices which are not positive definite will

significantly reduce the degree of parallelism of the processing. This reduction has two causes. First, since row interchanges may move the remaining diagonal elements of the identity
matrix to off-diagonal locations, the original matrix and its
inverse can no longer share a single array. Second, the rows to
be interchanged at each pivoting operation are, in general, different for each matrix. For these reasons, it appears that the
matrix inversion time for m matrices, using single precision
arithmetic and no iterative correction, would increase to, at
most, $(310 + 100m)d$ microseconds. In addition, the need for
separate subarrays for the original matrix and its inverse would
halve the maximum number of matrices which could be inverted at
one time.

VII. CONCLUSIONS

Several matrices may be inverted simultaneously on the MPP
by assigning each matrix to a separate square subarray of PEs.
A fairly straightforward Gaussian-elimination algorithm can provide a high degree of parallelism, especially if the matrices are
positive definite or are otherwise known not to require pivot-
row interchanges. For such cases, up to $[\text{Int}(128/d)]^2$ matrices, each d rows by d columns, can be inverted in less than
$300d$ microseconds.

Further enhancement of the matrix-inversion procedure is
facilitated by the existence of efficient algorithms for matrix
multiplication, so that numerical errors which accumulate during

Gaussian elimination can be readily removed by iterative correction. Each iteration of the correction process takes roughly one-half the time needed for the basic algorithm.

Another supporting algorithm permits using the Corner-Point Module to transfer blocks of inverse-matrix components (and other data) directly from the ARU to the MCU at rates up to 4 megabytes per second. This algorithm reformats sets of 16 contiguous planes such that, for each PE, 16 consecutive bits end up in a single plane, separated by distances equal to the spacing between the corner-point PEs.

In addition to the modules which specifically support matrix inversion, it has proved necessary to develop a number of new routines for moving data among PEs. These include subroutines to copy data from one row or column in each subarray into adjacent rows or columns and to transpose the rows and columns of each subarray. If iterative correction is used, the matrix multiplication algorithm also requires subroutines to skew matrices and rotate the data within a row or column.

ACKNOWLEDGMENTS

This work was supported by Goddard Space Flight Center under Contract NAS 5-27888, Task Assignment 80100.

The author thanks Byron Leas of Computer Sciences Corporation for testing and correcting the matrix inversion routine and supporting subroutines.

DATA STRUCTURES FOR IMPLEMENTING THE CLASSY ALGORITHM

ON THE MPP

Richard A. White
Computer Sciences Corporation
Silver Spring, MD 20910

Summary -- CLASSY, an adaptive maximum likelihood clustering algorithm, requires computing probability densities and gathering statistics for a large number of image samples. These procedures appear very well suited to the MPP; a straightforward adaptation of the serial version of the algorithm, however, quickly exhausts the MPP's 1024 memory planes. This report describes modifications to the algorithm which permit supporting up to 32 clusters and 21 image channels within the currently available MPP memory. Two types of modifications account for most of the memory savings: restructuring mathematical formulae to permit replacing floating-point arrays by limited-precision scaled-integer arrays; and recomputing some intermediate results instead of storing them. Somewhat unexpectedly, the analysis of processing times for each step revealed one step for which the memory allocation should actually be increased. Overall MPP processing time can be reduced roughly 40 percent by using extra memory to increase parallelism when summing statistical components over all samples.

I. INTRODUCTION

The CLASSY adaptive maximum-likelihood clustering algorithm was developed by Lennington and Rassabach [1], [2] for NASA's Johnson Space Center (JSC) as part of the Large Area Crop Inventory Experiment (LACIE). Instead of assuming a fixed number of clusters and finding the set of cluster statistics which maximizes some measure of goodness of fit, as is done by algorithms such as ISODATA and ISOCLS, CLASSY includes the number of clusters as an additional variable to be optimized.

The basic processing sequence for CLASSY is the alternation of a statistics-compilation phase with a decision phase. The statistics-compilation phase uses maximum-likelihood criteria to update the estimates of means, covariances, and probabilities for the multivariate normal distributions which approximate an existing set of clusters, and then compiles additional statistics needed by the decision phase. The decision phase splits single clusters whose skew and kurtosis values appear incompatible with a single multivariate normal distribution, and merges sets of two or more clusters when the likelihood function can be significantly increased by doing so or when their updated cluster means and covariances have become very similar. The decision phase also eliminates any cluster whose a priori probability has become so small that it no longer makes a significant contribution to the overall likelihood measure.

When implemented on a serial processor, the CLASSY algorithm spends most of its time in the statistics-compilation phase. Accordingly, the JSC version examined only a small, randomly chosen subset of the image samples during each iteration of the program. Subsequent iterations used additional subsets to refine the estimates of statistics. The time savings achieved by this approach, however, were partially offset by the extra mathematical complexity introduced by the need for continual updating of the previously computed distribution parameters to incorporate each small additional group of samples.

A parallel processor, on the other hand, can rapidly compile distribution statistics for a large number of image samples, using very straightforward mathematics. Hence the strategy for implementing CLASSY on the MPP is to use all of a large set of image samples to obtain, perhaps after several iterations, a close approximation to the distribution parameters which give a (local) maximum of the likelihood function for a particular set of clusters; only after convergence has been achieved will the mathematically complex and predominantly serial computations of the decision phase be entered.

Mih-Seh Kong of Computer Sciences Corporation [3] has modified the CLASSY algorithm to take advantage of the very high speed of the MPP for calculating distribution statistics. She found, however, that retaining the data structures used by the original version of the algorithm caused the storage capacity of the MPP Array Unit (ARU), which is 1024 bit planes, to be exceeded when more than about 10 clusters were used. For a larger number of clusters, part of the data would need to be stored in external memory, at the cost of greatly increased processing times due to the frequent data transfers to and from external memory.

Further examination of the CLASSY algorithm has shown, however, that the data structures can be modified to permit storing all required data for up to about 32 clusters within the available ARU memory. Part of the reduction in storage requirements is achieved by slightly restructuring the mathematical formulae and modifying the sequence of steps for compiling the statistics to permit taking advantage of the MPP's flexibility in assigning word lengths. In addition, some recomputation of intermediate values is required; this extra computation will add at most 10 percent to the total MPP processing time.

The discussion of the ARU data structures for CLASSY will begin by defining the cluster statistics which are to be calculated by the MPP, outlining the sequence of processing steps needed to compile these statistics, and examining each type of data which must be temporarily stored in the ARU in terms of the range and precision of its values and the amount of computation needed to calculate it. Then several of the individual processing steps will be examined to determine their requirements for working storage, taking into account some alternate algorithms which improve the balance between processing speed and storage requirements. Finally, the proposed allocation of image data and cluster statistics to the remaining ARU memory planes will be described.

II. CLUSTER STATISTICS TO BE COMPILED USING THE MPP

The CLASSY algorithm assumes that a set of multi-channel image measurements can be meaningfully grouped into an initially unknown number of clusters, for each of which the probability density function is a multivariate normal distribution, defined by a mean-value vector, a covariance matrix, and an a priori cluster probability. The distributions for different clusters may overlap, in which case measured image samples which lie in the overlap region are assigned partly to each of the overlapping clusters, in proportion to the values of the probability density function and the a priori probability for each cluster.

The statistics-compilation phase of CLASSY assumes a particular set of clusters and initial estimates of their means, covariances, and a priori probabilities. The initial estimates are updated by a series of iterative corrections until a reasonable approximation to a (local) maximum of the likelihood function is achieved. When convergence has been achieved, additional statistics are gathered, which are then used by the decision phase of CLASSY to decide whether some of the clusters in the trial set should be split, merged, or eliminated.

The various statistics which must be compiled are defined in Figures 1 through 3. The set of measurements for d spectral channels at each of N image samples are represented by a set of N sample vectors, as defined by Equation 1-1 (Figure 1). The probability density for cluster i at sample s is calculated using equations 1-2 and 1-3; the "relative cluster probability," which represents the relative probability that sample s belongs

A set of m multivariate normal distributions are to be fit to N sets of measurements, each of which consists of d channels. Let the measured values for sample s be represented by the vector

$$X_s = (x_{s1}, x_{s2}, \ldots, x_{sd})^T$$

(1-1)

For a given set of distributions described by the mean vectors μ_1 through μ_m and the covariance matrices Σ_1 through Σ_m, the probability density for X_s relative to distribution i is

$$\rho_{is} = (2\pi)^{-d/2} (\det \Sigma_i)^{-\frac{1}{2}} e^{-(Z_{is}^T \Sigma_i^{-1} Z_{is})/2}$$

(1-2)

where the displacement of sample s from the distribution is given by the vector

$$Z_{is} = X_s - \mu_i$$

(1-3)

The relative probability that sample s belongs to the distribution described by (μ_i, Σ_i) rather than to one of the other distributions is given by

$$P_{is} = a_{is} \, \rho_{is}/\rho_s$$

(1-4)

where values a_1 through a_m represent the *a priori* probabilities for distribution 1 through m, respectively, and the average probability density for sample s is given by

$$\rho_s = \sum_{i=1}^m a_i \, \rho_{is}$$

(1-5)

Figure 1. Statistics for a Single Multi-Channel Measurement

5090(57*)/84

The set of distributions which maximize the likelihood function over the N sets of measurements obey the relationships

$$a_i = (1/N) \sum_{s=1}^{N} P_{is}, \quad i = 1, 2, \ldots, m \tag{2-1}$$

$$\mu_i = (1/Na_i) \sum_{s=1}^{N} P_{is}X_s, \quad i = 1, 2, \ldots, m \tag{2-2}$$

$$\Sigma_i = (1/Na_i) \sum_{s=1}^{N} P_{is}Z_{is}Z_{is}^T, \quad i = 1, 2, \ldots, m \tag{2-3}$$

If the set of distributions is only an approximation to the maximum likelihood case, the approximations can be iteratively refined by repeated evaluation of equations (1-2), (1-4), and (2-1) through (2-3).

For non-overlapping distributions, convergence is fairly rapid. In particular, (2-1) immediately gives the new valus of a_i for a new set of μ_i and Σ_i. For overlapping distributions, on the other hand, (2-1) gives very slow convergence. Lennington and Rassbach (reference 1, equation 28) introduced a modified form of (2-1) which accelerates convergence when overlap is present. Their formula for the updated estimate a_i' in terms of the old value a_i can be written in the form

$$a_i' = a_i \frac{\displaystyle\sum_{P_{is}>a_i} (P_{is} - a_i)}{(1 - a_i)[a_i N - \displaystyle\sum_{s=1}^{N} P_{is}] + \displaystyle\sum_{P_{is}>a_i} (P_{is} - a_i)} \tag{2-4}$$

Figure 2. Cluster Statistics

5090(57'1/84

Measures of the deviation of the samples in a cluster from the multivariate normal distribution are derived from two statistics, the trace of the skew tensor,

$$S_i = (1/Na_i) \sum_{s=1}^{N} Z_{is} (Z_{is}{}^{T} \Sigma_i{}^{-1} Z_{is}) P_{is}$$

(3-1)

and the trace of the kurtosis tensor

$$K_i = (1/Na_i) \sum_{s=1}^{N} Z_{is} Z_{is}{}^{T} (Z_{is}{}^{T} \Sigma_i{}^{-1} Z_{is}) P_{is}$$

(3-2)

The logarithm of the likelihood ratio between a parent cluster i and the set of its m_i subclusters is given by

$$\ln \Lambda_i = -(m_i - 1)(2d + b) + \sum_{s=1}^{N} \ln\{(\sum_{j=1}^{m_i} P_{i_j s})/P_{is}\}$$

(3-3)

where b is a bias term, on the order of 1.

A measure of similarity between a parent cluster and its subclusters is

$$E_i = (1/N) \sum_{s=1}^{N} \{(P_{is}' - P_{is})/(P_{is}' + P_{is})\}^2$$

(3-4)

where the combined probability of the subclusters, normalized to the same *a priori* probability as the parent, is

$$P_{is}' = \{a_i/ \sum_{j=1}^{m_i} a_{i_j}\} \sum_{j=1}^{m_i} P_{i_j s}$$

(3-5)

Figure 3. Statistics to Support Split and Join Decisions

to cluster i rather than one of the other clusters, is then calculated using equations 1-4 and 1-5.

The relative cluster probabilities computed for all samples
are then used to compute new estimates of the mean-value vector
and covariance matrix for each of the m clusters using equations 2-2 and 2-3 (Figure 2). Although improved estimates for
the a priori cluster probabilities could be obtained using equation 2-1, each iteration of the calculation gives only a small
correction to the estimate when there is substantial overlap
between clusters. Lennington and Rassbach [1] showed that convergence can be significantly speeded using a modified expression for the priori cluster probability; this expression,
rewritten to facilitate evaluation using the MPP, is given by
equation 2-4.

To support the decision phase, two different sets of additional statistics are needed. If a given cluster has no subclusters, it is a potential candidate for splitting. The
decision whether or not to split the cluster, and if so, how,
requires the traces of the skew and kurtosis tensors, given by
equations 3-1 and 3-2 (Figure 3). If a cluster has already been
tentatively split into subclusters, then the likelihood ratio
between the parent and the combination of its subclusters, given
by equation 3-3, and a measure of similarity between parent and
subclusters, given by equation 3-4, must be computed. Equations 3-3 and 3-4 have been rewritten from the form used by
Lennington and Rassback for two reasons: (1) to make them depend on the relative cluster probabilities of each sample and

the a priori probabilities of the clusters, rather than on the probability density values; and (2) to use subcluster probabilities relative to all clusters, rather than just relative to the parent.

III. OUTLINE OF PROCESSING STEPS

The sequence of steps in each overall iteration of the CLASSY algorithm, starting with a new set of trial cluster parameters generated during the decision phase, can be summarized as follows:

1. Evaluate probability density function for each cluster at each sample.

2. Compute relative cluster probabilities for each sample.

3. Update estimates of a priori probabilities for each cluster.

4. Recalculate relative cluster probabilities for each sample using new a priori probabilities.

5. Update mean-value vectors and covariance matrices for all clusters using the new relative cluster probabilities.

6. Compute inverse covariance matrices.

7. Compute traces of skew and kurtosis tensors for each cluster which does not have subclusters.

8. Compute the subcluster likelihood ratio and similarity measure for each cluster which has subclusters.

9. Decide which clusters are to be split, joined, or eliminated, and compute initial estimates of parameters for new clusters.

Since the statistics computations can be performed very rapidly on the MPP, steps 3 and 4 will be repeated until stable values of the a priori probabilities are reached; only then will step 5 be performed. Similarly, steps 1 through 6 will be repeated until stable values of the mean-value vectors are approached.

For the first cycle through these nine steps, only one cluster will be defined, so the relative cluster probabilities for all samples will be equal to 1. Hence processing will begin with step 5, and no iterations will be needed before going on to steps 7 through 9.

IV. PROPERTIES OF DATA SETS USED IN ARU

Since the available ARU memory is insufficient to hold all the temporary data generated during the statistics-compilation phase of CLASSY unless the number of clusters is very limited, ways must be found to reduce the amount of ARU memory needed to store the data. Three options exist: (1) store the data outside of the ARU, (2) find more compact formats for the data, or (3) recalculate the values from other data already in memory.

With respect to the first option, the values which are computed and subsequently refined during the statistics-compilation phase can be divided into two categories: those values which are computed for every image sample and those, such as cluster parameters, which are independent of the individual samples.

The latter type, once they have been computed, will normally be extracted from the ARU bit planes via the Corner-Point Module, stored in Main Control Memory, and then reintroduced into subsequent computations via the Common Register. Hence no ARU memory planes are needed to store them, although some working storage may be needed while they are being computed. The elements of the inverse covariance matrices, however, are an exception. These matrices would occupy roughly half of Main Control Memory when the maximum numbers of clusters and spectral channels are used. Since this might leave inadequate space for program code and other data, 32 ARU memory planes are allocated for storing inverse covariance data, which will then be extracted via the Corner-Point Module as needed.

Sample-specific data, on the other hand, must either be stored within ARU memory or recalculated each time they are used; the time taken to copy to external memory and then retrieve a given value for each of the 16,384 samples would be much greater than the recalculation time for any but the most complicated calculations.

Accordingly, the search for ways to reduce ARU temporary storage requirements has three components: identifying those temporary sample-specific data sets which can be stored in compact form; identifying data which can be rapidly recomputed from other data; and then selecting the combination of compact data and recalculable data which gives the best trade-off between storage requirements and processing time.

In the following paragraphs, each of the sample-specific values defined in Figure 1 is examined in terms of the number of ARU memory planes needed to store it and the difficulty of re-calculating it.

A. IMAGE DATA

The sample vectors which contain the measured values in each channel for each sample are 8-bit values for current Landsat detectors and most other image sources. For a few detectors, such as the thermal IR channel for some meteorological satel-lites, additional bits are recorded. Although such measurements are typically unpacked into 16-bit computer words, it is very unlikely that these or future instruments will achieve more than 12 significant bits of accuracy (corresponding to an error on the order of 0.025 percent). Hence at most 12 memory planes per channel are needed to store the image data for 16,384 samples.

Since the image data represent the original measurements and are referenced repeatedly, they must be resident in ARU memory.

B. SAMPLE VECTORS RELATIVE TO CLUSTER MEANS

The vectors which give the differences between the measured image data for each sample and the mean values for each cluster are used in both linear and quadratic expressions in several different statistics. To store each value, one more integer bit is needed than for the image data, since the differences can be positive or negative. In addition, for 8-bit imagery, up to

7 fractional bits are needed to permit carrying mean values to 2 decimal places; less fractional precision would be warranted for 12-bit data. Hence, 16 memory planes are needed per component of these vectors.

Calculation of these values is very simple; it requires only taking the difference between the image data and the integer parts of the cluster means. For use in floating-point calculations, however, each value must first be converted from scaled-integer format to floating point and then normalized. This will take about 30 percent of the time needed for the subsequent floating-point multiplication. For quadratic expressions in the sample vectors, the computation time can be reduced by first multiplying the two values using integer arithmetic and only then floating the result.

C. PROBABILITY DENSITY VALUES

The probability density values cover a very wide dynamic range. The exponential function in equation 1-2 ranges in value from approximately 1 at the cluster center to a high negative power of 10 at locations many standard deviations away. Similarly, the determinant of the covariance matrix, in the denominator of equation 1-2, can range from much less than 1, for a very compact distribution, to a large power of 10. Hence the probability density values must be stored as floating-point numbers; the standard MPP floating-point format requires 32 ARU memory planes.

The probability densities are used to calculate initial values of the relative cluster probabilities for each sample (equation 1-4), and are needed again to recalculate these probabilities each time the a priori cluster probabilities are adjusted. The initial computation of the probability densities from the cluster means and covariances involves multiplying a vector by a matrix, taking a vector scalar product, and then evaluating the exponential function; repeating this calculation would be very time consuming. On the other hand, equation 1-4 can be inverted to retrieve the probability densities from the relative cluster probabilities and the average probability density for each sample (equation 1-5) using only two multiply or division steps per cluster. Thus, if the relative cluster probabilities are stored for all clusters, the probability densities can be reconstructed from them at moderate computational cost.

D. RELATIVE CLUSTER PROBABILITIES

The relative cluster probabilities for each sample are proportional to the a priori cluster probabilities, as is indicated by equation 1-4. Since experiments with both real and simulated data [2], [3] indicate that the final values of the a priori cluster probabilities obtained using CLASSY typically contain relative errors greater than 1 percent, the relative cluster probabilities for each sample will have, at best, comparable accuracy. Hence only 6 to 8 significant bits need be retained for the computation of the updated cluster means and covariances and the additional statistics used for split and join decisions. Since probability values are always between 0 and 1, they could be stored as scaled 8-bit integers.

However, the relative cluster probabilities are subject to repeated use for iterative updating of the a priori cluster probabilities, and, as will be proposed below, for recovering the probability densities. Accordingly, additional guard bits should be retained. A 12-bit scaled-integer format appears adequate.

The original calculation of the relative cluster probabilities involves summing the weighted floating-point probability density values for all the clusters to get the average probability densities given by equation 1-5, and then performing a multiplication and division for each cluster, as indicated by equation 1-4. For subsequent recalculations, using newly updated values of the a priori cluster probabilities, it is not necessary to go back to the original probability density values. Instead, equation 1-4 can be inverted to give the ratio of the probability density for a particular cluster to the average probability density in terms of the relative cluster probability and the previous value of the a priori probability. Since only the density ratio appears, the average probability density can arbitrarily be set equal to 1.0 and the relative density for each cluster calculated. Then correctly normalized values of the relative cluster probabilities are determined by recomputing the average density using equation 1-5 and inserting the result back into equation 1-4, together with the updated

a priori cluster probabilities. Since the new a priori probabilities are of limited accuracy, scaled integer arithmetic can
be used to compute the updated relative cluster probabilities.

This procedure for updating the relative cluster probabilities uses the probability densities twice: once to update the
average density using equation 1-5 and a second time to compute
the updated relative cluster probabilities from equation 1-4.
If the probability densities are not stored temporarily (which
would require up to 24 ARU memory planes per cluster), they will
need to be computed twice; this would add approximately 50 percent to the time taken to update the relative cluster probabilities.

E.   AVERAGE PROBABILITY DENSITY

When the relative cluster probabilities are updated using
the procedure outlined in the previous paragraph, the average
probability density for each sample does not need to be saved
between updates. Hence only temporary working storage need be
allocated.

V. WORKING STORAGE REQUIREMENTS

The available 1024 ARU memory planes must be divided between
data which remain permanently resident during the statistics
gathering phase and working storage used for temporary data during the individual computational steps.

Preliminary analysis of the processing algorithms shows that
three steps are the most demanding in terms of working storage;

accordingly, their storage requirements must be examined in detail. These three steps are the evaluation of the probability density function, the inversion of the covariance matrices, and the computation of skew and kurtosis.

The working storage requirements for these steps are somewhat dependent on the maximum numbers of clusters and spectral channels to be supported; but these maxima in turn depend on the number of memory planes taken up by working storage, as well as on trade-off decisions between saving intermediate results or recomputing them each time they are needed. Accordingly, target values for these parameters must be established before the working storage requirements can be evaluated.

A.   TARGET MAXIMUM NUMBERS OF CLUSTERS AND CHANNELS

As will be shown below, the working storage needed for initial computation of probability densities by evaluating the exponential function depends on the largest power of 2 not greater than the maximum number of clusters. It is sensible, therefore, to choose the target maximum number of clusters to be an exact power of 2; since 16 clusters would probably be too few for some image-classification problems, and 64 clusters would require three-quarters of the available memory planes just to hold the 12-bit scaled values of relative cluster probability, the target maximum number of clusters has been set to 32.

This maximum in turn leads to the requirement that up to 32 covariance matrices be inverted at one time. If each matrix is at most 21 by 21, then 36 matrices can be accommodated in one set of memory planes; for larger matrices, a single set of ARU memory planes could accommodate covariance data for at most 25 clusters, which is less than the desired number. Accordingly, the maximum number of spectral channels has been set to 21.

B. EVALUATION OF PROBABILITY DENSITY FUNCTION

As explained in Section IV-D, it is not necessary to save all the floating-point values of the probability density functions which, at 32 sets of 32 memory planes each, would use all of the 1024 ARU planes. Instead, only the 12-bit scaled integer representations of the relative cluster probabilities will be saved. Relative probability densities recreated from these 12-bit values will be used for subsequent calculations.

However, the initial evaluation of the exponential function in equation 1-2 leads to 32-bit floating-point results which must be summed over all clusters before the average probability density can be computed, and only then can the relative cluster probabilities be computed from the probability densities. At first glace, therefore, it appears that the time-consuming evaluation of the matrix-vector products and the exponential functions would need to be repeated for this latter step, unless the number of clusters was small enough (certainly less than 16) to permit temporarily storing the full set of 32-bit values.

Fortunately, the initial calculations of relative cluster probabilities for up to 32 clusters can be done while temporarily storing only five floating-point probability values.

The procedure is as follows. The probability density functions for the first two clusters are computed, their weighted sum (using the a priori cluster probabilities as weights) is calculated, and the cluster probabilities relative to this sum are computed. Since the relative cluster probabilities have a maximum value of 1 and the a priori probabilities are of limited accuracy, these values can be saved in only 12 bits each, rather than the 32 bits needed for floating-point values. The procedure is then repeated for the next two clusters, the weighted sums for the four clusters are combined, and each relative cluster probability is adjusted by multiplying by the ratio of its two-cluster sum to the four-cluster sum. Then the entire procedure is repeated for the next four clusters, and the probability values are adjusted to be relative to the eight-cluster sum. This process continues until all clusters have been incorporated. At any given time, 32-bit storage will only be needed for one raw probability density plus one multi-cluster sum of each type; additional working storage, however, will be needed for the current computation step.

The extra processing needed in this scheme will be approximately 1 floating-point division, 1 floating to integer conversion, and $\log_2 m$ 12-bit by 12-bit integer multiplies per cluster, where m is the number of clusters. For four image channels and more than 16 clusters, this will take only about 10 percent of the time needed to evaluate the density functions; for more channels or fewer clusters, the percentage will be less.

The total working storage requirements for evaluation of the probability density functions will then be as follows:

Partial (weighted) sum of densities	5 x 32
Accumulator for terms in matrix-vector products; final value of probability density	1 x 32
Scaled sample value relative to mean	1 x 16
Product of scaled sample values; current element of inverse covariance matrix (copied from Common Register); logarithm of determinant	1 x 32
Floating-point version of product of scaled sample values; second scaled sample value (16 bits)	1 x 32
Temporary storage for standard arithmetic and exponential functions	44
Total memory planes	316

C. INVERSION OF COVARIANCE MATRICES

The MPP can be used to invert the covariance matrices for all clusters simultaneously by assigning each covariance matrix to a separate subarray of ARU Processing Elements (PEs). Because the covariance matrices are always positive definite, and therefore well behaved, a simplified form of Gaussian elimination can be used, which does not require interchanging pivot rows or taking other special precautions against numerical instability. Inversion of positive-definite matrices on the MPP is discussed in greater detail elsewhere [4].

The time needed to invert a d by d matrix for each of m clusters, using standard single-precision floating-point arithmetic, is on the order of 270d microseconds; using the VAX-11/780, the time required (assuming optimized assembly language code) is on the order of $6md^3$ microseconds. Hence the

MPP will be faster than the VAX whenever, approximately, md^2 > 45. For example, inversion of covariance matrices for four-channel imagery (d = 4) will be faster on the MPP than on the VAX if three or more clusters are present. Since inversion on the VAX would also require additional time and complexity for transferring data between the MPP and the VAX, the MPP will always be used to invert the covariance matrices.

For 8-bit imagery, single-precision arithmetic should be adequate. This can be shown using the fact that, for a positive definite matrix, the condition number, which gives the maximum ratio between the relative errors in elements of the inverted matrix and the relative errors in the uninverted matrix, is the ratio between the largest and smallest eigenvalues (see, for example, [5], Section 7.2). Furthermore, the eigenvalues of the covariance matrix associated with a multivariate normal distribution are proportional to the square of the semi-axes of the ellipsoidal surfaces of constant probability density. In a coordinate system in which the semi-axes lie along the coordinate axes, the eigenvalues are simply the squares of the standard deviations along the axes.

Since the minimum standard deviation for a cluster is unlikely to be less than 0.5 (the code for splitting clusters is designed to ensure this) and the maximum for a sprawling cluster is very unlikely to exceed 50, the ratio of axes will almost certainly be less than 100. Hence the ratio of eigenvalues will be less than 10^4, so that the initial single-precision accuracy of the uninverted matrix, about 1 part in 10^7, will be reduced to, at worst, about 1 part in 10^3. Errors of this magnitude are less than the typical errors in the a priori cluster probabilities; single-precision arithmetic should, therefore, be adequate.

For 12-bit sample values, on the other hand, higher precision might be needed. This can be achieved in two ways: using standard MPP extended-precision arithmetic (30 significant bits, or about 1 in 10^9 accuracy), and/or using an iterative correction scheme [4].

The working storage requirements for single-precision matrix inversion are as follows:

Matrix to be inverted	1 x 32
Temporary storage for floating-point values	3 x 32
Masks used during inversion, for d by d matrix	2(d+1)
Matrix row and column numbers	$2\text{Int}[\log_2(d-1)+1]$
Temporary storage for standard arithmetic functions (computations of logarithms of determinant uses additional planes released upon completion of matrix inversion)	32
Total memory planes, for d = 21 channels	214

For inversion using the MPP 40-bit extended-precision arithmetic routines, 72 additional planes are needed (40 for the extended-precision version of the input matrix and 4 x 8 to extend each temporary-storage array), making a total of 286. The iterative correction procedure would require one additional set of planes for saving intermediate results, increasing the totals to 246 for standard precision and 326 for extended precision. Except when both iterative correction and extended precision are used, therefore, the matrix inversion can be accommodated by reusing the 316 planes temporarily allocated for the probability computations.

D. COMPUTATION OF SKEW AND KURTOSIS

The basic formulas for computing the contributions of each image sample to the cluster mean vectors, covariance matrices, and the traces of the skew and kurtosis tensors involve only a small number of arithmetic operations per component. Summing these components over all samples (i.e., over all ARU PEs), on the other hand, is surprisingly time consuming.

The most straightforward procedure is to sum the components for adjacent pairs of PEs to form two-sums, then combine pairs of two-sums into four-sums, and so on, until 16 partial sums, of 1024 elements each, are located at the PEs at the 16 ARU corner points. Then the partial sums are normalized (if they are floating-point values), extracted via the Corner-Point Module and the Common Register of the PE Control Unit, and combined into the final sum in the Main control Unit. This procedure involves 10 addition steps to form the partial sums, the equivalent of a further addition to perform the normalization and extraction, and additional ARU cycles for moving data between PEs.

Using this procedure, the summation of vector, matrix, and tensor components over all PEs will represent between about 50 percent (for 2 to 4 image channels) to more than 60 percent (for 16 or more channels) of the total ARU cycles needed by the CLASSY algorithm. Accordingly, total processing times could be significantly reduced by using a more efficient summation method.

The obvious approach is to perform the summations for groups of components. Specifically, the contribution of each image sample to component 1 is computed and saved in temporary storage. Then the contributions to component 2 are computed. At this point, the component 1 value on each even-numbered PE is moved to the neighboring odd-numbered PE, and the component 2 value on each odd-numbered PE is moved to the neighboring even numbered PE. A single addition operation then forms two-sums for both component 1 and component 2 at the same time. Similarly, the formation of four-sums is postponed until two sets of two-sums, representing components 1 through 4, are available. After several such cycles, the intermediate sums for all components in the group can finally be combined into totals using addition steps in which some PEs do not contain meaningful data. Using the Main Control Unit to finish the addition is no longer advantageous when the groups contain more than about four components; instead, the final sum for each component will be formed at a single PE.

Using this approach, forming sums for groups of 8, 16, or 32 components will take approximately 2.1, 3.5, or 5.9 times as long, respectively, as forming the sum for a single component; the corresponding average summation times per component are about 26, 22, or 19 percent, respectively, of the time for a single component. Larger groups yield only minor further reductions.

The skew and kurtosis components can be computed and summed in groups of 16 using no more working storage than is required for the evaluation of the probability density function; this group size will reduce total ARU cycles for CLASSY by roughly 40 percent. Although increasing the group size to 32 would permit a small further reduction in processing time, it would require allocating 32 more memory planes for working storage, thereby reducing storage available for other data. The loss of data storage space is not worth the time saved.

Using summation in groups of 16, the working storage requirements for the skew and kurtosis computations are as follows:

Storage for partial sums	5 x 32
Scaled sample value relative to mean	1 x 16
Accumulator for terms in matrix/vector products; product of scalar product and relative cluster probability	1 x 32
Current element of matrix inverse (copied from Common Register); skew component	1 x 32
Second scaled sample value (16 bits); product of scaled sample values; floating-point version of product; floating-point version of sample value relative to mean; kurtosis component	1 x 32
Temporary storage for standard arithmetic functions	44
Total memory planes	316

VI. PROPOSED ARU MEMORY ALLOCATION

Given the target values of 32 clusters and 21 image channels, the maximum working-storage requirement has been found to be 316 memory planes for both the probability density evaluation step and the skew and kurtosis step, while matrix inversion requires fewer planes even if extended-precision arithmetic and iterative correction are needed. In addition, 50 planes are used by the MPP executive software (Control and Debug Module, CAD), 32 planes are needed to store the elements of the inverse covariance matrices, and 32 planes will be set aside for contingencies. This leaves 594 of the total 1024 planes available for storing data between processing steps.

As noted in Section IV, two sets of data (the 12-bit relative cluster densities and the raw image values) cannot be recreated except at considerable cost in I/O or recomputation. For the target 32 clusters and 21 image channels, these data sets require 384 and 168 planes, respectively, for 8-bit image data. Thus, only 42 planes remain unallocated.

Accordingly, it is not feasible to save either the sample vectors relative to the cluster means or the probability density values; they must instead be recomputed each time they are needed. The estimated extra time taken by these recomputations is less than 10 percent of the estimated total processing time.

A. ARU MEMORY ALLOCATION FOR 8-BIT IMAGERY

The resulting allocation of ARU bit planes for 8-bit image values can be summarized as follows:

Image Data, 21 channels (8 bits each)	168 planes
Unallocated	42
Relative Cluster Probabilities, 32 clusters	384

Inverse Covariance Matrices	32
Unallocated (reserved for contingencies)	32
Temporary Working Storage	316
Executive System (CAD)	50

B. ARU MEMORY ALLOCATION FOR 12-BIT IMAGERY

The 42 unallocated memory planes would permit extending the precision of image values to 10 bits while retaining a full 21 channels. For 12-bit imagery, however, the maximum number of channels must be reduced.

If the increased precision of the image data does not require using both extended-precision arithmetic and interative correction for inverting the covariance matrices, up to 17 channels could be supported, with 6 memory planes left unallocated.

However, if the image values actually extended over the full 4096 levels supported by the 12-bit format, there might be some very elongated clusters for which the condition number of the covariance matrix exceeded 10^6. Under these circumstances, extended-precision arithmetic might not give sufficient accuracy, so iterative correction would also be needed. This would reduce the maximum number of image channels to 16.

C. ARU MEMORY ALLOCATION FOR MORE THAN 32 CLUSTERS

More than 32 clusters could be accommodated within the currently available 1024 memory planes if the number of image samples was reduced to 8192 instead of 16384. In this case, only half the PEs (for example, the odd-numbered ones) would contain image data; the other half could provide storage for additional relative cluster probabilities.

Although the computation of the probability density values would require storing additional partial sums, the required storage could be divided between the even- and odd-numbered PEs, so the amount of working storage needed for this step need not increase. On the other hand, the number of inverse covariance matrices to be stored in ARU memory planes would increase in proportion to the total number of clusters, with the result that additional planes would need to be allocated for this function.

Using 8192 samples of 8-bit imagery, it would be possible to support maximum values such as 64 clusters with 32 channels or 93 clusters with 16 channels. For 12-bit imagery, 64 clusters could be used with 25 channels.

VII. CONCLUSIONS

Two modifications of the CLASSY statistics-compiling procedure account for most of the reduction in MPP storage requirements.

The first of these is the restructuring of the mathematical formulae to define most of the statistics in terms of the relative cluster probabilities for each image sample instead of the probability densities. Because of their limited dynamic range and accuracy, the relative cluster probabilities can be saved in a scaled-integer format which occupies only 12 memory planes per cluster. The wide dynamic range of the density values, in contrast, would require using a floating-point format taking

32 planes per cluster. An additional benefit of restructuring the formulae is that a number of floating-point arithmetic steps can be replaced by much faster integer arithmetic.

The second modification trades off added processing time against reduced storage by initially summing probability densities only over subsets of the clusters, computing sample probabilities relative to the subsets, and then updating the relative probabilities as more clusters are added to the partial sums. This procedure reduces the number of sets of 32 planes each needed for temporary storage of floating-point density values from 32 to 5; the extra time needed for updating the relative cluster probabilities is at most 10 percent of the time needed to compute the densities.

Other reductions in storage requirements are achieved by such obvious measures as recomputing, rather than saving, the differences between sample values and the cluster means and by carefully allocating memory planes for intermediate results in each computation so as to ensure maximum reuse of each set of planes.

The analysis of trade-offs between recomputing values or using extra planes to store them led to one unanticipated result: the summation of variables over all samples (i.e., over all PEs) was found to account for at least half the total processing time. This summation time can be sharply reduced by allocating extra memory planes to permit partial summations over groups of variables. In other words, in this case the trade-off analysis dictates actually increasing the memory allocated for temporary working storage to achieve major savings in processing time.

ACKNOWLEDGMENT

This work was funded by Goddard Space Flight Center under Contract NAS 5-27888, Task Assignment 80100.

REFERENCES

[1]. R. K. Lennington and M. E. Rassbach, MATHEMATICAL DESCRIPTION AND PROGRAM DOCUMENTATION FOR CLASSY, AN ADAPTIVE MAXIMUM LIKELIHOOD CLUSTERING METHOD, Lockheed Electronics Company, Inc., April 1979.

[2]. R. K. Lennington and M. E. Rassbach, "CLASSY--An Adaptive Maximum Likelihood Clustering Algorithm," PROCEEDINGS OF THE NINTH ANNUAL MEETING OF THE CLASSIFICATION SOCIETY, May 1978.

[3]. M.-S. Kong, IMPLEMENTATION OF THE CLASSY PROGRAM ON THE MASSIVELY PARALLEL PROCESSOR, Computer Sciences Corporation, August 1983.

[4]. R. A. White, "Inversion of Positive Definite Matrices on the MPP" (included elsewhere in this volume).

[5]. G. Strang, LINEAR ALGEBRA AND ITS APPLICATIONS, Academic Press, Inc., 1976.

LANDSAT-4 THEMATIC MAPPER DATA PROCESSING WITH THE MASSIVELY PARALLEL PROCESSOR

Rudolf O. Faiss
Goodyear Aerospace Corporation
1210 Massillon Rd.
Akron, Ohio, 44315

ABSTRACT

The Massively Parallel Processor (MPP) is a new supercomputer system with a 4000 MOP rating. To achieve its speed, the system's primary computational engine employs 16K processing elements (PEs) that communicate with a 2 megabyte cache-like memory by way of channels that have a composite bandwidth of 20,000 megabytes per second. The primary components of the main computing engine are organized according to a single instruction stream, multiple data stream (SIMD) architecture. Since its delivery to the NASA Goddard Space Flight Center, it has been undergoing tests to determine its applicability for a wide variety of problems. This paper discusses how the MPP was used to convert LANDSAT-4 Thematic Mapper (TM) sensor World Reference System (WRS) scene data from sensor collection space coordinates to standard mapping space coordinates (e.g., Space Oblique Mercator (SOM) or Universal Transverse Mercator/ Polar Stereographic (UTM/PS)). A processing time on the order of 20 seconds is required to treat the pixels of such a scene (nominally, 250 million single band pixels). The paper concludes with a discussion of the changes that would be required to transform the NASA MPP test bed system into a real time production system.

INTRODUCTION

BACKGROUND

The MPP was conceived by NASA to solve severe processing problems likely to be encountered by remote sensing programs. After MPP concept evolution by NASA, Goodyear Aerospace Corporation (GAC) was awarded the contract to design, fabricate, deliver, and install the MPP. The MPP was accepted at NASA's Goddard facility in May, 1983.

The MPP has a processing power rating of 4000 MOPS. To achieve this power, it employs a SIMD architecture to organize the activity of 16K PEs. The hardware, system software, and architectural characteristics of this system are disclosed in a number of articles (see Shaefer 1982, Batcher 1983, Gilmore 1983, Burkley/Michelson 1983) as well as in MPP program reports available through NASA).

Operations to validate the MPP were initiated shortly after installation of the MPP at NASA. During the validation period, a number of demonstration programs were developed to test the MPP's realizable processing power, its general applicability (e.g., its ability to execute scientific processing tasks related to such diverse topics as fluid flow analysis, factoring, etc., as well as remote sensing tasks), and the general utility of its system software. Results of some of this work are found in published articles (see Strong 1983), U. of Illinois reports, and NASA reports. The positive flavor of the results has sparked widespread interest in the MPP.

In the fall of 1983, NASA began the assembly of an MPP testbed for testing the utility of the MPP for performing full scale applications. By the end of December, 1983, hardware and software interface connections that link the MPP and VAX of the MPP testbed system had been installed. NASA is currently executing testbed evaluation programs on this system. When usage rules have been established (scheduled for Sept., 1984), NASA intends to make the testbed operational.

OBJECTIVE OF PAPER

The objective of this paper is to familiarize readers with the NASA MPP interim testbed and to provide a base for making more critical assessments of the testbed system as well as the MPP itself. Assessments made here are based on work performed to use the testbed to convert LANDSAT-4 TM WRS scene data to a standard mapping space form.

ORGANIZATION OF PAPER

Preceding discussion establishes the basis for the work reported here. The succeeding discussion treats the work itself. In order, it includes the problem statement, describes the hardware to be used, and describes the strategy for solving the TM problem. It then discusses overall observations made during the course of designing and implementing the TM problem solution algorithm; the conclusion utilizes the observations to make preliminary recommendations for enhancing testbed performance.

PROBLEM STATEMENT

The Earth surface brightness function sensed by the TM is sampled at fixed time intervals at the node points of a pixel index (p) and sweep index (J) grid that is tied to the TM telescope's observation space. Because neither the sampling grid nor the observation space of the collected data are of standard form and because the sampling grid is further distorted from a regular form as the result of TM telecope "look" angle perturbations (mirror jitter), the utility of the collected data is diminished for most users. To provide data of high utility, the description of the brightness as a function of the collection space coordinates (p,J) must be converted to a description in terms of standard map projection space (e.g., the SOM, UTM, or PS mapping space) coordinates, (x,y). In such form, the scene data can be conveniently compared to a variety of previously acquired, location-dependent data sets (e.g. culture, political boundaries, roads, drainage, etc.).

The solution to the scene conversion problem is subject

to a number of supplementary conditions:

1) To convert scene data to the standard form with sufficient accuracy, the perturbation data provided by jitter sensors must be used to correct nominal sample post positions that are computed using measurement data supplied by the LANDSAT's primary position/orientation sensors.

2) An implicit description of the non-linear relationship between the collection (input) space coordinates and the standard mapping (output) space coordinates must be acceptable; the implicit description of the relationship is a set of 32 input/output space coordinate pairs developed from measures obtained from the primary position/orientation sensors.

3) The scene brightness at each grid point of the 28.5 meter mesh output space grid must be interpolated using a weighted sum of nearby input space brightness samples.

4) A full 300 megabyte WRS scene (nominally, 6500*6000 pixels by 7 color bands) must be treated so as to establish the manner of flow of the large amounts of brightness data through the testbed hardware.

5) Input (Output) data was to be supplied (generated) on NASA standard form and format tapes.

The testbed has insufficient RAM memory to concurrently store the data of a complete WRS scene. The solution of the auxiliary problem of partitioning the scene data and establishing the process order for the various types of scene subsets is a prerequisite for solving the primary scene conversion problem.

SOLUTION HARDWARE

This section discusses the resources of the NASA MPP testbed that affect the correction and conversion problem solution strategy. How the hardware affects the TM data correction/conversion program design is discussed immediately following this section.

TESTBED BLOCK DIAGRAM

The efficient conversion of a WRS scene from an input space coordinate description to the final output space description requires knowledge of the processing resource to be used to execute the conversion. For the effort discussed here, the NASA MPP testbed of Figure 1 is used. In the figure, MPP components lie to the right of the DR 780 interface; VAX components lie to the left of it. The VAX is a well known mini and will not be discussed here; the MPP is discussed in the references so only a brief discussion of it is included here.

MPP CHARACTERISTICS

The top right 1/4 of the figure shows the elements of the MPP that are key to its high speed processing power and data throughput capability. The stager (I/O buffer) memory is a permutation memory that can be populated to 64 megabytes (the testbed's stager is 1/32 populated). It connects to the array unit (ARU) which comprises 3 parts: the 16K PE set, the array memory (a cache-like data memory that is directly connected to the PE set via a 16K bit wide channel), and a small (128*128 bit) intra system I/O buffer that handles the bandwidth transition (BT) for data moves between the stager and array memory.

Figure 1. NASA MPP Testbed

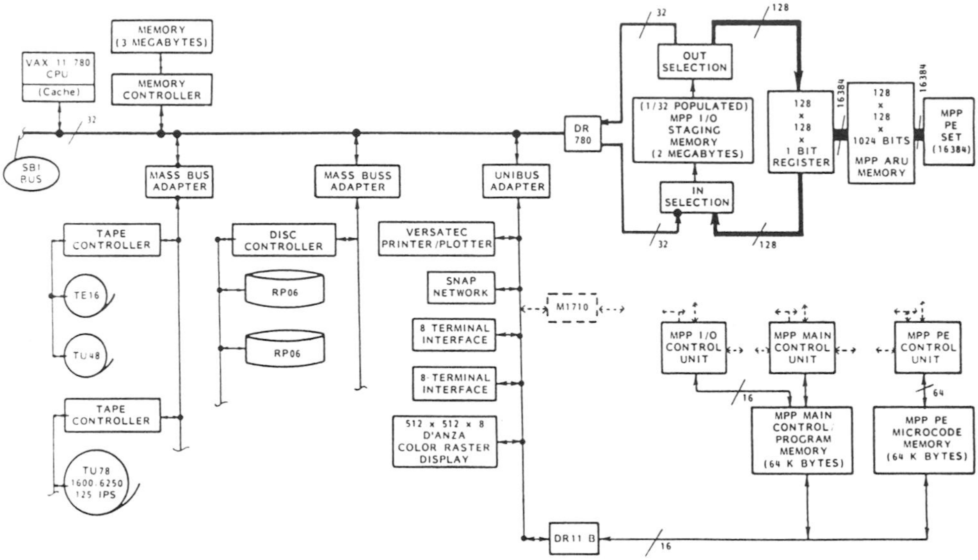

The array memory, 1/64 populated (2 megabytes) in the testbed, is laid out as a 3-D stack of 1024 bit planes (b); the 16K bits of each plane are arranged in a square 128 row (r) by 128 column (c) matrix pattern. Bits of the 1024 planes that are at a common (r,c) grid point location are connected to a particular PE; the 16K PEs are laid out in the same type of square 128 by 128 plane as the array memory bit planes so each has an associated set of 1024 PEs. The PEs have direct communication paths to adjacent row/column neighbors.

CHANNEL BANDWIDTHS. The slashes marked on channel lines of the figure indicate the data bit widths of a channel. Since the basic cycle time of the MPP is 100 nanoseconds, the bandwidth per bit is 10 megabits/second (1.25 million bytes/sec=mbyts) per bit channel. Thus, the bandwidth between the DR-780 and stager is 40 mbyts (each way), between the stager and BT buffer is 160 mbyts (each way), and is 20,000 mbyts on the common (but wide) channel to which the PEs, array memory, and BT buffer memory attach.

MPP CONTROL SECTION. The control section of the MPP (lower right 1/4 of the figure) comprises three asynchronous control units, namely, the I/O, Main, and PE control units. The I/O controller's (IOCU) primary task is synchronizing data flow between the various MPP elements including the MPP side of interfaces. The PE control unit (PECU) delivers instructions to each of the 16K PEs each cycle time. The Main control unit (MCU) orchestrates MPP activity. It keeps the PECU busy (by setting up PECU tasks and putting them in the PECU task queue), interacts with the IOCU, and interacts with the host.

TESTBED MPP/VAX INTERFACES

Three interfaces link the MPP to the VAX; in each case, the VAX channels throttle data moves through the interface.

The DR 780, a nominal 8 megabyte/second interface, provides the primary data connection between the MPP's primary I/O buffer (staging memory) and the main bus (SBI bus) of the VAX; WRS input and output scene data flow through this interface.

The DR11B, a nominal 1 megabyte/second interface, provides a connection between MPP control memory elements and a VAX Unibus; ancillary WRS scene data is passed to MPP control elements through this connection.

Finally, the M1710 interface provides a connection between MPP control registers and a VAX Unibus; the interface is used to accomplish intersystem control activity and for debug purposes.

TESTBED TM DATA INTERFACES

The ability of the testbed to receive raw or transmit refined remotely sensed data is limited. The testbed has neither the ability to directly intercept transmitted space craft sensor data nor the ability to read ground telemetry station high density tapes (HDTs) used to record such data. The 6250 BPI CCT drive shown in Figure 1 is the device used for inputting (and outputting) TM data.

PROGRAM DEVELOPMENT

The design of the testbed TM WRS scene geometric correction and coordinate conversion program depended on many factors. Three stand out. They are 1) the character of the solution algorithm, 2) the character of the data sets treated- input, transitional, output- and 3) the resources of the testbed. Their impact is examined here.

SELECTED TWO PHASE LAS CONVERSION ALGORITHM

A variety of algorithms can be employed to convert the perturbed sampled brightness data of the TM to a corrected, standard output space grid form. The TM data jitter correction and mapping transformation algorithm presently used by NASA's LANDSAT ASSESSMENT SYSTEM (LAS) was selected for implementation on the MPP testbed system. The intent of the choice was twofold. First, it was intended to exhibit that quite complex algorithms can be restructured to make efficient use of the resources of the MPP. (To provide the brightness function with higher spatial frequency power and continuity characteristics, GAC modified certain lower level steps of the LAS algorithm. The modifications employ higher order polynomials for data fitting and so demand more computations per scene than were required by the LAS algorithm.) Secondly, it was intended to show that the MPP could maintain a high degree of computational efficiency even when the various MPP-resident data entities are not

treated in the same way at each PE.   (The non-linear
character of the equations linking collection space and
output space coordinates shows up in the MPP-targeted
implementation as a need to move data differently at each PE
location; common lock-step data moves are the exception
rather than the rule.)

The LAS algorithm accomplishes the error correction and
coordinate space conversion task in two phases rather than
in a single phase.   In the first phase, brightness is
determined for the sample posts of an x,J intermediate space
grid by performing a one dimensional warp of the input
brightness data (in the sweep direction, J=constant).
Jitter and sensor offset effects are removed during the
first phase warping process.   The intermediate space
brightness is defined as a function of the point (x,J)
coordinates.

In the second phase, a nominally cross-sweep direction
(x=constant), one dimensional warp of the intermediate space
brightness data completes the warp needed to develop
brightness at the sample posts of an x,y output space grid.
Brightness data are moved along lines of constant "x"
(roughly, in a direction orthogonal to the sweep direction).
The output space brightness is defined as a function of the
point (x,y) coordinates.

(The LAS processing algorithm is highly compatable with
the form and order of the ancillary and scene data of the TM
LANDSAT-4 CCT-AT input tapes.   The testbed TM software

processing sequence was set up to make use of the natural form, format, and order of the tape data.)

PHASE 1 DESCRIPTION. Phase 1 of the algorithm develops the brightness (b) and output space y values for each of the (x,J) sample posts of an intermediate (middle) space coordinate system that uses the input space "J" coordinate axis as one of its axes and the output space "x" axis as the other (axis). The sample posts of the midspace are established over the general region of the WRS scene- at the intersections of 6967 x=integer lines and 5984 J=constant detector trace lines. For the midspace grid point, (x0,J0), which is at the intersection of the x=x0 (x0=integer) line with the trace line at J=J0, the input space coordinates are p0 and J0 where p0 is computed as a known function of (x0,J0); the brightness value found at (p0,J0) is the same as that at (x0,J0). Since the value "p0" determined by the function is not generally an integer, interpolation is used to establish a brightness value at the (p0,J0) point. Samples with indices [p0]-1, [p0]-0, [p0]+1, and [p0]+2 are used as inputs to a cubic convolution interpolation procedure that yields the interpolated brightness.

The y0 coordinate of the output space point that equates to the (x0,J0) midspace grid point is computed in the same manner as p0; it, too, is a known function of (x0,J0). The calculation of y0 establishes the output space point (x0,y0) that corresponds to the midspace point (x0,J0). Since the three points, (p0,J0), (x0,J0), (x0,y0)-input, intermediate, and output space points, respectively—all designate the location of the same physical point, the brightness is the same at all these locations. In general, although the output space point (x0,y0) lies along the output space x=x0 grid line, it does not lie on an output space grid point; phase 2 processing develops the output space grid point brightness values from the brightness values of sets of midspace grid points that lie along the x=constant output space grid lines.

PHASE 2 DESCRIPTION. After the brightness values of the midspace grid posts have been established, phase 2 processing commences to establish the brightness at the grid sampling posts of the output space system.

The locations of the sampling posts of the output space WRS scene (5965 y values by 6967 x values) are established by the intersections of the x=integer and y=integer lines (unit=28.5 meters). To compute the brightness value at an output space post with the integer coordinates (x0,y0), the midspace posts that lie along the x=x0 line are identified; from this set of midspace posts, those which are nearest and straddle the output post (in the "y" direction) are identified. The brightness and y coordinate values of these midspace posts are used to interpolate the brightness at the output sample post. Phase 2 interpolation procedures differ from those of Phase 1. They are modified to account for the variations of swath boundary spacing caused by cross-swath jitter.

BAND SEQUENTIAL PROCESSING

The band sequential order of WRS scene brightness data stored on the LANDSAT-D LAS CCT-AT tape determined the order in which the data from the different spectral detector sets would be treated. The MPP program was designed to accomplish full WRS scene correction/conversion for one spectral band at a time.

ONE PASS PROCESSING

Band processing using a two pass procedure appeared attractive from the standpoint of software structure. (Such a procedure would create the full WRS midspace scene for the band prior to initiating the development of any output scene pixel values.) Yet, a one pass processing procedure was implemented. When adequate memory is available in a system, such a procedure halves the load on the data channels of the system.

ASSIGNMENT OF PROGRAM TASKS TO RESOURCES

The basic rule for assigning program tasks to the MPP or VAX of the testbed system was obvious: if a task required many processing operations of the same type, it was assigned to the MPP. As a result, the MPP was assigned all the pixel data processing tasks. The VAX was assigned the tasks related to keeping the MPP supplied with new input data, receiving processed output data from the MPP, and developing ancillary data needed by the MPP during the course of mainline processing.

DATA SEGMENTATION

The random access memory (RAM) resources of the testbed are not large enough to hold the data of a single band WRS scene. Analysis of the resources of the testbed resulted in the decision to segment the band samples into stripes, segments, and patches. Stripes group the samples into 4 sets. About 30 segments comprise a stripe, and exactly 14 patches comprise a segment. The break down above is used for input, middle, and output space versions of a scene.

THE ELEMENTAL PROCESSING UNIT: THE "PATCH". Because of the layout of the MPP PEs, the grid sample post pattern of a patch was defined to be 128 single band pixels in the along swath (or "x") direction and 256 single band pixels in the cross swath (or "y") direction .

PATCH MAPPING INTO MPP ARRAY MEMORY. The topological mapping of patch sample posts into the physical MPP array memory is convenient. An input space patch contains the band data of 256 consecutive trace lines of forward and backward sweeps. Each line contains the 8 bit band brightness samples of 128 consecutive pixels. The forward sweep data are stored into 8 planes of the MPP array memory (i.e., into an 8 bit "field"); the backward sweep data are stored into a second 8 bit "field". Respectively, each row and column index pair (r,c) of the array memory corresponds to a traceline index and pixel index (grid point) of the input patch data.

THE "SEGMENT". A segment comprises 14 contiguous patches in the along-swath (or "x") direction. This gives the sement a 1792 (along-swath, along-"x") by 256 (cross-swath, along-"y") grid point rectangular shape.

THE "STRIPE". Stripes of the middle and output space are composed of segments that have been butted along their long edge. Their along-"x" width is 1792 pixels; their cross-swath (or along-"y") dimension is nominally about 30*256. Adjacent stripes butt perfectly. The input space stripe is only roughly rectangular. Segments stacked to form the stripe are overlapped by 32 trace lines and are slightly offset from segment to segment. Input space stripes overlap.

ORDER OF DATA PRODUCTION

Output scene data are produced a stripe at a time, beginning with the leftmost (lowest "x" index side) stripe. Within a stripe, the topmost (lowest "y" index side) segment data are produced first. Finally, within a segment, the leftmost patch data are produced first.

DATA FLOW

To optimize data flow during the course of processing, multiple I/O buffers are employed within the MPP and VAX memories. In the VAX environment, concurrent data flows are

maintained between the input tape and VAX memory, between
the RP06 disc and VAX memory, between the DR 780 and VAX
memory, and between the DR11B and VAX memory.   In the MPP
environment, concurrent data flows are maintained between
the MPP stager and ARU memory, between the MPP stager and DR
780, and between the MPP MCU memory and the DR11B.

MPP PROCESSING TASKS

Within the MPP, phase 1 and 2 error correction and/or
coordinate conversion processes are executed to completion
for a band patch subset of the total WRS scene.   Completion
of processing for a full scene occurs when all band patches
of all segments of all stripes of all bands of a scene have
been processed.

PHASE 1 "PATCH" PROCESSING.   During phase 1 processing,
MPP operations develop a midspace patch from input space
patches.   To implement phase 1 of the LAS algorithm,
midspace pixels are individually mapped to MPP PEs. Each of
a pixel's midspace location coordinates, $x0$ and $J0$, is
associated with an MPP array column and row index,
respectively. Using coefficient data (developed in the VAX
and sent to the MCU memory of the MPP) to define the
non-linear relationships that define "p" and "y" in terms of
the "x" and "J" midspace grid point variables, the "p0" and
"y0" values are developed (in parallel) for the midspace
patch gridpoints using scalar:vector and vector:vector
arithmetic routines.   After these coordinate values are

corrected for distortion, both static (geometric and sample time phasing) and dynamic (jitter), a processing intensive operations set, brightness processing for the midspace grid point is initiated.

Input space patches are loaded into the ARU memory so that the corresponding trace lines of the input and midspace patches lie in common MPP row locations; brightness values of input space patches need be moved only in the MPP row direction to get them to where they belong in the midspace grid. Each MPP row and column location provides the (p0,J0) location in input space that holds the brightness required for that (midspace) location. Because the input data is assigned to the MPP ARU memory so that the data for a given "J" value (e.g., "J0") lies in the same ARU array row for both the midspace and input space point, at a PE, the difference between the "p0" value computed for the PE's midspace grid point and that of the input space "p" value assigned to the same PE is the distance (in units of PE intervals) input brightness data must be shifted (along a row) in order to move it to the PE's midspace point.

Within the MPP ARU, processing operations slide all brightness data of 2 or 3 (along-swath) consecutive input patches over the grid of a midspace patch in the along swath (column) direction. As the input brightness data move by the full set of midspace gridpoints, the data are tapped and stored in association with the midspace points whenever required input brightness values arrive at such points. The tap-off point for each midspace patch grid point is determined from the computed "p"-direction fetch distance; prior to any moves of the input patches (and during the moves), each midspace grid point knows where the input brightness "interpolation" sample (a set of 4 samples) lies that must be moved to its location. (Because the move distance computed is usually not an integer, the four nearest input space brightness values (rather than a single value) are moved to a midspace point. A cubic convolution interpolation procedure uses these values to estimate brightness at the non-integer distance .)

After the input brightness sample sets suitable for establishing the "interpolation" sample value are present at all the midspace patch grid points, the interpolated brightness is computed for these points.

PHASE 2 "PATCH" PROCESSING. During phase 2 processing, MPP operations are aimed at creating output space brightness patches from the midspace patch created during phase 1. Within the MPP array unit, processing operations slide the brightness data of the midspace patch over the grid of an output space patch in the "y" (row) direction. As midspace brightness data moves by the set of output space gridpoints, the data are tapped and stored in association with the output space points whenever required midspace brightness values arrive at such points. In this case, for each output space patch point, the interpolation procedure adapts to the variations in inter-sweep distance that are the result of cross-swath jitter displacements.

VAX PROCESSING TASKS

For the TM task, the VAX has been programmed to execute the role of process executive. As the executive, its primary job is that of a data flow manager. When the MPP calls for input imagery data, it handles the management of the input imagery database and supplies the appropriate chunk of data. When the MPP requests to disgorge output imagery data, the VAX handles the management of the output imagery database and appropriately stores the chunk of data.

The VAX handles all testbed peripherals through its own channel set. Input from tape is dissected as required; output to tape is re-assembled as necessary.

Concurrent to its role as a data flow manager, the VAX generates polynomial coefficients that define the character of the jitter. When this ancillary data are required to support MPP patch processing, these coefficients are written to the MPP MCU memory.

General initialization tasks (e.g., the loading of the MPP domain programs) and termination tasks are ihandled or initiated by the VAX.

PROGRAM FINDINGS

The MPP requires about 20 seconds of MPP processing time

to perform the geometric correction of all the pixels of a TM WRS scene. The processing time is faster than real time. The   observed 2 orders of magnitude slowdown between wallclock time and the 20 second MPP processing time had been predicted from the start of the GAC effort. The VAX channels, peripherals, interfaces ,and software induce severe data flow bottlenecks and latencies that account for the slowdown.

The limited size of the testbed MPP stager and array memory (1/32 and 1/64 populated, respectively) forced the use of patch processing sequences that were somewhat inefficient. Considerable time was required to re-calculate coefficients and to develop pixel output values for overlap regions.

CONCLUSIONS

The MPP proved itself to be an exceptionally capable processor for performing TM geometric corrections. It has the architectural and processing power attributes needed for treating the tasks of advanced remote sensing systems.

For the MPP to provide TM geometric correction throughput capability that matches its processing speed, it needs to have direct access to high speed data sources and sinks. The data source (or sink) can not reside in a VAX environment; VAX channel bandwidth capabilities are inadequate to support the data rates that are required to keep the MPP busy. A solution to the source/sink bottleneck problem would be to provide direct high speed data channels between the MPP and high speed source/sink peripherals of a system. In such case, the VAX (or other host), would be used as the controller of the interface between the peripherals and the MPP.

The TM problem could have been performed more efficiently if both the MPP stager and array memory address space had been populated with about 4 times as much memory. For a system set up to directly handle downlinked data in real time, growth of the array and stager memory would be mandatory.

The MPP's ability to perform the TM problem processing extremely fast and efficiently, even while performing a significant number of tasks that demanded individualized action from different PEs, suggests that the MPP would be useful for treating a wide class of problems .

The TM program employed assembly language modules to develop control fields that determined the activity of individual PEs. MPP HOL development effort should be expanded to determine how control field type processing should be handled in an HOL programming environment.

ACKNOWLEDGMENTS

The author wishes to thank his GAC colleagues- Robert Messner, Douglas Smith, and Richard Lott- for their significant effort; also, the author wishes to thank David Fischel, James Fisher, and Jim Strong of NASA for their willing support and cooperation.

REFERENCES

Batcher, K.E. 1983, Architecture of the MPP: Proceedings of the Second Annual IEEE Society Workshop on Computer Architectures for Pattern Analysis and Image Database Management

Burkley, J.T. and Mickelson, C.T. 1983, MPP: A Case Study of a Highly Parallel System: Proceedings of the AIAA Conference on Computers in Aerospace #4

Fischel, D. , 1982, Thematic Mapper Geometric Correction Operator (unpublished NASA Internal Document), NASA/GSFC, Greenbelt, MD.

Gallopoulos, E.J. and McEwan, S.D. 1983, Numerical Experiments With The Massively Parallel Processor: Proceedings of the 1983 International Conference on Parallel Processing, pp 29-35

Gilmore, P.A. 1983, The Massively Parallel Processor (MPP) A Large Scale SIMD Processor: 27th Annual Technical Symposium of the SPIF

LANDSAT-D Assessment System Library Computer Compatible Tape (LASLIB- CCT/LAS-CCT) Tape Format Document For Thematic Mapper, 1982, WBS No. 10T031, NASA Contract NASA S-24350, Task Assignment 38100

Lynch, D., Strong, J. P. 1983, The Massively Parallel Processor- Its Here!: 12th Annual Applied Imagery Pattern Recognition Workshop

Schaefer, D.H., Fischer, J.R., Wallgren, K.R. 1982, The Massively Parallel Processor: Journal of Guidance, Control and Dynamics, Volume 5, Number 3, pp 313-315

FLUID DYNAMICS MODELING[a, b]

E. J. Gallopoulos
Department of Computer Science
University of Illinois
Urbana, Ill. 61801

Introduction -- The MPP was designed as a machine to support high-speed processing of satellite imagery. After preliminary work at the University of Illinois and at
NASA GSFC its use in problems in other areas involving large scale-computations was
sought. In this chapter we will describe some of these problems. The way these are
mapped on the architecture will also be exposed and estimates for the performance of
some of these algorithms will be given.

BACKGROUND

The area of Fluid Dynamics makes the scientist encounter not only the most complicated mathematical problems but also such formidable computational requirements
that the use of the most powerful computers is necessarily demanded. As a result,
national laboratories engaged in research in these areas have traditionally been the primary users of the new supercomputers. It must be said that although historically the
concept of centrally controlled arrays which constitutes one aspect of the MPP design
was conceived for enabling the fast numerical solution of partial differential equations
using mesh-relaxation techniques, this was certainly not the case with other aspects of
the design.

---

[a]Research supported in part by NASA under contract NAS5-26405.

[b]A first version of this paper appeared in [1].

The computational problems that are most often encountered require the fast processing of arrays of data in the context of matrix calculations, the solution of discretized partial differential equations and data transformations. It is therefore necessary to design algorithms for these problems which will exploit the architecture to the utmost degree. Some of the most important attributes of the MPP architecture which the programmer must always keep in mind as potential blessings or curses to his effort in writing efficient code for the MPP are the serial-by-bit operating mode, the availability of the shift-register, the staging-memory, the very small local memory per PE, the mesh-connected network and the grid-like geometry of the processor collection. The close observation of these attributes more often than not leads to what a purist would call inelegant programming but which nevertheless is as efficient as possible. This will account for the many special purpose routines, written in PEARL or MCL and which can be found in some of the packages written for the MPP.

ITERATIVE METHODS

Iterative methods for solving the large systems of linear equations arising from the discretization of partial differential equations are not difficult to implement on the MPP. Modifications to such methods to run efficiently in processor array environments like the Illiac IV, the DAP and the MPP can be found in [3]. A great advantage of using iterative schemes for such an architecture is that only local interactions are involved at each step. Only local routing of data is needed and interprocessor communication is kept at a minimum. It must be said however that iterative schemes can suffer from slow convergence rates. The algorithms that have been written to run on the MPP implement the Jacobi, Gauss-Seidel, SOR, Line SOR, and Cyclic Chebychev iterative methods. More details about the MPP implementations can be found in [2].

PROBLEM DESCRIPTION

The first large-scale problem that was considered for MPP implementation was the solution of a form of the Navier-Stokes equations suitable for weather prediction in meteorology. The physical processes occurring in the atmosphere and as a result their mathematical formulations are non-linear. Even with the occasional simplifications, the arising equations cannot be solved analytically and require good numerical techniques.

It has been found that the so called shallow-water equations contain the essential numerical aspects of the large scale prediction equations. These are strictly two-dimensional and thus refer to phenomena at a single fluid layer.

The spherical polar coordinates (λ, ϕ) where λ is the longitude and ϕ the latitude are chosen, as the most natural reference system for motions around the globe. At time t and at position (λ, ϕ) the dependent variables for the model are the height h of the isobaric atmospheric surface under consideration equal to $h_T - h_B$, and the eastward and northward velocity components u and v respectively. The meaning of the variables can be better understood if one regards as independent variables the longitude and latitude - which as soon as they are frozen they specify an atmospheric column - and as the third independent variable (kept fixed for the one level model) not the altitude but the pressure. This is possible since there is a monotonic relationship relating the two and can thus be used interchangeably [4]. The height then becomes a dependent variable. The equations are then

$$\frac{\partial h}{\partial t} = \frac{-1}{a\cos\phi} \left[\frac{\partial hu}{\partial \lambda} + \frac{\partial hv\cos\phi}{\partial \phi} \right] \tag{1a}$$

$$\frac{\partial hu}{\partial t} = \frac{-1}{a\cos\phi} \left[\frac{\partial(hu)u}{\partial \lambda} + \frac{\partial(hv\cos\phi)u}{\partial \phi} \right] - \frac{gh}{a\cos\phi}\frac{\partial h_T}{\partial \lambda} + (f + \frac{u\tan\phi}{a})vh \tag{1b}$$

$$\frac{\partial hv}{\partial t} = -\frac{1}{a\cos\phi} \left[\frac{\partial(hu)v}{\partial \lambda} + \frac{\partial(hv\cos\phi)v}{\partial \phi} \right] - \frac{gh}{a}\frac{\partial h_T}{\partial \phi} - (f + \frac{u\tan\phi}{a})uh \tag{1c}$$

where a, g and f are the radius of the earth, the gravitational constant and the Coriolis parameter respectively. The first equation comes from the law of mass conservation and the last two from the law of momentum conservation. They can be found in this form in [5]. For a model where bottom orography is not included, $h_B = H$, a constant, and thus the h_T variable above can be replaced by h. This is the system that must be solved, given suitable boundary and initial conditions. The equations are written in flux form, using the time derivatives of the height-velocity products. It is thus possible to retain some of the conservative properties of the continuous set when going to the discrete schema. It is known that this is a very desirable feature of a finite-difference scheme. Apart from the intuitive modeling accuracy that is preserved the most important benefit is the reduced possibility of encountering the phenomenon of non-linear instability described in [6]. The characteristic speeds for the above system correspond to i) a pair of fast moving gravity waves having phase speeds of order of magnitude $\sqrt{gH}$ and to ii) a slowly moving Rossby wave which is of most importance for large scale meteorological processes.

COMPUTATIONAL GRID AND DISCRETIZATION. A latitude-longitude grid with constant angular increments $\Delta\lambda$ and $\Delta\phi$ was used (fig. 1). The grid is non-staggered (all variables are defined at each node.) Each node lies at the intersection of selected latitude and longitude circles. The grid system is shifted by $\dfrac{\Delta\phi}{2}$ next to the poles. Hence the polar singularity which arises from the $a\cos\phi$ term in the equations above is avoided. For m longitude and n latitude circles

$$\Delta\lambda = \frac{2\pi}{n}, \quad \Delta\phi = \frac{\pi}{m},$$

the first and last latitude circles lying next to the north and south poles respectively, correspond to $\phi = \pm\left(\dfrac{\pi}{2} - \dfrac{\Delta\phi}{2}\right)$. Boundary conditions are doubly periodic as with the GLAS model. In the East-West direction for both scalar and vector elements $s(\lambda + 2\pi,\phi) \equiv s(\lambda,\phi)$. In the North-South direction, when variables are needed across the poles, the values are taken from the first grid point encountered by moving along the

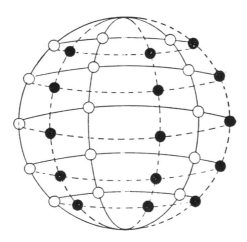

Fig. 1. Latitude-Longitude Grid

same latitude circle 180° around the pole. To keep the equations consistent the signs of the vector variables and the trigonometric functions must be changed when combined across the poles [7]. Hence $\vec{v}(\lambda,\pm(\frac{\pi}{2}+\frac{\Delta\phi}{2})) \equiv -\vec{v}(\lambda+\pi,\pm(\frac{\pi}{2}-\frac{\Delta\phi}{2}))$ and $s(\lambda,\pm(\frac{\pi}{2}+\frac{\Delta\phi}{2})) \equiv s(\lambda+\pi,\pm(\frac{\pi}{2}-\frac{\Delta\phi}{2}))$. For the solution of the system, a set of initial conditions for h, u, v at all locations must be available. For model testing, the conditions used were derived analytically as in [8], instead of extracting them from a weather map.

The objective is to write finite-difference expressions and discretize the space derivatives $(\frac{\partial}{\partial\phi}, \frac{\partial}{\partial\lambda})$ on the right-hand side of the equations (1). Then a time differencing scheme is applied to integrate one step ahead in time and update the variables. The explicit leapfrog scheme is frequently used in numerical weather prediction models, giving

$$S^{(n+1)} = S^{(n-1)} + 2\Delta t(\frac{\partial S}{\partial t})_{t=n\Delta t} \tag{2}$$

where for notational simplicity S is the vector of unknowns $[h,hu,hv]^T$ defined at each grid point.

The relevant theory [9] imposes an upper bound on the timestep that one could use to avoid the phenomenon of linear instability. Roughly, the finer the resolution, the smaller that bound. In [5] a stability criterion is shown for the model. Due to the converging meridians at the poles a latitude-longitude grid forces a time step much smaller at the polar regions than at the equator. As a result that minimum time step should be used. An alternative is to use a split-grid where the number of grid-points per latitude circle would be a function of the latitude. Such a scheme had been proposed in [10, 11] and others. It can be shown however [12] that this would produce excessive truncation errors near the poles as the truncation errors increase with latitude and certainly depend on the grid-point distance. A more acceptable way to overcome this constraint is to filter the unstable waves. We discuss this later. Since second-order differences are used for both the time and space discretizations the scheme is of second order in space and time. To start the computations data from two time levels are needed since the chosen time-differencing scheme use information from the two previous time levels. This is achieved by using a simple forward time scheme for a fractional time step and then proceeding.

MPP IMPLEMENTATION. The steps taken to develop the algorithm were the typical ones which the MPP users would also follow. At first the program was written using the tools provided in the simulator environment. The debugging was also done on the simulator and initial performance measurements were taken. At a later stage the actual MPP implementation followed. As is mentioned in chapter 15 the simulator's overhead and the sequential processing done by the host machine makes infeasible the simulation of a 128×128 ARU. Therefore a 32×32 ARU was simulated. Each PE and PE memory contained the variables and constants for the corresponding node. The northmost (southmost) PE row corresponded to the longitude circle immediately to the south (north) of the North (South) pole.

All the code was written in MCL and PEARL. The routines for the elementary arithmetic and data communication operations had been developed at the University of Illinois.

The variable elements that are only functions of position like the Coriolis force component f, $\tan\phi$, $\cos\phi$ etc. were all precalculated before the start of the integration loop since they are constant (with respect to time) arrays. The time dependent variables h, u, v and their combinations are also defined at each point. Hence the above values are stored in each PE memory at fixed locations and their corresponding type declaration in Parallel Pascal is

PARALLEL ARRAY [1 .. N, 1 .. N] OF REAL

where N is the number of rows (columns) of the grid and corresponding ARU systems. The scalar data is either global to the problem and used in the actual equations (1) or is used for counting purposes. To the former category belong g, Δt, $\Delta\phi$, $\Delta\lambda$, a, Ω etc. and to the latter all the variables keeping track of the number of steps and simulated time since the last important event (reinitialization, filtering etc.) The limited available memory per PE (only 1024 bits) forces the programmer to look for ways to economize as much space as possible by using the Main Controller memory when appropriate. The availability of scalar-array arithmetic routines avoids wasting time and PE memory space for broadcasting and storing scalar operands. In order to avoid unnecessary repetition of floating-point operations some constant arrays and scalars can be combined from the initiation of the computations with the appropriate scale factors (e.g. Δt, $\Delta\lambda$ etc.) Thus by storing in the ARU precomputed constant data, the number of required floating operations, which are expensive, is reduced. The available East-West ARU topology readily provides for the East-West periodicity, the first and last PE columns corresponding to $\lambda = 0$ and $\lambda = 2\pi - \Delta\lambda$ respectively. The situation is more complicated for the simulation of the periodicity across the poles, as that cannot be mapped to the available interconnection topologies of the ARU. To combine the appropriate elements, the variable arrays would have to be rotated (using the same East-West interconnection) by $\frac{N}{2}$ columns. When the simulator system is used $N = 32$ and the cycle count is underestimated for these routing operations.

The corresponding angular increments for the simulated and the real ARU are $\Delta\lambda = 2\Delta\phi \approx 11°$ and $\Delta\lambda = 2\Delta\phi \approx 3°$ respectively. To compare, a currently used GLAS model utilizes $\Delta\lambda = 5°$ and $\Delta\phi = 4°$ whereas an "ultrafine" version has $\Delta\lambda = 3°$ and $\Delta\phi = 2.5°$. We thus see that the MPP dimensions are adequate for the described problem. Hence no 'dimensional sacrifice' need be done to size down the problem for a parallel implementation, an unfortunate practice in some examples demonstrating the usefulness of parallel computers.

The operations applied at each grid point (PE) for the derivation of the spatial differences are local operations. The only place where this is not so is at some of the calculations for the latitudinal differences. For the scheme used, which is of 2^d order, only elements from the immediate neighbors are needed. For a more accurate 4th order scheme, like the one used in [13] the elements involved for a calculation at PE(i,j) would lie in the surrounding PEs at distances of at most 2.

The inner loop of the code would go through the following steps in order to derive the new values at $t=(n+1)\Delta t$ out of known data at the two previous time steps:

1) From the available values for h, u, v at time level n use the discrete form of equations (1) to approximate the space derivatives and by adding the λ and ϕ contributions at each grid point (PE) derive an approximation to $2\Delta t(\frac{\partial S}{\partial t})$ for the current time level.

2)   Apply (2) to derive the values at the new time level. This only needs one addition per component of the S vector.

3)   Update the variables and counters.

Figure 2 shows the flowchart for the entire program.

The PE memory restriction of 1K bits was observed: only 680 bitplanes have been used and these could be further reduced down to 600. By going from the simulator to the real system a drastic reduction to the time step used for the integrations is required in order to satisfy the CFL criterion. This is because of the much higher resolution achieved by the latter system. We have used $\Delta t = 200sec$ for the case N = 32, and $\Delta t \approx 10$ seconds for N = 128. Alternatively, since the time constraint is relaxed by going to a coarser grid and if the high resolution in the latitude is not needed, the number of longitude circles can be reduced (e.g. halved.) Since the North-South interconnections are not used, two independent simulations could be run concurrently (using the same global constants but different initial conditions). The one system would lie in the upper half of the ARU (using half of the PE rows) and the other would lie in the lower half. At the end of each computation cycle results for both systems would be simultaneously obtained.

In order to avoid the excessive accumulation of energy in the short wavelengths [6], a filtering procedure [14] was used. Such a filter applied in the East-West direction to an array variable q at location (i, j), repeatedly calculates $\dfrac{q_{ij+1} - 2q_{ij} + q_{ij-1}}{4}$ and then combines the result with the original array values q_{ij}. As explained above, things are slightly more complicated in the North-South direction. This filtering results in the elimination of $2\Delta x$ waves where Δx is the East-West grid distance which may introduce the

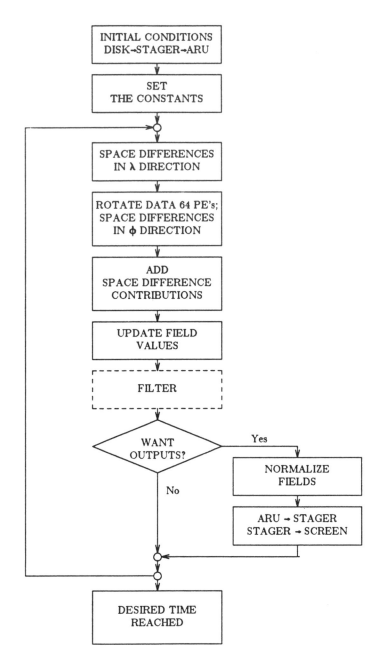

Fig. 2: MPP Program Flow for the Shallow-Water Equations.

instability. This procedure was applied every hour on h, u, v, eight times in each direction resulting in a 16th order filter. The MPP implementation of the above operator is very efficient in the zonal direction, taking full advantage of the parallelism. The absence of over-the-poles connections introduces considerable delays due to the communication necessary when the operator is applied in the North-South direction.

In a Parallel Pascal environment

```
            CONST
              order = 8 ;
              N = 128 ; (* the ARU size *)
            TYPE
              arr = PARALLEL ARRAY[1 .. N, 1 .. N] OF REAL ;
            VAR
              i : INTEGER ;
              q, qsv, temp : arr ;
            BEGIN
              qsv := q ;
              FOR i := 1 TO order DO
                BEGIN
                  temp := q - ROTATE(q, 0, 1) ;
                  q := ROTATE(temp, 0, -1) - temp ;
                  q := q/2 ;
                  q := q/2
                END;
              q := qsv - q;
            END;
```

The repeated divisions by 2 should be done by special purpose routines. The bit-serial nature of the arithmetic makes divisions and multiplications by 2 and its powers considerably faster than if using the floating point division routine. In the libraries we used, the floating-point division routine for IBM single-precision format consumed 1031 PCU cycles whereas the special-purpose division by 2 consumed 266 PECU cycles. Moreover, it has been noted that an even better rate of 75 cycles can be achieved by letting the routine consist only of PEARL instructions [15].

FOURIER FILTERING. Filtering sets of data samples in order to exclude undesirable noise effects is a frequent requirement for many applications including the one described in this chapter. Such filtering can be done efficiently by means of the Fast Fourier Transform. In order for the most elementary linear stability criterion to be met, the upper bound on the time step that can be used at points nearest to the poles is about 80 times less than the maximum stable time step at the equator, unless the high-latitude unstable short wave components of the height and velocity fields are eliminated. The filtering problem can then be defined as follows: At selected latitudes the field is analyzed to its components in the frequency domain. Depending on the amount of filtering that is needed each of the components is either left unaffected or is multiplied by some weight factor (which can be zero.) Finally, the (filtered) field is reconstructed from the modified components. Both the analysis and synthesis are done by means of a forward/inverse FFT pair developed for the MPP using the tools described in chapter 15, in particular the Parallel Pascal Translator. At the time of this writing, there are no performance results from runs on the MPP available. This implementation differs from the FFT package described in [16]. The data is in floating-point rather than fixed-point representation. The root-of-unity multipliers used at each step of the algorithm are calculated on the fly by means of trigonometric identities. Since each ARU row corresponds to one latitude, one FFT is done per row, in parallel for all rows. The forward transform generates the components in scrambled order using a Decimation-in-Time algorithm. The inverse transform takes its inputs in scrambled order and generates the results in the natural order using a Decimation-in-Frequency algorithm. Additional routines exist for the descrambling operations if needed. The FFT algorithms repeatedly combine elements that are at distances 64, 32, ..., 1 PE's apart. Hence the time spent for interprocessor communication becomes very important. Details about the algorithms can be found in [2].

DESCRIPTION OF RESULTS The resulting simulation corresponded to east to west moving wave patterns for h, u, v. Due to the choice of the initial conditions and the filtering used, the gravity waves had a very small effect on the development of the wave patterns. It is hard to appreciate the results just by looking at vast computer printouts. Hence a color graphics display was used to depict the qualitative structure of the solutions.

For the real MPP, the initial constant and variable arrays were generated and stored in the VAX disk. From there, they were moved to the host and then to the ARU through the Stager. This necessitated a format conversion of the initial input arrays from VAX to IBM format (which was the MPP format for floating-point numbers at the time.) This time consuming stage will be eliminated when efficient VAX format floating-point arithmetic routines for the MPP will become available. Since PE memory space was available, the initial arrays were saved to facilitate comparisons. Moreover the color display memories were used as temporary storage of the initial arrays: moving data from there to the array was faster than moving data from disk to the array. Hence, whenever the simulation had to be restarted using the same initial conditions, less time was necessary for the data transfer. After the initiation of the computations and at selected time intervals, the calculated height and velocity fields were being scaled to integers ranging from 0 to 255 (8 bits) with each number corresponding to a color. The scaling and integer transformations occur at each grid point and full advantage of the parallelism is taken. Thus even for this output oriented consideration the MPP can be used very efficiently. The integration of the fields was thus followed as an evolution of color patterns on the display.

MPP TIMINGS. The number of consumed cycles, as they were estimated from the simulator, for each routine was given in [1]. The elementary routines used had been written at Illinois using the environment described in chapter 15. The floating-point operations were written for the IBM single-precision representation. A main step, consisting of calls to the procedures to do the space derivative calculations (by far the most time consuming routine amongst the frequently called ones) and to update the fields takes about 43,000 PECU cycles, or for 100 ns/cycle there are about 230 iterations/sec. With a 200sec time step and excluding any overhead, we get that 1 day is simulated in about 2 seconds. For a 10 second time step, one day needs 50 seconds.

PERFORMANCE COMPARISONS. As long as we are interested in particular problems and not general evaluations a good strategy is to simply compare the timings for their solution on the examined machines [17]. Even this however may not be a fair criterion since the fastest algorithms for each machine would possess different numerical properties. Dimensions also would probably be chosen to suit the machine (magic numbers like 64 or 128 for the Cray, the DAP or the MPP) rather than the modeler. The DAP [18] array is 1/4 of the MPP array and also has considerably slower MFLOP rates. As a result, for this problem it would not compete with the MPP. On the other hand the currently used DAPs have 4K bits of memory per PE (to be extended to 16K) and hence it could be used to model a multi-level model, or one containing more equations, without the constraints imposed by frequent I/O exchanges which might be needed for the MPP in its initial memory configuration. Experiments on the CRAY-1 [19] for a similar model with a resolution of $\Delta\lambda = \Delta\phi = 12°$ required 8.5×10^{-4} sec/step, whereas with $\Delta\lambda = \Delta\phi = 4°$ the integration required 4.97×10^{-3} sec/step. The $\Delta\lambda = 2\Delta\phi \approx 11°$ resolution achieved with the MPP simulator took about 4.3×10^{-3} sec/step. As the parallelism is almost fully exploited and redundancy is kept at a minimum by going to the full ARU this timing estimate would only increases slightly but the available resolution becomes $\Delta\lambda = 2\Delta\phi \approx 3°$ which is superior to the finer resolution in the Cray model above. Therefore a better resolution and comparable or better timing per timestep is achieved with the MPP. Moreover, it is possible to have concurrent integrations of multiple initial data sets.

CONCLUSIONS.

The initial experiment demonstrated that the MPP can be used to solve problems with intensive floating-point computations very effectively. In the earlier form of this paper it was mentioned that since the MPP gives much better performances for integer computations it would seem worthwhile to investigate the possibility of using fixed or block floating point arithmetic in the computations. The nature of the field values however is such that such a task might be very cumbersome.

The performance results extrapolated from the simulator rates for the real MPP were found to be remarkably accurate. This strengthens the claim made in chapter 15 that the simulator can be used for giving accurate performance estimates even without simulating IO. Were IO to be much more intensive however, that would not be the case any longer.

The use of the MPP makes efficient and possible the simulation of General Circulation models over the entire globe with adequate horizontal resolution. Consequently the modeler doesn't have to worry about imposing artificial lateral boundary conditions. A complete model would have multiple vertical levels. It would also take account of thermal phenomena which here were ignored, by incorporating more equations. A 4th order space-differencing scheme would be preferable. For multiple level simulation the PE memory becomes inadequate. The addressing capability of the PE index registers is for 64K bits per PE memory and a future system could contain such memory. At this time, when more storage area is needed, one will have to use its SM as an immediate active buffer area. A few of the not too frequently used arrays for a large model could be stored in the stager and brought in the ARU under some paging policy designed to minimize interference with the computations. A preliminary theoretical study of the problems related with memory allocation and management for the SM can be found in [20]. Real or various analytical initial data would be gathered in a data base and from there it would initialize the MPP arrays. Multiple concurrent simulations could then be run as suggested above or a single fine-grid simulation could be instigated and the results at selected time steps would be displayed. For long predictions, periodic updating of the variables could be done by utilizing newly observed data.

The experiment which we described was the first attempt to use the MPP for problems outside the area of Image Processing. The results were found to be encouraging and more work is currently under way to test the performance of other algorithms for the MPP. We mention here the solution of the same equations with a 4th order differencing scheme and the solution of the driven-cavity problem [2].

REFERENCES

[1] E. Gallopoulos and S. D. McEwan, "Numerical Experiments with the Massively Parallel Processor," PROC. OF THE 1983 INTERNATIONAL CONFERENCE ON PARALLEL PROCESSING, August, 1983, pp. 29-35.

[2]. E. J. Gallopoulos, PROCESSOR ARRAYS FOR PROBLEMS IN COMPUTATIONAL FLUID DYNAMICS, Ph. D. thesis, (in preparation,) Department of Computer Science, University of Illinois at Urbana-Champaign.

[3] D. Hockney and J. Jesshope, PARALLEL COMPUTERS, Adam Hilger, 1982.

[4] Akira Kasahara, "Computational Aspects of Numerical Weather Prediction and Climate Simulation," METHODS IN COMPUTATIONAL PHYSICS, Academic Press, 1977.

[5] M. Grimmer and D. B. Shaw, "Energy-Preserving Integrations of the Primitive Equations on the Sphere," QUART. J. ROY. METEOR. SOC., 1967, pp. 337-349.

[6] N. Phillips, "An Example of Nonlinear Computational Instability," THE ATMOSPHERE AND SEA IN MOTION, Rockefeller Inst. Press, 1959.

[7] D. L. Williamson, "Difference Approximations for Fluid Flow on a Sphere," NUMERICAL METHODS IN ATMOSPHERIC MODELS, GARP Publication, 1979.

[8] Norman Phillips, "Numerical Integration of the Primitive Equations on the Atmosphere," MONTHLY WEATHER REVIEW, September, 1959, pp. 333-345.

[9] R. D. Richtmyer and K. W. Morton, DIFFERENCE METHODS FOR INITIAL-VALUE PROBLEMS, Wiley(Interscience), 1967.

[10] A. B. Carroll and R. T. Wetherald, "Application of Parallel Processing to Numerical Weather Prediction," JACM, July, 1967, pp. 591-614.

[11] M. Graham and D. L. Slotnick, AN ARRAY COMPUTER FOR THE CLASS OF PROBLEMS TYPIFIED BY THE GENERAL CIRCULATION OF THE ATMOSPHERE, Department of Computer Science, University of Illinois at Urbana-Champaign, Report UIUCDCS-R-75-761, December, 1975.

[12] Frederick G. Shuman, "On Certain Truncation Errors Associated with Spherical Coordinates," JOURNAL OF APPLIED METEOROLOGY, August, 1970, pp. 564-570.

[13] E. Kalnay-Rivas and D. Hoitsma, DOCUMENTATION OF THE 4TH ORRDER BANDED MODEL, Laboratory for Atmospheric Sciences, NASA Goddard Space Flight Center, Technical Memorandum 80608, December, 1979.

[14] R. Shapiro, "Smoothing, Filtering and Boundary Effects," REV. GEOPHYS. AND SPACE PHYS., May, 1970, pp. 359-387.

[15]. D. L. Slotnick, Neil B. Coletti et al, RESEARCH IN THE APPLICATION AND DESIGN OF A MASSIVELY PARALLEL PROCESSOR, Department of Computer Science, University of Illinois at Urbana-Champaign, Seventh Quarterly Progress Report, September, 1982.

[16]. Neil B. Coletti, IMAGE PROCESSING ON MPP-LIKE ARRAYS, Department of Computer Science, University of Illinois at Urbana-Champaign, May, 1983.

[17] D. Parkinson and H. Liddell, "The Measurement of Performance on a Highly Parallel System," IEEE TRANSACTIONS ON COMPUTERS, January, 1983, pp. 32-37.

[18] P. M. Flanders, D. J. Hunt, S. F. Reddaway, and D. Parkinson, "Efficient High Speed Computing with the Distributed Array Processor," HIGH-SPEED COMPUTER AND ALGORITHM DESIGN, Academic Press, 1977, pp. 113-128.

[19] R. L. Gilliland, "Solution of the Shallow Water Equations on the Sphere," JOURNAL OF COMPUTATIONAL PHYSICS, September, 1981, pp. 79-94.

[20] A. P. Reeves and J. D. Bruner, THE LANGUAGE PARALLEL PASCAL AND OTHER ASPECTS OF THE MASSIVELY PARALLEL PROCESSOR, School of Electrical Engineering, Cornell University, December, 1982.

DATABASE MANAGEMENT

Edward W. Davis
Department of Computer Science
North Carolina State University
Raleigh, North Carolina 27695-8206

Introduction --Although the MPP was originally motivated by requirements related to image processing, it is a fully programmable machine and can be used for other, quite distinct, applications. Database management is one such potential application. The relational model is used here as a basis for examining selected database management functions.

DATABASE SYSTEMS

New digital computer architectures offer the potential for improved solutions to computer based applications. The massively parallel processor represents a new architecture with such potential. MPP system design supports the processing, interprocessor communication, memory, and input/output bandwidth performance needed for large database systems. Previous work related to parallel architectures and database systems has had positive results [1]-[3], thus, it is reasonable to examine database management as an application where the MPP's highly parallel properties are potentially advantageous.

The relational model has been selected for its applicability to parallel processing, its mathematical foundations, and its recognition as a model which is better than the hierarchical and network models in many respects [4]-[5]. Relational

database systems can be implemented on conventional uniprocessor computing equipment. They do not require any unique functional capability. However, database system performance can be
affected greatly by features of the underlying computer architecture. As a result, several machines have been designed
specifically for database applications. Four examples are RAP
[2], DBC [6], DIRECT [7], and NON-VON [8].

The MPP design has features that nicely support the relational database model. Essentially, the massive parallelism
can be used to great advantage for fundamental relational
operations. Processing in the MPP array unit takes place in
SIMD fashion. All enabled processing elements, (PEs), execute
the same instruction on distinct data items. Processing is
enabled or disabled within each PE according to the state of a
mask register. Masking allows selection of a subset of PE's to
take part in further processing; a feature that is very useful
in query and update functions on databases.

Since processing elements and their memories are one bit
wide units, processing takes place in bit-serial fashion. Since
each PE in the entire array can operate simultaneously, a 128
by 128 plane of bits can be processed in parallel. If an
instruction requires a data memory access, each PE accesses the
given location in its own random access memory. Thus the data
streams to be processed in parallel must be mapped onto
addresses in parallel memories.

RELATIONAL DATABASES IN THE MPP

THE RELATIONAL MODEL

An important feature of the relational model of data is that the user's view involves just one data structure: the relation. Essentially a relation is a tabular structure consisting of rows called "tuples" and columns called "attributes". A database is made up of one or more relations. Operations on the data structures result in modification of attribute values or construction of new relations. The functions performed are updates and queries. An update can include modification of values as well as tuple insertion or deletion. A query is a search of attributes to identify or select certain tuples.

Figure 1 is an example database in relational form adapted from the Date text [5]. This very small example is used to illustrate the tabular nature of relations. The databse concerns suppliers of parts. The S relation contains information about suppliers, P contains information about parts, and SP provides an association between suppliers and parts based on supplier numbers and part numbers from their relations.

RELATIONS IN MPP MEMORY

Processing parallelism in the MPP occurs when an operation takes place on a bit plane distributed over many processors. That is, the same operation is performed on many data items.

S:	S#	SNAME	STATUS	SCITY
	S1	SMITH	20	LONDON
	S2	JONES	10	PARIS
	S3	BLAKE	30	PARIS
	S4	CLARK	20	LONDON
	S5	ADAMS	30	AKRON

P:	P#	PNAME	COLOR	WT	PCITY
	P1	NUT	RED	12	LONDON
	P2	BOLT	GREEN	17	PARIS
	P3	SCREW	BLUE	17	ROME
	P4	SCREW	RED	15	LONDON
	P5	CAM	BLUE	12	PARIS
	P6	COG	RED	19	LONDON

SP:	S#	P#	QUANTITY
	S1	P1	300
	S1	P2	200
	S1	P3	400
	S1	P4	200
	S1	P5	100
	S1	P6	100
	S2	P1	300
	S2	P2	400
	S3	P2	200
	S4	P2	200
	S4	P4	300
	S5	P5	400

FIGURE 1. A RELATIONAL DATABASE

Database queries involve operations on attribute fields of tuples in relations. Since a given operation occurs on the same attribute of many tuples, parallel processing has great potential. A relation stored with one tuple per PE will have a parallelism factor limited only by the number of tuples in the relation (its cardinality) or by the number of PE's. In the MPP, the 16,384 PE's represent the hardware limit on parallelism.

A good data structure for a relation will have an individual tuple stored in the memory of an individual PE. Such a mapping places the same attributes of each tuple in the same memory locations for parallel, bit plane accessing. If tuple length exceeds the realized memory size, a single tuple can be mapped into more than one PE memory. Alternatively, selected attribute fields can be stored in a PE memory, rather than an entire tuple.

MPP MEMORY HIERARCHY

Primary data memory capacity in the MPP ranges from two megabytes in the first realization to 128 megabytes as a design limit. Primary memory is supported by a hierarchy of memory components. The staging memory provides up to 64 megabytes of solid state memory backing the primary and operating with a 160 megabytes per second I/O rate. It has been designed to handle access to rows and columns of multidimensional data structures. For example, the staging memory can provide columns of attributes as needed for array unit I/O, and it can provide rows of tuples as may be needed for host or peripheral interfacing.

The next level in the memory hierarchy is devices peripheral to the MPP such as a disk memory system. All levels of the hierarchy provide physical storage for relations that is very similar to the user's logical view.. On disks, a relation is a file with tuples as records. Transfers between disk and staging memory are sequences of tuples. The close fit of the user's view of relations to their physical storage simplifies the conceptual design of a relational database system for the MPP.

DATABASE FUNCTIONS

This section describes implementation of selected database functions in the MPP and provides a performance comparison with an abstract conventional uniprocessor. Processing operations on data in primary memory are considered, as well as treatment of larger databases using the memory hierarchy.

Some assumptions are made in order to provide a basis for performance comparisons. Both the MPP and the uniprocessor are assumed to have the same execution cycle time. In the MPP an execution cycle is a bit level operation in each PE. In the conventional machine it is a word level operation, regardless of the word length. The second assumption is that primary memory available for data storage is equivalent in each machine. That is, the conventional machine has two megabytes of primary memory in addition to that used for the operating system and programs. This amount is necessary to match the minimum MPP configuration.

QUERIES

Implementation and performance of queries on a database resident within PE array memory is considered first. At the design limit of 64K bits per PE, memory capacity exceeds a billion bits. Although a few bit planes may be reserved for system use, none of the space is used for program storage.

Finding tuples that satisfy a query corresponds to the "select" operation in relational terms [5]. The horizontal subset of the original relation that results from a select operation will be indicated by a flag bit in each PE. Further processing could involve retrieving information from selected tuples, counting selected tuples, creating new relations, etc.

SINGLE RELATION QUERIES. A query on a single attribute of one relation is the simplest query. It is implemented as a comparison between a single comparand and the attribute field of all tuples. Tuples with attributes that satisfy the search criterion are indicated by setting a flag bit in PE memory. The operation is a comparison of a scalar value with all elements of a vector. The MPP design supports this operation as a single instruction. Using the database from figure 1, suppose the query is to find all suppliers in London. The single instruction to achieve this is:

EQSA,S   'LONDON',S.SCITY,RESULT

The instruction will perform an equality comparison between a scalar and an array in PE's enabled by the flag bit symbolically labeled S. Flag bit S identifies PE's holding the supplier relation. The scalar value is 'LONDON'. The vector is the field in memory defined for attribute field SCITY in relation S. PE's with tuples satisfying the search will set the bit called RESULT.

At the microprogram level in the array, the instruction is a loop whose iteration count depends on attribute field bit length. Response time is proportional to this field length, but independent of the number of tuples. In a conventional uniprocessor, the processing also involves looping. Since comparisons would occur sequentially, the iteration count is dependent on the number of tuples. That is, uniprocessor response time is proportional to the number of tuples but independent of attribute field length. These notions of performance hold when the relation fits in primary memory of the MPP with one PE per tuple, and in the uniprocessor with one word per attribute field.

Based on items that determine query response time, a first order performance evaluation suggests that the MPP will be faster than the uniprocessor whenever the number of tuples in a relation exceeds the number of bits in the attribute field. Figure 2 is a graph of relative query timing for a 32 bit attribute field. It shows the performance difference resulting from increasing parallelism as the number of tuples increases.

Logical combinations of single attribute queries can be achieved in the MPP by logical operations between bit plane results of individual queries. Response time is proportional to the total field length of all attributes queried plus the number of logical operations. In a uniprocessor, a sequence of queries is also carried out. While the first query must examine the appropriate attribute in all tuples, the second attribute need be examined only in tuples where the first search was successful. Additional attributes need to be searched only on remaining candidate responders. Response time for the uniprocessor is proportional to the total number of tuples plus the numbers which satisfy subsequent searches.

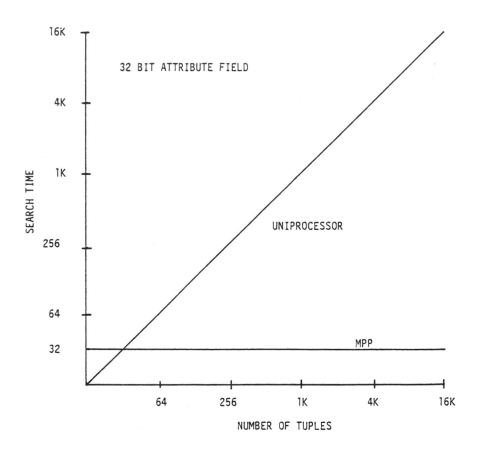

FIGURE 2. SIMPLE QUERY TIMING COMPARISON

Another type of query, involving multiple attribute fields within a relation, is the comparison between pairs of attributes. This can be characterized as a comparison of corresponding elements of two single dimensional arrays. An MPP application program needs just one instruction to carry out an array to array search, with execution time proportional to the field lengths.

MULTIPLE RELATION QUERIES. Queries mentioned above were limited to a single relation. Responses could be completely determined from information in the relation. Database queries typically need to be able to combine information from several relations in operations such as union, intersection, and join. These are more complicated queries for both the MPP and uniprocessors.

The join is illustrated with an example taken from the database in figure 1. Suppose the query is to find all suppliers of bolts. The supplier relation, S, does not specify what is supplied. The parts relation, P, does not identify the supplier of each part. The relation SP associates supplier and part numbers but does not give the type of parts being supplied. An outline of a method used in the MPP to satisfy the query, that is, find all suppliers of bolts, is given here.

```
Search P.Pname for 'BOLT', flagging all responders.
While responders remain do:
        Retrieve one responder's P.P# and reset its flag.
        Search SP.P# for the retrieved P.P# value.
        Logically OR responders into a result bit plane.
End.
```

In the method above, both parallel and sequential operations are used. The first search is in parallel over all parts in order to find the part numbers of bolts. The loop takes one part number at a time and searches relation SP in parallel to find tuples with that part number. These tuples identify suppliers of bolts. Flags are set to mark responding tuples. Iterations of the loop occur sequentially. Resolving responders and retrieving one can be done with a minimum value search on P.P# and some scalar operations.

A very similar method can be used in a uniprocessor. It is necessary to sequentially search all tuples of P.PNAME for 'BOLT', followed by a search of SP for each tuple representing a bolt.

An abstraction of the two methods to achieve a "join" is given in figure 3. Symbols R, r, and n refer to relations, the number of tuples in a relation, and the number of bits in an attribute field, respectively. Numbers 1 and 2, when used with R or r, distinguish the two relations involved in the operation; when used with n they refer to attribute field lengths, in bits. Timing is indicated as being proportional to field lengths or to the number of tuples. Expressions for timing of a join operation are as follows:

MPP: $n1 + (n1 + n2) *$ (number of responders from R1)

Uniprocessor: $r1 + r2 *$ (number of responders from R1)

For large databases, r will certainly be much greater than n, yielding a longer "join" time for the uniprocessor.

METHOD	ACTION	TIMING	
MPP:	Search relation R1	O(n1)	
	Min search on R1	O(n1)	For each
	Scalar operations	minimal	responder
	Search R2	O(n2)	from R1
Uniprocessor:	Search relation R1	O(r1)	
	Scalar operations	minimal	For each
	Search R2	O(r2)	responder
			from R1

FIGURE 3. THE "JOIN" OPERATION

RESULT RETRIEVAL

Ultimately it will be necessary to retrieve results of queries. When an attribute value from a relatively large number of tuples must be output, an I/O bit plane provides a parallel, high bandwidth path. The plane consists of the S register bit from each PE, as shown in array unit hardware diagrams later in this book.

Output of attribute values is done in bit serial, word parallel fashion. The method is to move one bit of the attribute from each selected tuple out of the PE array in parallel, then iterate the process through all bits of the attribute. Output of one bit plane requires a PE memory access to load the I/O plane, followed by right shifting out of the array. The shift count depends on the position of selected tuples in the array. If all selected tuples are in the rightmost column, a single shift completes the output. In the worst case, a selected tuple may be located in the leftmost column, requiring

128 position shift. Output time, at 100 nanoseconds per shift,
is thus based on the column position of tuples selected for
output as well as the number of bits in the field. Figure 4 is
an output timing graph which shows the effects of column position and field length, n.

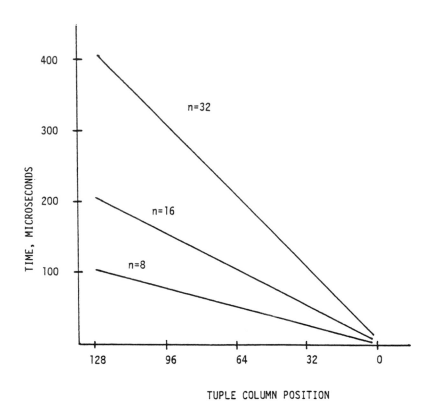

FIGURE 4: ATTRIBUTE OUTPUT TIMING

Using the I/O plane method, output time is independent of the number of selected tuples in the columns being output. Output of an n-bit attribute from one tuple can take as long as 12.9 n microseconds, based on one memory access and 128 shifts, all at a 100 nsec rate. However, many more attribute values could be output in the same time. An effective output rate can be determined as a function of the percentage of tuples selected.   Figure 5 shows the effective rate under the assumption that result attributes are distributed over all PE columns, requiring a full 128 position shift. The figure shows that the effective 32 bit attribute output time is about 800 nanoseconds when 3% of all tuples are selected.

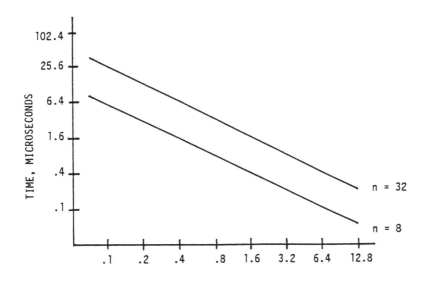

SELECTED ITEMS, % OF TOTAL

FIGURE 5: EFFECTIVE ATTRIBUTE OUTPUT TIMING

UPDATE OPERATIONS

Databases are dynamic. The capability to change information in a database by adding new information, removing that
which is no longer needed, and changing existing information is
necessary. This section is concerned with the dynamic nature
of a database from the viewpoints of managing relational data
structures and modifying their content.

Increasing the size of a relation by inserting tuples is a
straightforward process in the MPP. The definition of a relation is a set of tuples, with no implied order among set
members. Query processing also does not depend on an ordering.
Again, the user's logical view of a relation matches the MPP
architecture. A tuple can be inserted by simply appending it
to the existing relation and setting a flag bit to indicate PEs
storing tuples belonging to a given relation. If the number of
relations, R, is large it may be better to assign an address
using $\log(R)$ bits rather than R individual flags. The penalty
is that identification time is $O(\log R)$ instead of $O(1)$.

Since either flags or addresses can identify tuples
belonging to a particular relation, it is not necessary for a
relation to be stored in contiguous PEs. Tuples to be deleted
need only to have their identifying bits reset. Tuples to be
inserted can use any available PE with no consideration of ordering. That is, they can fill PEs that have had tuples
deleted, without applying any special compression routines.

Parallelism, as discussed for query processing, can also be used for modifying attributes of tuples. The MPP is capable of performing arithmetic and logical operations on data in all enabled PEs in parallel. Modification of an attribute field by a single value is similar to a simple query. It is a scalar-to-array operation. Timing relationships are similar to the query case with MPP timing proportional to the field length and uniprocessor timing proportional to the number of tuples to be modified. Functional operations between fields in a relation are implemented as array-to-array operations. Corresponding elements in each array are functionally combined for all tuples simultaneously. The processing is bit serial but tuple parallel.

VERY LARGE DATABASES

Prior sections have considered primary memory resident databases. For larger databases, I/O involved in moving the database between secondary memory and the PE array must be considered. Movement of large amounts of data will be via the high bandwidth, S register I/O plane.

In the MPP, processing and I/O can be almost totally overlapped in time. Processing uses data paths that are independent of those used for I/O. When the staging memory is operating at its normal transfer rate of 100 nsec per 128 bit column of data, a 128 by 128 bit plane can be input in 12.9 microseconds. The time is based on 128 shifts and one memory write, each taking 100 nsec. For an n bit field the input time is 12.9 n microseconds. This time holds for any number of tuples up to the 16K PE array size. For more than 16K the input process must be repeated once for each integral multiple of 16K. Thus MPP input time for a set of r tuples of length n bits is:

t(MPP) = 12.9(n)(ceiling (r/16384)) microseconds

To arrive at a performance evaluation, input time for a uniprocessor is comparably defined. Assume input occurs at a 100 nsec rate for each 32 bit item. Input time for an r tuple relation with tuple lengths up to 32 bits is 100 r nsec. For lengths greater than 32 bits, the input process must be repeated. Thus uniprocessor input time for r tuples of length n bits is:

t(uniprocessor) = 0.1(r)(ceiling (n/32)) microseconds

Figure 6 is a graph of input timing under the assumptions given. Since the graph uses the number of tuples as the independent axis, it shows discrete changes in MPP timing at 16K steps. If the graph was against field length, n, the uniprocessor plots would be for a specific length and would show discrete changes at 32 bit steps.

In figure 6 it can be seen that MPP input performance, relative to the uniprocessor, improves as the number of tuples increases. The break even point is near 4000 tuples for 32 bit items. If the time equations for both machines are equated, values of r and n that that satisfy the equation can be plotted. The graph, plotted in figure 7, divides the space into a

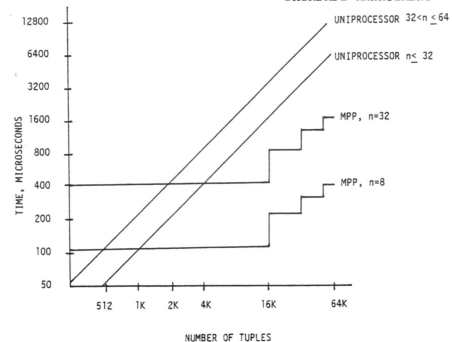

FIGURE 6:   INPUT TIMING COMPARISON

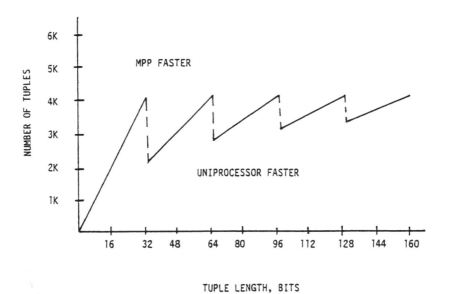

FIGURE 7:   INPUT TIMING BREAKEVEN DIMENSIONS

lower part where the uniprocessor is faster and a higher part where the MPP is faster. The figure shows that MPP input is faster than uniprocessor input, regardless of tuple length, when the number of tuples exceeds 4128. MPP input performance is well suited to large relations.

Emphasis in this section has been on input data movement. Due to staging memory and I/O plane design, output can occur at the same time as input. The only difference from a pure input process is that one memory access is used to load the I/O plane with output data prior to shifting in new data. Right shifting the S register to input data from the left simultaneously outputs data on the right. The additional memory access used for output adds 100 nsec to the total I/O time. That is, one bit plane can be output and a different plane input in a total time of 13.0 microseconds.

FINAL COMMENTS

The MPP may have certain advantages over a high performance conventional uniprocessor for relational database query and update operations. Parallelism in the architecture is useful in achieving high speed processing and I/O rates as needed for this application. The primary data memory organization is well suited for tabular data structures, as used in relational systems. The close correspondence of the database implementer's logical view with the machine's physical structure will simplify database system design and software development.

REFERENCES

[1]. R. Moulder, "An Implementation of a Data Management System on an Associative Processor," AFIPS PROCEEDINGS OF THE NATIONAL COMPUTER CONFERENCE, Vol. 42, 1973, pp. 171-176.

[2]. E. A. Ozkarahan, S. A. Schuster, and K. C. Sevcik, "Performance Evaluation of a Relational Associative Processor," ACM TRANSACTIONS ON DATABASE SYSTEMS, Vol. 2, June 1977, pp. 175-195.

[3]. G. T. Capraro and P. B. Berra, "A DATA BASE MANAGEMENT MODELING TECHNIQUE AND SPECIAL FUNCTION HARDWARE ARCHITECTURE," Rome Air Development Center, Griffiss AFB, New York, TR-79-14, January 1979.

[4]. E. Babb, "Implementing a Relational Database by Means of Specialized Hardware," ACM TRANSACTIONS ON DATABASE SYSTEMS, Vol. 4, March 1979, pp. 1-29.

[5]. C. J. Date, AN INTRODUCTION TO DATABASE SYSTEMS (3rd ed.), Addison-Wesley, 1981.

[6]. J. Banerjee, D. K. Hsiao, and R. I. Baum, "Concepts and Capabilities of a Database Computer," ACM TRANSACTIONS ON DATABASE SYSTEMS, Vol. 3, December 1978, pp. 347-384.

[7]. D. J. DeWitt, "DIRECT- A Multiprocessor Organization for Supporting Relational Database Management Systems," IEEE TRANSACTIONS ON COMPUTERS, Vol. 28, June 1979, pp. 395-406.

[8]. D. E. Shaw, "THE NON-VON SUPERCOMPUTER," Department of Computer Science, Columbia University, August 1982.

LIST BASED PROCESSING ON THE MPP

Jerry L. Potter
Mathematical Sciences Department
Kent State University
Kent, Ohio 44242

Introduction -- The Massively Parallel Processor (MPP) is a Single Instruction Multiple Data (SIMD) type of computer with 16,384 processing elements. This type of computer has been studied extensively for computationally intensive applications such as image processing. In these applications the MPP is customarily used as a hardware DO LOOP. That is, in one pass through the algorithm, 16,384 results are calculated in parallel instead of just one.

There are many non-numerical computationally intensive tasks in data base management and artificial intelligence which could also benefit from the MPP's computer power. This chapter describes how the MPP can be used for searching list based data bases used in many AI applications.

BACKGROUND

One reason for the wide spread use of list based languages such as LISP is that they facilitate the development of sophisticated pattern matching algorithms used for searching grammars, production rules, and data bases. Unfortunately, programs written using lists for data structures and program control tend to result in slow program execution. If Lisp and similar languages using lists are to be used in practical applications with non-trivial data bases and for extended periods of time, the speed of execution of programs written in these languages must be improved.

Several research efforts have concentrated on developing special computers which would allow "real time" list processing. Most projects which attempt to improve the speed of execution of LISP programs are based on traditional sequential architectures. Greenblatt's [5] LISP Machine is essentially a traditional general purpose computer with special purpose microcode customized for LISP and list processing. Baker's [2] design depends on a specialized instruction set for linked list processing. Bonar's [4] approach uses content addressable memories for real time lisp execution. His implementation is essentially a linked list data structure developed for conventional sequential architectures implemented in content addressable memories.

This chapter describes an alternative implementation of list data structures which take advantage of the MPP's SIMD parallelism. The implementation not only allows simple list operations such as CAR, CDR and CONS but pattern matching operations to be executed in parallel.

LINKED LIST STORAGE

The tree representation of the list (A B (C D)) is shown in Figure 1. Figure 2 shows a typical linked list implementation. See Weissman [8] for more details on implementing lists for LISP.

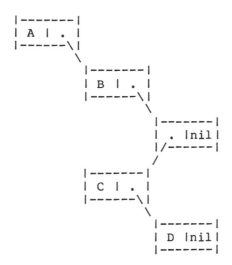

Figure 1 - Tree Representation of (A B (C D))

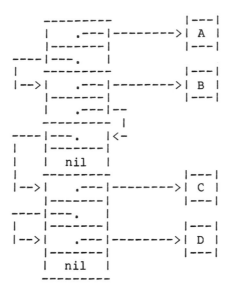

Figure 2 - Linked List Implementation of (A B (C D))

CAR and CDR are two basic functions in Lisp. They allow the programmer to traverse trees or equivalently to extract sublists from lists. CAR is the instruction to traverse down the tree to the left sibling of a node.   In list notation the result is the sublist produced by extracting the left most element of the list. CDR causes a traverse down the tree to the right sibling.   The sublist produced by a CDR is composed of the remainder of the list after the first element has been extracted. Thus the CAR of the list (A B (C D)) is A.   While the CDR is (B (C D)). CAR and CDR functions are frequently applied sequentially. The sequence is abbreviated by writing simply A or D in sequence to represent CAR or CDR (Execution is inside out or right to left.) and then adding a single C and R as in CADDAR.   CONS (construction) is the inverse of CAR.   It inserts a new element at the beginning of a list.   Thus the CONS of A and (B (C D)) is (A B (C D)).

LIST STORAGE

Linked list storage techniques require that sequences of CAR and CDR functions (henceforth called CDAR functions) be executed. The data representation shown in Figure 3 enables CDAR functions to be executed in parallel allowing direct parallel searching for any list or sublist. With this representation, all CDAR functions can be executed in real time. (Real time is when each elementary operation is bounded by a constant independent of the number of list cells in use Baker[2].)

Let 0=CAR, 1=CDR, left justify with 1 fill, then
L = (A B (C D)) can be stored as:

```
       LIST    CDAR
       NAME    CODE     ATOM
       --------------------
      | L  | 01111111 | A |
      |------------------|
      | L  | 10111111 | B |
      |------------------|
      | L  | 11001111 | C |
      |------------------|
      | L  | 11010111 | D |
      |------------------|
```

Figure 3 - CDAR Encoding

The code illustrated in Figure 3 is designed such that numeric range searches can be used to search for sublists. Thus if the list (A B (C D)) is to be processed by the function CADDR, the function sequence is first converted into the CDAR code 110 (The order of code application is from left to right). Then, the lower bound of the search is obtained by adding zero fill, the upper bound by adding one fill. Thus in this example, the CADDR of the list shown in Figure 3 is obtained by selecting all elements greater than or equal to 11000000 and less than or equal to 11011111. These elements, C and D, form the sublist (C D) (See Potter [6] for additional details on storing lists in SIMD computers). The CAR and CDR functions are of course, special cases of the more general CDAR function.

The CONS function is also easy to implement using the CDAR codes. If the list L1 = (B (C D)) is stored in the MPP's array memory as shown in Figure 4a, and the atom A is to be CONSed to it, the process is simply one of appending a zero to the front (left) of the CDAR code for A, appending a 1 to the front of the codes for L1, and changing the list name of L1 (See Figure 4b). If a new list is being generated, the elements of L1 and L2 would be copied before modification and both list names would be changed.

LIST NAME	CDAR CODE	ATOM
|L1|	01111111	B
|L1|	10011111	C
|L1|	10101111	D
|L2|	11111111	A

LIST NAME	CDAR CODE	ATOM
|L1|	01111111	A
|L1|	10111111	B
|L1|	11001111	C
|L1|	11010111	D

a - Lists (B (C D)) and A   b - List (A B (C D))

Figure 4 - Effects of CONS

The next atom in a list can be found simply by searching for the next largest code number. In the MPP this is done by restricting the minimum function to the responses of a search for all codes larger than the current atom code and with the same list name. Note that the data elements consisting of the list name, CDAR code and atom can be stored in any order and at any location in the array. Elements from the same list do not need to be stored contiguously.

Figure 5 is a PDL representation of the algorithm for generating the CDAR code for a list from the conventional Lisp list input. For simplicity, it is assumed that the input string has been scanned and the items have been broken out and stored in the array memory field ITEM in a manner such that index I will reference them in the proper order. (See "Programming the MPP" elsewhere in this book for background information on the PDL.)

```
PROCEDURE SCAN
TYPE
      CDARRECORD = RECORD
            CDARCODE: CODETYPE
            ATOM: ATOMTYPE
            LISTNAME: NAMETYPE
            END
VAR
CDARMEMORY: ARRAY[1..m] OF CDARRECORD
NODECT:  ARRAY[1..n]  OF INTEGER (* NODE COUNT AT EACH LEVEL *)
(*                                                       *)
(*  RIGHTSHIFT SHIFTS THE SECOND ARGUMENT RIGHT          *)
(*  ONE BIT AND SHIFTS THE FIRST ARGUMENT INTO           *)
(*  THE LEFT MOST BIT                                    *)
(*                                                       *)

FUNCTION GENERATE
CONST
      ACODE = 0
      DCODE = 1
BEGIN (* GENERATE *)
GENERATE := 11111111 (* SET GENERATE TO ALL ONES *)
DO K := LEVEL TO 1
  GENERATE := RIGHTSHIFT(ACODE,GENERATE)
  DO L := NODECT(K) TO 1
    GENERATE := RIGHTSHIFT(DCODE,GENERATE)
  ENDDO
ENDDO
END (* GENERATE *)
(*

BEGIN  (* SCAN *)
LEVEL := 0
J := 1
DO I = 1 TO ENDI
  CASE ITEM(I) OF
  LEFTP:
      LEVEL := LEVEL + 1
      NODECT(LEVEL) := 0
  ATOM:
      CDARCODE(J) := GENERATE
      ATOM(J) := ITEM(I)
      LISTNAME(J) := NAME
      J := J + 1
      NODECT(LEVEL) := NODECT(LEVEL) + 1
  RIGHTP:
      CDARCODE(J) := GENERATE
      ATOM(J) := NIL
      J := J + 1
      LEVEL := LEVEL - 1
      NODECT(LEVEL) := NODECT(LEVEL) + 1
  ENDDO
END. (* SCAN *)
```

Figure 5 - CDAR Code Generation Algorithm

The algorithm contains a scan and a generate procedure. The scan procedure identifies the next item in the list. If the item is a left parenthesis, the level of the tree is incremented by one and the number of nodes on that level is initialized to zero. If the item is an atom, the appropriate CDAR code is generated and associated with the atom. After the code and atom have been associated, the count of the nodes on the current level is incremented. If the item is a right parenthesis, the level count is decremented and the number of nodes on the lower level is incremented.

The effect of the CDAR code generation function is to generate a string of code for each sublist in the list. The code consists of a one for each atom in a sublist terminated on the right with a zero. The codes for the sublists are concatenated from right to left with one fill on the right.

LIST SEARCH

The previous section described how list structures can be built and "parsed" using CDAR codes. The list name and CDAR code uniquely identify every atom in the data base. That is, the list name identifies the list and the CDAR code identifies the position of the atom in the list. The CDAR code is unique since it encodes the sequence of CAR's and CDR's needed to extract the atom from the list. The uniqueness property of the CDAR encoding technique allows it to be used for list searching and pattern matching.

SEARCH BY ATOM. Search by atom is the simplest type of search. In this type of search, the sequential controller broadcasts the name of the atom to the PEs.   The PEs search the atom field of their respective memories for an exact match.   If one or more matching atoms are found, the corresponding CDAR codes and list names can be retrieved.

SEARCH BY STRUCTURE.   Since the CDAR code preserves the structure of the list, the list can also be searched by structure.   That is, it is possible to search for the atom or sublist that exists in a given list position.   Since an atom is a single entity, its position can be described by a single CDAR code.   However, a sublist can be any arbitrary sequence of atoms and sublists, thus its position must be delineated by a set of lower and upper CDAR code bounds.

It is important to realize that the lower and upper bounds required to delineate a sublist in a list only describe the list position itself.   They do not in any way describe the structure of the sublist.   For example in Figure 6, the bounds 10000000 and 10111111 identify the second position of the lists and delineates both the sublists (B) and (B (C)).

ATOM	CDAR CODE	ATOM	CDAR CODE
A	01111111	A	01111111
B	10011111	B	10011111
C	11011111	C	10100111
D	11101111	D	11011111

(A (B) C D)   (A (B (C)) D)

Figure 6 - List Position

The bounds can be manipulated to delineate successive list positions. For example, the bounds 10000000 and 10111111 can be modified by adding a one on the left and deleting a one on the right to produce 11000000 and 11011111 which delineates the 3rd position of a list. The sequence of bounds shown in Figure 7 delineate the second position of the top level list, the second position of the list nested at the second position of the top level and the second position of the list nested at the second position of the list nested at the second position of the top level.

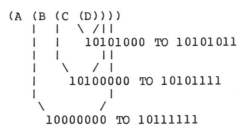

```
(A (B (C (D))))
 |  |   \ /||
 |  |    10101000 TO 10101011
 |  |       ||
 |   \   /  |
 |    10100000 TO 10101111
 |           |
  \         /
  10000000 TO 10111111
```

Figure 7 - Nested Lists

The CDAR codes for the bounds illustrated above can be broken into three portions, the initial or left portion, the central or pattern portion and the fill or right portion. To generate the sequence of bounds that selects positions in a list, the initial portion is set to nil, the central portion is set to the pattern for CAR (zero) and the fill portion is set to zeroes for the lower bound and ones for the upper bound. If the length of the CDAR code is m and the length of the pattern is n, then the initial length of the fill portion is m-n and m-n+1 different bounds can be generated as follows:

```
INITIAL = ""
PATTERN = "0"
LOWFILL = "00000000"
HIFILL  = "11111111"
FOR I = 1 TO m-n+1
LOWER(I) = TRUNCATE(INITIAL+PATTERN+LOWFILL,m)
UPPER(I) = TRUNCATE(INITIAL+PATTERN+HIFILL,m)
INITIAL = INITIAL+"1"
ENDFOR.
```

The sequence of limits in Figure 7 is generated by repeating the pattern for selecting the second element of a list (10 for CADR) from one to [m/n] times as follows:

```
INITIAL = ""
PATTERN = "10"
LOWFILL = "00000000"
HIFILL  = "11111111"
FOR I = 1 TO [m/n]
LOWER(I) = TRUNCATE(INITIAL+PATTERN+LOWFILL,m)
UPPER(I) = TRUNCATE(INITIAL+PATTERN+HIFILL,m)
INITIAL = INITIAL+PATTERN
ENDFOR.
```

UNANCHORED SEARCHES. When a pattern is to be tried in all positions as described above, it is said to be an unanchored search. Unanchored searches can be quite complex and time consuming if all positions of all possible sublists are to be searched. See Potter [7] for a more complete discussion of unanchored searches.

ANCHORED SEARCHES. Frequently it is desirable to anchor the search pattern to a fixed position in the input. Searches can be anchored by list structure and/or atom matches. Thus a search by atom is a trivial anchored search. That is, the search is completed as soon as the anchor is found. If a complex search contains constants, they can be used to anchor the pattern reducing the number of combinations that need to be processed for the remainder of the search. To anchor a search by list structure, the structure is encoded as a CDAR pattern and used as the left or initial portion of the lower and upper bounds. Complex search combinations can be generated, as for example, if a searched is to be anchored not to the top level list structure but to an embedded list structure.

MATCH OPERATORS. Match operators are required to allow the user to generate useful match patterns. Two of the most useful match operators are ? and *. The ? operator will match any single atom or sublist. The * operator will match any number of atoms and/or sublists. Frequently, it is desirable to save the atoms and sublists matched by an operator in a variable. This is denoted by appending a variable name to the operator, as in ?A or *A.

PATTERN MATCHING. The algorithm to match a pattern with operators consists of:

1) Using constants and search by name to anchor the pattern,

2) Using the anchor bounds found in 1) to generate the remaining bounds in the pattern,

3) Searching the list for bound matches, and

4) Verifying the match requirements.

As an example of pattern matching, assume that the sentence:

The big green pyramid is on the red block.

is to be processed.   The sentence is first preprocessed to
determine the parts of speech and is put in list form, resulting
in:

((det the) (adj big) (adj green) (noun pyramid) (verb is)

(prep on) (det the) (adj red) (noun block)).

Figure 8 shows the CDAR form of this list.   Simple noun   phrases
can be found by the pattern shown in Figure 9.

ATOM	CDAR CODE	ATOM	CDAR CODE
DET	001111111111	IS	111101011111
THE	010111111111	PRED	111110011111
ADJ	100111111111	ON	111110101111
BIG	101011111111	DET	111111001111
ADJ	110111111111	THE	111111010111
GREEN	110101111111	ADJ	111111100111
NOUN	111001111111	RED	111111101011
PYRAMID	111010111111	NOUN	111111110011
VERB	111100111111	BLOCK	111111110101

Figure 8 - CDAR Storage

ATOM	CDAR CODE
DET	001111111111
?A	010111111111
*B	101111111111
NOUN	110011111111
?C	110101111111

((DET ?A) *B (NOUN ?C))

Figure 9 - Simple Noun Phrase Pattern

The   first   step   of   the algorithm is   to   search   for   the
constants DET and NOUN to anchor the pattern.   A search by atom
with   DET   results   in   anchoring   DET   to   001111111111   and
111111001111.   A search by atom with NOUN results in anchoring
NOUN to 111001111111 and 111111110011.

In step 2 of the algorithm, the bounds for all operators are generated from the anchor values. The operator bounds are generated on the basis of their position in the pattern. The anchor's pattern code is simply replaced by the operator's pattern code (i.e. 00 for DET is replaced by 010 for A?) with zero fill for the lower bound and one fill for the upper bound, as below:

	FIRST ?A MATCH BOUNDS	SECOND ?A MATCH BOUNDS
LOWER	010000000000	111111010000
UPPER	010111111111	111111010111

Similarly substituting 1100 for NOUN with 11010 for ?C produces:

	FIRST ?C MATCH BOUNDS	SECOND ?C MATCH BOUNDS
LOWER	111010000000	111111110100
UPPER	111010111111	111111110101

The bounds for *B are determined by the bounds of the elements which surround it in the pattern (i.e. ?A and NOUN). Thus

    LOWER *B = UPPER ?A + 1 and
    UPPER *B = ANCHOR NOUN - 1.

Since there are two sets of bounds for each of ?A and NOUN, there are four sets of bounds for *B and the pattern as a whole.

	?A BOUNDS	*B BOUNDS	NOUN ANCHOR
LOWER	010000000000	011000000000	111001111111
UPPER	010111111111	111001111110	
LOWER	010000000000	011000000000	111111110011
UPPER	010111111111	111111110010	
LOWER	111111010000	111111011000	111111110011
UPPER	111111010111	111111110010	
LOWER	111111010000	111111011000	111001111111
UPPER	111111010111	111001111110	

The last set of bounds is impossible in that ?A would have to match an element to the right of NOUN, but all other combinations are legal.

The third step is to search the list for the matches, resulting in the three sets of bindings shown below:

```
A :: THE
B :: (ADJ BIG) (ADJ GREEN)
C :: PYRAMID

A :: THE
B :: (ADJ BIG) (ADJ GREEN) (NOUN PYRAMID) (VERB IS)
     (PREP ON) (DET THE) (ADJ RED)
C :: BLOCK

A :: THE
B :: (ADJ RED)
C :: BLOCK
```

The last step of the algorithm is to check that each ? operator (i.e. A and C) matched one and only one atom or sublist. All three sets of bindings meet this requirement.

The semantic meaning of these pattern matches will require additional analysis. However, their syntax as determined by the pattern for NOUN PHRASE is correct.

CONCLUSION

Preliminary analysis of the CDAR encoding technique implies that for the specific case of 2000 lists with 4 atoms and two levels of structure each, assuming that one fourth of the lists partially match, at least a 64 to 1 speed up in pattern match searching is possible. It is important to realize that this time savings estimate is only a snapshot for a single instance of a single pattern match, and that in general, this savings can be magnified significantly since in many pattern matching applications all lists in a set must be matched against all other lists in the set resulting in exponentially increasing search times as the size of the sets increase. In SIMD parallel computers such as the MPP, search times in these instances tend to only increase linearly since n+1 lists can be searched in the same amount of time as n lists. In worst case situations, time may increase exponentially, but with a much smaller exponent than in sequential systems.

While this chapter has concentrated on lists as they would be used in a LISP implementation, it is important to remember that these fundamental list storage and matching techniques are applicable to all areas of computer science where data searching and retrieval are important such as in Natural Language Processing, Information Storage and Retrieval, and Rule Based Production Systems. Moreover, direct implementation of pattern matching in such applications as a high level language such as PROLOG is straight forward and easy to implement efficiently in the MPP.

REFERENCES

[1]. Aho, A. V. and M. J. Corasick, "Efficient String Matching: An Aid to Bibliographic Search," COMMUNICATIONS OF THE ACM, 18, 1975, pp. 333-340.

[2]. Baker, Henry G.,"List Processing in Real Time on a Serial Computer," COMMUNICATIONS OF THE ACM, April, 1978, pp. 280-294.

[3]. Bobrow, Daniel G. and Douglas W. Clark, "Compact Encodings of List Structure," ACM TRANSACTIONS ON PROGRAMMING LANGUAGES AND SYSTEMS, October, 1979, pp. 266-703.

[4]. Bonar, Jeffrey G. and Steven P. Levitan, "Real-time LISP Using Content Addressable Memory," IEEE, 1981, pp. 112-

117.

[5]. Greenblatt, R. THE LISP MACHINE, Working Paper 79, MIT
      Artif Intell Lab, Cambridge, Mass., Nov., 1974.

[6]. Potter, J. L., "Alternative Data Structures for Associative
      Devices," PROCEEDINGS OF THE INTERNATIONAL CONFERENCE ON
      PARALLEL PROCESSING, August 1983.

[7]. Potter, J. L., "Disparity Based Scene Analysis," in
      Proceedings of the 1983 NATO ASI on Computer Architecures
      for Spatially Distributed Data, Cetraro, Italy.

[8]. Weissman, C., "Lisp 1.5 Primer," Dickenson Publishing
      Company, Inc., Belmont, California, 1967.

PART II

HARDWARE

THE MASSIVELY PARALLEL PROCESSOR SYSTEM OVERVIEW

Kenneth E. Batcher
Digital Technology Department
Goodyear Aerospace Corporation
Akron, Ohio 44315

Introduction -- The Massively Parallel Processor (MPP) was developed by Goodyear Aerospace Corporation for NASA Goddard Space Flight Center under contract NAS5-25942. The MPP is a high speed digital processor designed to solve two-dimensional data processing problems such as those encountered in the processing of satellite imagery. It is flexible and programmable to handle a large range of problems with a wide variety of data formats.

To handle two-dimensional data processing problems at high speed the array unit of the MPP is organized with a number of 16384-element planes (conventional computers are organized with a number of words with only 64 or less bits per word). Each plane is a square with 128 rows and 128 columns. Instructions operate on a whole plane of data in parallel.

The array unit can treat data of arbitrary precision. Black-white images are stored and processed as arrays of single-bit picture elements (pixels), images with 256 grey levels are stored and processed as arrays of 8-bit pixels, etc. Each band of a multi-spectral image can be given its own pixel length independent of the other bands. Arrays of floating-point data can also be stored and processed. The precision of intermediate and final results can be adjusted to fit the range

of expected values.   An array of 16,384 pixels with N bits per
pixel is stored on N planes of the array unit.

Since   planes   of data   are   treated   in   parallel   the
MPP   has   a very high processing rate   as   can   be   seen   from
the   following   table   of   addition,   subtraction,   and
multiplication speeds:

```
+--------------------------------------++-----------------+
|                                      ||                 |
|               Operation              || Processing Speed |
|                                      ||     (MOPS)      |
+======================================++=================+
|   Addition or subtraction:           ||                 |
|      8-bit fixed-point (9-bit result) ||      6553       |
|     12-bit fixed-point (13-bit result) ||      4428       |
|     16-bit fixed-point (17-bit result) ||      3343       |
|        32-bit floating-point          ||       470       |
+--------------------------------------++-----------------+
|   Multiplication:                    ||                 |
|      8-bit fixed-point (16-bit result) ||      1861       |
|     12-bit fixed-point (24-bit result) ||       910       |
|     16-bit fixed-point (32-bit result) ||       538       |
|        32-bit floating-point          ||       291       |
+--------------------------------------++-----------------+
```
            MOPS = millions of operations per second

SYSTEM OVERVIEW

Figure 1 is a block diagram of the hardware elements of the
MPP.   The   bulk   of the processing power is in   the   Array   Unit
(ARU).   The   ARU is controlled by the Array Control Unit   (ACU).
Items   of   data   are sent to the ARU   and   taken   from   the   ARU
through the Staging Memory.   Users control the MPP from terminals
on a front-end   computer.   A   switch   in   the ACU selects   the
front-end   computer - either the Program and Data Management Unit
(PDMU)   or   the host computer. The PDMU is a Digital   Equipment
Corporation (DEC) PDP-11/34A minicomputer while the host is a DEC

VAX 11/780 computer. Not shown in figure 1 are two external interfaces connected to the ARU.   There are no devices connected to these interfaces at this time.

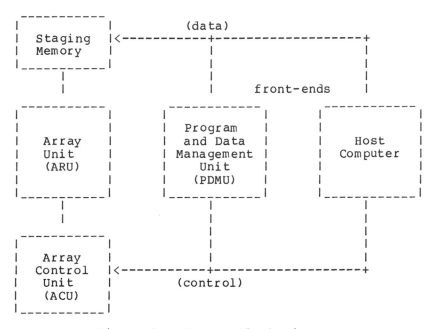

Figure 1.   System Block Diagram

All MPP front-end software is originally written to run on the PDMU. Parts of it will be transported to the host as time goes on. The system software modules used by the application programmers will be transported first - special-purpose software such as hardware diagnostics will be transported last .   Thus,   as the software is transported the usage of the PDMU will decrease and the usage of the host will increase. Eventually,   the host will be in control all of the time except possibly for running hardware diagnostics when faults are discovered.

There are two interfaces between the front-end computer and the MPP: a control interface to the ACU to load MPP programs and execute them, and a data interface to the staging memory.

CONTROL INTERFACE

The control interface allows the front-end computer to load a main application program into main control memory, to load array processing routines into PE control memory, and to initiate execution of the application program in the MCU. The interface also allows users at terminals on the front-end computer to trace execution of the program, dump memories, and perform other tasks necessary to debug the program.

The PE control memory and the main control memory are accessed through a DEC DR-11B direct memory access interface. Access to other hardware in the MPP is through a DEC M1710 Interface Foundation Module.

DR-11B DIRECT MEMORY ACCESS INTERFACE

After it is set up the DR-11B can transfer a block of 16-bit words between the memory of the front-end and either the PE control memory or the main control memory of the MPP. The front-end computer can directly access four registers in the DR-11B: a word count register, a bus address register (holding the address of a buffer in the front-end memory), a status and command register, and a data buffer register.

Another address register holds the address of data in the PE control memory or the main control memory. This register is accessed through the M1710 interface foundation module.

M1710 INTERFACE FOUNDATION MODULE

The M1710 interface foundation module is a DEC-built module that has been customized for use with the MPP. It allows the front-end computer access to various registers in the MPP and allows the MPP to interrupt the front-end computer when a significant event occurs.

IO PAGE REGISTERS. The M1710 module responds to sixteen word addresses in the IO page of the front-end computer. Four of these words relate to the DR-11B interface, another three words relate to the MPP power sequencer, and another two words relate to the mailbox. The other seven words are spare locations.

The IO page words that relate to the DR-11B interface allow the front-end to set up and read the MPP address of DR-11B data, to read the status of the DR-11B, and to see the last byte transferred over the interface.

The three words that relate to the power sequencer allow the front-end to power up the MPP cabinets, to power down the cabinets, and to monitor the status of the MPP power supplies.

The two words that relate to the mailbox are used to access internal registers in the MPP. One word is used as a mailbox address and the other word holds data being transferred to or from the MPP. The MPP registers that are accessible include the MCU, IOCU, and PECU registers. Levels in the call queue are also accessible. The front-end can also send and receive data on the stager command bus (SCB) through the mailbox.

INTERRUPTS.   The   M1710   module   can   send   interrupts   to sixteen   different   interrupt   vectors   in   the   front-end   computer. All   interrupts   occur   at   bus   request   level   5   (BR5).   The interrupts   are   prioritized   within   the   M1710   interface   as follows:

    Power fail/Power on   (highest priority)
    MCU Error
    PECU Error
    IOCU Error
    Staging Memory Error
    Spare
    Spare
    Spare
    Power Sequencer Data Ready
    MCU Call
    MCU Breakpoint
    PECU Breakpoint
    IOCU Programmed Interrupt
    Staging Memory Done
    Performance Monitor Timer Overflow
    Performance Monitor Event Overflow   (lowest priority)

An MPP driver is added to the operating system of the front-end to handle the interrupts and allow user programs in the front-end to communicate with the MPP.

DATA INTERFACE

The   data interface transfers data between the   front-end computer   and   the   staging   memory   in   the   MPP.   The interface to the   PDMU   uses   a DR-11B module.   The   interface   to   the   host computer uses a DR-780 module.

PDMU DATA INTERFACE

A   DR-11B   direct   memory   access   interface   is   used   to transfer data between the staging memory and the PDMU.   This DR-11B module is just like the module   used to   load the MPP control

memories   - after   it   is set up with a word count and   a   start
address of a buffer in the PDMU,   the   module   moves   a block of
words into or out of the staging memory.   Before this transfer
occurs the staging memory control units should have been set   up
through the SCB using the mailbox.

HOST COMPUTER DATA INTERFACE

A   DEC   DR-780   General   Purpose   Interface   is   used   to
transfer data between the staging memory and the host   computer.
The DR-780   interface   is   considerably faster   than   the DR-11B
interface   used in the PDMU - it can transfer data   at   about   6
megabytes per second.   The   DR-780   has   two   interconnects: a
data interconnect and a control interconnect.

The data interconnect is four bytes wide and is connected to
an input port and an output port on the staging memory. A block
of data can be moved over this interconnect either from the host
computer to the staging memory or from   the staging memory   to
the host computer.   The transfer rate is about 6 megabytes per
second.

The   control interconnect is one byte wide and is connected
to   the   SCB.   The DR-780 must compete with the IOCU and   the
M1710 module to be granted access to the SCB.   After   it has
obtained access to the SCB, the staging memory can be set   up
using   the   control   interconnect.   Alternatively,   the host
computer can set up the staging memory through the M1710 module
the same way that the PDMU sets up the staging memory.

SUMMARY

Figure 1 shows the topology of the Massively Parallel Processor. The three major components, the Array Unit (ARU), the Array Control Unit (ACU), and the Staging Memory, are described in separate chapters. The VLSI design of the Array Unit's processing elements are covered in the last chapter of this section.

ARRAY UNIT

Kenneth E. Batcher
Digital Technology Department
Goodyear Aerospace Corporation
Akron, Ohio 44315

Introduction -- The Array Unit (ARU) is designed to handle two-dimensional processing problems so it is organized as a number of two-dimensional planes rather than as a number of words or bytes (see figure 1). Each plane has 128 rows and 128 columns so it can hold 16,384 data bits. Each plane also has 4 spare columns to bypass faulty hardware - the spare columns are not normally used. The four edges of each plane are called the north, east, south, and west edges, respectively. In figure 1 the west edge of any plane is on the left side, the east edge is on the right side, the south edge is out of the page, and the north edge is into the page.

The array unit contains one S-plane, 1024 memory planes, and 35 processing planes, for a total of 1060 planes. A plane of data can be transferred en masse between the S-plane and a memory plane or en masse between a processing plane and a memory plane in one machine cycle. The nominal machine cycle time in the MPP is 100 nanoseconds (10 million machine cycles per second).

As with conventional computers, the ARU can be programmed at different levels. Low-level program modules contain instructions that specify how each data plane is transferred to and from memory, between processing planes, etc. - these modules are analogous to assembly language routines in a conventional

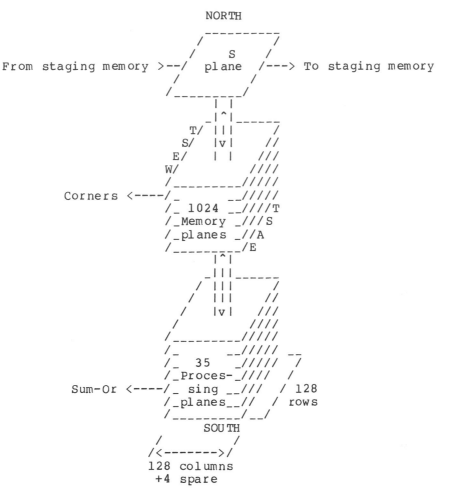

Figure 1 - Array Unit (ARU)

computer.   High-level   programs   contain   instructions   that
specify how memory planes or arrays of memory planes are to be
combined   and   processed - these programs are analogous   to
high-level   language   routines in a conventional computer (e.g.,
FORTRAN). High-level programs make calls to low-level modules to
perform   the   micro-steps of each high-level operation   - the

complexities of S-plane and processing plane manipulations are not programmed in a high-level program. Readers not concerned with the details of low-level programs may want to skip over items S-PLANE and PROCESSING PLANES.

S-PLANE

The S-plane handles data input and output for the ARU. On input it accumulates a plane of data column by column and then transfers the data plane en masse to a memory plane. On output the S-plane receives the contents of a memory plane en masse and then transfers the plane out column by column. The S-plane can handle input and output simultaneously.

A plane of data is moved from the staging memory to the ARU as follows. The staging memory splits the plane up into 128 columns with 128 data bits per column. Each column is sent to the west edge of the S-plane in turn. The east edge of the data plane is transferred first and the west edge of the data plane is transferred last. All data bits in a column are transferred simultaneously. A column is transferred every machine cycle. When the S-plane receives a new data column it shifts all the columns it has accumulated one place to the east and inserts the new column along its west edge. After 128 column transfers the first column received (the east edge of the data plane) will be at the east edge of the S-plane and the last column received (the west edge of the data plane) will be at the west edge of the S-plane. The data plane of 16,384 bits is then transferred en masse to a memory plane in one machine cycle.

A plane of data is moved from the ARU to the staging memory as follows. First a plane of data is moved en masse from a memory plane to the S-plane in one machine cycle. Then the data plane is shifted to the east. Each shift takes one machine cycle. As each column is shifted out at the east edge of the S-plane it is transferred to the staging memory. All 128 data bits in a column are transferred simultaneously in one machine cycle. The first column sent out will be the east edge of the data plane and the last column sent out will be the west edge of the data plane. The staging memory then re-assembles the data plane.

The simultaneous transfer of an input data plane and an output data plane takes place as follows. First the output data plane is moved en masse from a memory plane to the S-plane. Then the output plane is shifted column by column out of the east edge of the S-plane while the input plane is shifted column by column into the west edge of the S-plane. After 128 shifts the complete output data plane has been moved out of the S-plane into the staging memory and the complete input data plane has been moved from the staging memory to the S-plane. The input data plane is then moved en masse from the S-plane to a memory plane in one machine cycle.

The input and output ports of the S-plane are each 128 bits wide and can transfer a column of data every machine cycle for a rate of 1280 megabits per second (160 megabytes per second). When input and output are performed simultaneously the total IO rate is 320 megabytes per second.

Note that while the S-plane is shifting columns of data in and/or out through its ports there is no interference with the memory planes or the processing planes of the ARU. The only interference occurs when the S-plane transfers a data plane en masse to or from a memory plane. It takes one machine cycle to move a data plane en masse to or from a memory plane while it takes 128 machine cycles to shift a data plane column by column through an S-plane port so memory contention occurs less than 1% of the time (less than 2% of the time for simultaneous input and output).

The shifts and en masse data transfers of the S-plane are controlled by the Input-Output Control Unit (IOCU) in the ACU (See Chapter on the ARRAY CONTROL UNIT). Programmers can avoid the complexities of S-plane programming by using the Input-Output instructions in Main Control Language (MCL).

MEMORY PLANES

The ARU has 1024 memory planes. Like every other plane in the array unit, each memory plane has 128 rows and 128 columns so it can store 16,384 data bits. Thus, the 1024 memory planes can store 16,777,216 data bits (over 2 megabytes). Memory planes are given addresses in the range of 0 to 1023. The number of memory planes may be increased at a future date so each memory plane address is 16 bits long to allow up to 65536 memory planes to be addressed.

Any memory plane of 16,384 data bits can be randomly accessed and sent to the S-plane or to one or more processing planes in one machine cycle. A plane of 16,384 data bits can be transferred en masse from the S-plane or a processing plane to any memory plane in one machine cycle.

Each memory plane contains 2048 parity bits in addition to the 16,384 data bits.   A status bit in the array control unit controls parity generation and checking in the ARU memory planes.   If the ACU status bit is set to the 1-state then parity bits are generated whenever a data plane is written into a memory plane and the parity bits are checked whenever a memory plane is read. This will detect most errors in the memory planes.   If the ACU status bit is cleared to the 0-state then parity bits are neither generated nor checked.   Parity generation and checking may increase the read and write cycle times of the memory planes slightly.

Arrays of data are usually stored vertically across several memory planes.   For example, a 128 x 128 two-dimensional array of 16-bit items will be stored in 16 consecutive memory planes. The first memory plane will store the most significant bit of every item while the last memory plane will store the least significant bit of every item.   Such an array will be processed plane by plane rather than item by item as in a conventional computer.   The whole array of 16,384 items can be read from memory and sent to the processing planes in 16 memory cycles (1.6 microseconds).   In a conventional computer a similar array would be read from its memory item by item in 16,384 memory cycles.   It is this ability to access data arrays by planes rather than by items that gives the MPP its large processing power.

To store satellite imagery in the ARU, an image can

be sectioned into sub-images with 128 lines by 128 pixels in each sub-image. If pixels have 256 grey levels, for example, then a sub-image of 8-bit pixels is stored across eight memory planes in the ARU and processed plane by plane. Since this uses only eight of the 1024 planes available, one could store several sub-images in the ARU at one time.

The staging memory can re-format data many different ways (See chapter on the STAGING MEMORY). This gives a user many different choices for data layouts in the ARU memory planes. For example, a 256-line by 256-pixel image can be split vertically and horizontally into four quadrants: upper left, upper right, lower left, and lower right. Each quadrant occupies a set of consecutive memory planes in the ARU. Alternatively, the staging memory can separate even lines from odd lines and even pixels from odd pixels to create the following four arrays: even pixels of even lines, odd pixels of even lines, even pixels of odd lines, and odd pixels of odd lines. Each array occupies a set of consecutive memory planes in the ARU. In either case the same number of memory planes is used. In some cases the first arrangement can be processed faster and in other cases the second arrangement can be processed faster.

Sixteen of the 16,384 data bits in a memory plane are called the corner elements or corners. The 16 corners of a memory plane can be transferred to the ACU. The memory plane is sectioned into 16 sub-planes with each sub-plane containing 32 rows and 32 columns - the corner elements are the data bits located in the southeast corners of the sub-planes (see figure 2).

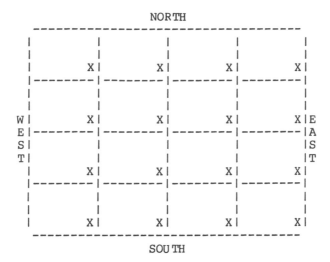

Figure 2.   Corner Elements of a Memory Plane

The   corner   elements   can be used to   help   compute   the
statistics of an array. First the statistics of each 32 X 32 subarray   are   accumulated   and   stored   in   the   corner   elements.
Then   the   ACU reads the sub-array statistics   from   the   corner
elements and computes the statistics of the whole array.

An   MPP   software module (CAD) uses the last   fifty   memory
planes   (planes   974 through   1023)   for element addressing   and
for   temporary storage of processing planes (See the CONTROL   AND
DEBUG MODULE in the chapter on MPP SOFTWARE).   Also certain array
operations   stack   temporary data   planes on a stack starting   at
memory   plane   973 and working down through   memory   planes   972,
971,   etc.   To   minimize the chance of a   conflict,   application
programmers   should   lay out their data arrays at the   beginning
of   ARU   memory   -   memory planes 0, 1, 2, etc.

PROCESSING PLANES

There   are   35   processing planes in the ARU.   Thirty   of the processing planes are in a planar shift register. The other five processing planes are called the G-plane, P-plane, A-plane, B-plane, and C-plane, respectively. Like all other planes in the ARU, each processing plane has 128 rows and 128 columns and holds 16,384 data bits.

Several processing plane operations can be executed simultaneously in one machine cycle time. The processing planes and the operations that can be performed on them are discussed in the following sub-items.

G-PLANE. The G-plane is used to mask activity in the other processing planes. Most of the operations on the other processing planes have two modes: unmasked and masked. When an unmasked operation is performed on a processing plane it is performed on all 16,384 bits of the processing plane. When a masked operation is performed on a processing plane it is only performed on a subset of the processing plane. Where a bit of the G-plane is set to the 1-state, the operation is performed on the corresponding bit of the processing plane. Where a bit of the G-plane is cleared to the 0-state, the corresponding bit of the processing plane is not disturbed.

Activity masking is akin to conditional branching in a conventional computer. As an example, suppose we want to clear all negative items of an array to the zero state and leave the non-negative items undisturbed. With a conventional computer, we would traverse the array item by item. The sign of each item is tested with a conditional branch instruction and if the item is negative we would clear it, otherwise we would leave it undisturbed.   With   the   ARU,   we   transfer   the   sign   plane   of the   array   of   items   to   the   G-plane.   Then   we   do   a   masked-clear operation   on   the   array   to   clear   those   items   with   sign   bits   set   to the   1-state.

The   P-plane   and   the   G-plane   are   compared   in   hardware   to develop   a   third   plane,   PEQG.   A   bit   in   the   PEQG-plane   is   in   the 0-state   where   the   corresponding   bits   in   the   P-plane   and   the   G-plane   are   in   opposite   states   -   a   PEQG   bit   is   in   the   1-state   where the   corresponding   P-plane   and   G-plane   bits   are   in   the   same state.   The   PEQG-plane   can   be   copied   into   certain   processing planes   and   stored   in   any   memory   plane.

The   PEQG-plane   can   be   used   to   perform   a   masked   negate operation   in   two   machine   cycles.   In   the   first   cycle   the complement   of   a   memory   plane   is   loaded   into   the   P-plane   (See   the section   on   the   P-PLANE)   and   in   the   second   cycle   the   PEQG-plane   is stored   back   into   the   memory   plane.   This   will   complement (negate)   the   memory   plane   where   G   =   1   and   leave   the   memory   plane undisturbed   where   G   =   0.

The   G-plane   can   be   loaded   with   data   from   any   memory   plane, the   P-plane,   the   B-plane,   the   C-plane,   or   the   PEQG-plane. Copying   the   PEQG-plane   into   the   G-plane   complements   the   G-plane where   the   P-plane   is   in   the   0-state   and   leaves   the   G-plane undisturbed   where   the   P-plane   is   in   the   1-state.

P-PLANE.   The   P-plane   is   used   for   logic   and   routing operations.   P-plane   data   can   be   sent   to   any   memory   plane, the   G-plane,   the   P-plane,   and   the   A-plane.

Logic   Operations.   A   logic   operation   combines   two   source

planes to form a result plane.   One source plane is the P-plane.
The other source plane can be any memory plane, the B-plane, the
C-plane, or the P-plane. The result plane is stored into the
P-plane.   Each bit of the result plane is a logical function
of the two corresponding source plane bits.   Any of the
sixteen Boolean functions of two variables can be used for the
logic function. The functions are:

$$P \longleftarrow D \qquad P \longleftarrow P \mathbin{\&} D \qquad P \longleftarrow P \vee D \qquad P \longleftarrow P + D$$

$$P \longleftarrow \overline{D} \qquad P \longleftarrow P \mathbin{\&} \overline{D} \qquad P \longleftarrow P \vee \overline{D} \qquad P \longleftarrow P + \overline{D}$$

$$P \longleftarrow P \qquad P \longleftarrow \overline{P} \mathbin{\&} D \qquad P \longleftarrow \overline{P} \vee D \qquad P \longleftarrow 0$$

$$P \longleftarrow \overline{P} \qquad P \longleftarrow \overline{P} \mathbin{\&} \overline{D} \qquad P \longleftarrow \overline{P} \vee \overline{D} \qquad P \longleftarrow 1$$

where P represents a bit of the P-plane, D represents the
corresponding bit of the other source plane,   "<--" represents
the   replacement   operation, "&" represents the logical-and
function, "v" represents the inclusive-or function, "+"
represents the exclusive-or function, 0 represents the 0-bit, 1
represents the 1-bit, and a line over a variable
represents logical negation (complementation). A logic
operation can be masked or unmasked.   If the operation is
unmasked then the operation is performed on all 16,384 bits of
the P-plane.   If the operation is masked then the operation is
only performed where the corresponding bit of the G-plane is in
the 1-state - the P-plane bit is not disturbed where the
corresponding bit of the G-plane is in the 0-state.

One use of logic operations in image processing is to mark
those pixels with grey levels above, below, or equal to a
threshold. The memory planes in the array of grey levels are

logically combined in the P-plane until the P-plane contains the
desired marks - an N-plane grey level array can be searched with
N   logic operations.   After the marks are developed in the P-
plane they may be stored in memory or transferred to the G-plane
to mask subsequent operations on the pixels.

Routing Operations.   A routing operation shifts the data in
the P-plane in an of four directions: north, east, south, or
west.   Each   routing step moves the P-plane a distance of one
column or one row.   To move the data in the P-plane a distance
of H columns east or west and V rows north or south requires H+V
routing steps.   Each routing step takes one machine cycle.

A routing step can be masked or unmasked.   An unmasked
routing step moves all 16,384 P-plane bits simultaneously a
distance of one column or one row.   A masked routing step moves
some of the bits, duplicates some, deletes some, and leaves
others undisturbed - where the G-plane bit is in   the   1-
state, the corresponding P-plane bit copies the P-plane bit
of its nearest neighbor: north, east, south, or west.   Where the
G-plane bit is in the 0-state, the P-plane bit is not
disturbed during a masked routing step.

A topology register in the ACU selects the treatment along
the north and south edges of the P-plane. When a north or south
routing step is performed we can either stitch the north and
south edges of the P-plane together or we can separate them.
When the north and south edges are stitched together the north
end of each column is stitched to the south end of the same
column.   If the edges are stitched together then a shift to the

north will copy the data along the north edge of the P-plane into the P-plane bits along the south edge - similarly, a shift to the south will copy the south edge into the north edge. If the north and south edges are separated then a shift to the north will introduce 0-bits along the south edge of the P-plane and the data on the north edge will be lost - similarly, a shift to the south will remove data along the south edge and introduce 0-bits along the north edge.

The topology register also selects the treatment of the east and west edges. We can either stitch the east and west edges together or we can separate them. When the east and west edges are stitched together we can either stitch the west end of each row to the east end of the same row or we can move the stitching by one row so the west end of each row is stitched to the east end of its neighbor row to the north. When the east-west stitching is moved by one row we can either stitch the west end of the north edge to the east end of the south edge or separate these two P-plane bits.

Thus, we can select eight different P-plane topologies for routing operations. Since routing of any memory or processing plane goes through the P-plane, the topology of all ARU planes is the same as the topology of the P-plane. The topologies are numbered from 0 through 7 as follows:

Topology 0:   All four edges are separated and the P-plane looks like a 128 by 128 square island surrounded by an infinite sea of 0-bits.

Topology 1:   The north and south edges are stitched together and the east and west edges are separated to make the P-plane look like a finite cylinder with an east-west axis, 128 elements around the circumference, 128 elements along the axis, and with a semi-infinite cylinder of 0-bits on either side.

Topology 2:   The cylinder of topology 1 can be rotated to a
north-south orientation by separating the north and south
edges and stitching the east and west edges together.

Topology 3:   The north and south edges are stitched together
and the east and west edges are stitched together so the P-
plane looks   like   a torus (doughnut) with 128 elements
around the major circumference and 128 elements around the
minor circumference.

Topology 4:   A cylinder like topology 2 except the stitching
of the east and west edges is moved by one row so the rows
around the cylinder are connected together in a long 16,384-
element spiral that wraps around the cylinder 128 times (the
ends of the spiral are separated).

Topology 5:   A torus like topology 3 except that the east-
west stitching is moved by one row so the rows are
connected together in a long 16,384-element spiral that wraps
around the minor circumference of the torus 128 times (the
ends of the spiral are separated).

Topology 6:   A cylinder like topology 4 except that the the
two ends of the long spiral are stitched together so   the
spiral   looks   like   the circumference of a circle with
16,384 elements.

Topology 7:   A   torus like topology 5 except that the
ends of the spiral are stitched together to make the spiral
look like the circumference of a circle with 16,384 elements.

Note   that the long spiral of topologies 4 through 7 can be
used to change   the two-dimensional P-plane   into   a   one-
dimensional line   or circle containing 16,384 bits.   This is
convenient for processing large one-dimensional arrays. We can
shift the elements of a one-dimensional, 16,384-element array
up or down one place at a time using east-west routing steps or
128 places at a time using north-south routing steps.   End-off
shifting is performed using topology 4 while end-around shifting
is performed using topology 7.

PLANAR SHIFT REGISTER.   The ARU contains a planar shift
register with a programmable depth.   The depth of the planar

shift register can be set to 2, 6, 10, 14, 18, 22, 26, or 30 planes. Like every other ARU plane, each plane in the planar shift register contains 128 rows and 128 columns and can hold 16,384 data bits. Thus, the planar shift register holds 32,768 data bits when its size is set to the minimum value and 491,520 data bits when its size is set to the maximum value.

A shift step in the planar shift register causes an en masse movement of its data from plane to plane. Let the planes in the planar shift register be numbered from 1 to N where N is the number of planes. For I in the range of 2 to N, a shift step moves the data of plane I-1 to plane I. Plane 1 receives data from the B-plane. The data in plane N can either be loaded into the A-plane or discarded. A shift step moves every data bit in the planar shift register a distance of one plane. All movement is between corresponding bits of the planes - a data bit in a given row and column of a plane moves to the same row and column of the next plane. Each shift step takes one machine cycle.

Shift steps can be masked or unmasked. An unmasked shift step affects every data bit in the planar shift register. A masked shift step shifts a subset of the data bits. In a masked shift step the data bits located at the intersection of column X and row Y are shifted from plane to plane only when the G-plane bit at the intersection of column X and row Y is set to the 1-state - where the G-plane bit at the intersection is in the 0-state, no movement along the intersection occurs.

The planar shift register is useful for temporary storage of intermediate results. It has a role akin to an accumulator register in a conventional computer. As the result of an arithmetic operation is formed plane by plane in the B-plane it can be shifted into the planar shift register and used through the A-plane in a subsequent operation. Alternatively, we could store the result in a set of memory planes but this would require using memory write cycles to store the result and memory read cycles to use the result later. Intermediate results can be shifted into the planar shift register and used later on while other data planes are read from memory.

When the planar shift register holds an array of 16,384 N-bit numbers, the most-significant data plane is in plane 1 and the least-significant plane is in plane N of the shift register. Each shift step shifts the numbers one place toward the least-significant end and is akin to a shift right instruction in a conventional computer. A masked shift step shifts some numbers (those where the corresponding G-plane bits are in the 1-state) and leaves the other numbers undisturbed. Masked shift steps are useful to align floating-point fractions, normalize floating-point results, and in other processing operations where different elements of an array must be shifted different amounts.

Another use for masked shift steps is to change the constant routing of the P-plane into a variable routing. As discussed above, P-plane routing steps move all data bits of the P-plane the same distance. Masked routing steps can be employed to perform some variations in the move distance -

masked planar shift register shifts can be employed to perform other variations. One can route the P-plane a number of times while copying the plane to the B-plane and shifting the copies into the planar shift register. Each plane of the planar shift register will contain a copy of the P-plane routed a different distance. Using masked shift steps one can make each element of the A-plane choose which copy of the P-plane to read so some elements will read the P-plane bit that was four rows away, for example, while other elements will read the P-plane bit that was seven rows away, etc. Programming of image magnification, image reduction, image warping, and geometric correction operations can use this technique.

A-PLANE. The A-plane receives the output of the planar shift register - it can be considered to be a one-plane extension to the depth of the planar shift register. The A-plane can also be loaded with data from any memory plane, the P-plane, the B-plane, the C-plane, or the PEQG-plane. The A-plane can also be cleared to the all-zero state.

The shift, load, and clear operations of the A-plane can be masked or unmasked. An unmasked A-plane operation affects all 16,384 data bits in the A-plane. A masked A-plane operation only affects those A-plane bits where the corresponding G-plane bits are in the 1-state. As discussed in B-PLANE and C-PLANE, the A-plane is a source plane for arithmetic operations.

B-PLANE. The B-plane is the sum plane in arithmetic operations. A half-add operation puts A + C into the B-plane (A + C is the exclusive-or of corresponding A-plane and C-plane bits).   A full-add operation puts A + P + C into the B-plane (A + P + C is the exclusive-or of corresponding A-plane, P-plane, and C-plane bits.) As discussed in a subsequent paragraph, the carry plane of the half-add and full-add operations is put into the C-plane.

As mentioned in MEMORY PLANES, arrays of data are usually read from ARU memory, processed, and stored in ARU memory in a series of plane operations (each step transfers or processes one plane of the array at a time). When a data array contains numerical data the least-significant plane is processed first and the most-significant plane is processed last. Arithmetic is performed sequentially bit-plane by bit-plane. This is like many computers of the 1950's that performed arithmetic bit by bit starting with the least-significant bit and ending with the most-significant bit - the main difference is that the ARU processes bit-planes of 16,384 data bits each whereas computers of the 1950's processed single-bit items.

Addition and subtraction of data arrays are performed in the ARU in the following manner. Bit-planes of one source array are loaded into the A-plane least-significant plane first (from memory or from the planar shift register). Bit-planes of the other source array are loaded into the P-plane (the planes are complemented when subtracting). The initial carry plane in the C-plane is cleared to an all-zero state for addition or set to an all-one state for subtraction. A series of full-add operations will form the bit-planes of the result array in the

B-plane where they can be stored in memory or sent to the planar shift register. B-plane data can also be sent to the G-plane, P-plane, and the A-plane.

The full-add and half-add operations can be masked or unmasked. A masked operation only affects those B-plane and C-plane bits where the corresponding G-plane bit is in the 1-state.

C-PLANE. A half-add operation stores the logical-and of the A-plane and the C-plane into the C-plane. A full-add operation stores the carry function of the A-plane, the P-plane, and the C-plane into the C-plane - the carry function bit equals 1 where two or three of the corresponding bits of the A-plane, P-plane, and C-plane are in the 1-state. If a half-add or full-add operation is masked then a C-plane bit is not affected where the corresponding G-plane bit is in the 0-state. Performing addition and subtraction with full-add operations was discussed in B-PLANE.

Two other operations affecting the C-plane clear the C-plane to an all-zero state and set the C-plane to an all-one state. These are used to initialize the carry plane before adding or subtracting.

C-plane data can be sent to a memory plane, the G-plane, the P-plane, and the A-plane.

SUM-OR OUTPUT. The ARU generates a status bit which is sent to the ACU. The status bit is generated from a source plane. If all 16,384 bits of the source plane are in the 0-state then the status bit is in the 0-state. If one or more of the

16,384 bits of the source plane is in the 1-state then the status bit is in the 1-state. Thus, the status bit is a logical inclusive-or of all 16,384 bits in the source plane - the status bit is called the Sum-Or. The source plane for the Sum-Or can be any memory plane, the P-plane, the B-plane, the C-plane, or the PEQG-plane. When the PEQG-plane is used as the source plane the Sum-Or status bit will be in the 0-state if the P-plane is the complement of the G-plane - the status bit will be in the 1-state if the P-plane equals the G-plane in one or more places.

ARU PACKAGING

The S-plane and the processing planes are implemented with 2,112 custom VLSI integrated circuits. Each integrated circuit contains a 2-row by 4-column section of all planes. The memory planes are implemented with 4,752 standard bi-polar RAM integrated circuits - each RAM circuit contains 4 data bits or 4 parity bits of all 1024 memory planes.

Twenty-four VLSI circuits and 54 RAM circuits are packaged on one printed-circuit board to make up a 16-row by 12-column section of the ARU planes. The 128-row by 132-column ARU requires 88 printed-circuit boards. Another 8 boards are used for the topology switches around the edges of the P-plane, to distribute the control signals from the ACU, and for the Sum-Or tree. The 96 boards are packaged in one cabinet together with the power supplies for the ARU. Forced-air cooling is used.

ARRAY CONTROL UNIT

Kenneth E. Batcher
Digital Technology Department
Goodyear Aerospace Corporation
Akron, Ohio 44315

Introduction -- The Array Control Unit (ACU) controls operations in the Array Unit (ARU). The ACU also performs the arithmetic on any scalars (single data items) required to support operations on data arrays in the ARU. As shown in figure 1, the ACU is split into three independent control units: the Processing Element Control Unit (PECU), the Input-Output Control Unit (IOCU), and the Main Control Unit (MCU).

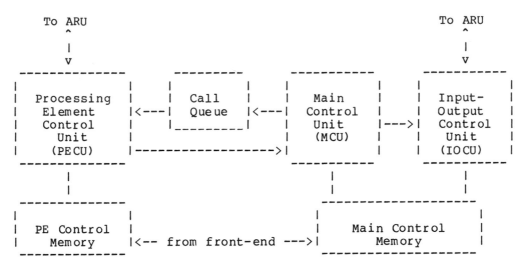

Figure 1 - Array Control Unit

The PECU controls operations in the processing planes of the ARU. Each PECU instruction specifies the processing plane operations for one machine cycle - many simultaneous operations may take place in one machine cycle. Sets of PECU instructions are grouped together into array processing routines which are stored in PE Control Memory. An example of an array processing routine adds the contents of one ARU memory array to the contents of another ARU memory array.

Execution of an array processing routine occurs when the MCU calls the routine. The call enters the Call Queue and when the PECU receives the call it jumps to the called routine. The Call Queue can stack up to 16 calls - calls are sent to the PECU in strict first-in-first-out order. Whenever the PECU completes one array processing routine it immediately jumps to the next called routine (if the call is waiting in the Call Queue).

Some array processing routines develop scalar results from ARU memory arrays. An example is the routine to find the maximum value stored in an array. After being developed in the PECU these results are sent to the MCU over a separate path.

The IOCU controls S-plane operations in the ARU. It shifts the S-plane whenever the staging memory is ready to transfer a column of data to and/or from the ARU. When a plane of data has been shifted in and/or out of the S-plane, the IOCU controls the transfer of another ARU memory plane. The IOCU executes a series of IO commands grouped in an IO program which is stored in Main Control Memory. It starts execution when called upon by the MCU.

The MCU runs the main MPP application program which is stored in Main Control Memory. A typical application program contains array operations, IO operations, and scalar operations. Array operations are executed by the PECU when the MCU initiates them by putting calls into the Call Queue. IO operations are executed by the IOCU when the MCU initiates IO programs. The MCU performs all scalar operations itself. All three control units operate simultaneously to allow overlapping of the three types of operations.

The MCU is programmed in an assembly language called Main Control Language (MCL). The language includes mnemonics to make calls to a library of standard array processing routines executed by the PECU and to initiate standard IO programs in the IOCU. An application program can be coded completely at the MCL level if the array operations and IO operations are standard. Non-standard array operations are coded at the lower level of the PECU assembly language, PRL. These routines can be added to the library of PECU routines and MCL mnemonics to call them can be added to the library of MCL macros to expand the set of standard array operations.

PE CONTROL MEMORY

The PE control memory holds the instructions for the PECU. It is loaded from the front-end computer with the set of PECU routines required to run the main application program. The PE control memory contains 65,536 bytes (the size can be expanded at a later date). The bytes are addressed with 16-bit addresses ranging from 0 to 65535. A parity bit is added to the eight bits of each memory byte to detect errors. Each PECU instruction contains 64 bits so the PECU accesses the PE control memory in 8-byte groups. The PE control memory can hold up to 8192 PECU instructions. The PECU can read an instruction every machine cycle; since it never modifies its own code it can not write into the memory. The front-end computer loads PECU routines into the PE control memory as a block of 16-bit words through a direct memory access interface.

PROCESSING ELEMENT CONTROL UNIT (PECU)

The processing element control unit (PECU) controls operations in the processing planes of the ARU. The processing planes and their operations are described in the chapter on the Array Unit. Each PECU instruction is 64 bits long and may contain several processing plane operations and PECU operations which are executed simultaneously. Processing plane operations operate on the application program data in the ARU while PECU operations handle the associated overhead within the PECU itself. By merging several operations within each PECU instruction users can bury much of the overhead so most instructions perform useful work on the problem data in the ARU.

Execution of a PECU routine begins when it is called by the MCU through the call queue (see the subsection on CALL QUEUE). Each call contains the entry point address of the routine and a number of call parameters. Most array processing routines can be applied to data arrays located anywhere in ARU memory so some of the call parameters specify array locations. If the routine works with data arrays of variable length then other call parameters specify the lengths of the arrays. Routines that combine array data with scalar data (e.g., a routine to add a scalar to every element of an array) will receive the scalar data in other call parameters. The location of the scalar data within the call is sometimes specified with another call parameter. Call parameters are stored in the PECU registers before the first instruction of the called routine is executed so they can be used immediately by the first instruction.

The PECU contains eight index registers, a 64-bit common register for scalar data, a topology register, a program counter, a subroutine stack, and an instruction register. These are described in subsequent sub-items.

INDEX REGISTERS

The PECU contains eight index registers to hold addresses of ARU memory planes, lengths of data arrays, loop counts, and the index of a scalar data bit. Each index register holds 16 bits and is given a label in the range of R0 through R7. Any index register can be used to hold the length of a data array or a loop count. The index of a scalar data bit can only be held in R0. The address of an ARU memory plane or an ARU data array can be held in any index register except R0. When an array processing routine is called from the call queue each index register is initialized with a call parameter before the first instruction of the routine is executed. The eight call parameters are given labels in the range of Q0 through Q7 - index register Rn is initialized with call parameter Qn.

Index register operations modify the contents of the registers. The operations are specified by eight operation fields in each PECU instruction. Each operation field is 2 bits long and specifies the operation for a particular index register. Code-0 in an operation field indicates a no-op; the associated index register is not disturbed. Code-1 and code-2 specify incrementing by unity and decrementing by unity, respectively; the associated index register has +1 or -1 added to its contents. Code-3 in an operation field applies a special index operation to the associated index register. There are four code-3 operations:

> Load an immediate value, K, into the index register (K is in a 16-bit field of the PECU instruction).

> Add K to the contents of the index register (K can be positive or negative).

> Re-initialize the index register with its corresponding call parameter (load Rn from Qn).

> Load the index register from a neighboring index register; R7 from R0, R0 from R1, R1 from R2, etc.

One of the code-3 operations is selected by another field in the PECU instruction and applied to all index registers with code-3 in their operation fields.

Two PECU operations test the contents of any index register and either branch (jump) if the contents equal zero or branch if the contents do not equal zero. These are useful to count the number of executions of a loop of instructions. Processing plane operations use index register R1, R2, ..., or R7 to address ARU memory planes. Index register R0 can be used to address a particular bit in the common register. As shown in the discussion of the common register, the addressed bit, W, has several purposes.

COMMON REGISTER

The 64-bit common register of the PECU is used to store scalar data. Scalars are used by array processing routines such as routines to add a scalar to an array or to multiply an array by a scalar. Other routines such as a routine to find the maximum value in a data array generate scalar data in the common register.

When an array processing routine is called from the call queue the common register can be initialized with a call parameter before the first instruction of the routine is executed. This is the way that the MCU sends scalar data to the PECU. Alternatively, the common register can be left undisturbed so the previous PECU routine can pass scalar data to the called routine. The choice is specified by a bit in the call to the routine.

The contents of the common register can be returned to the MCU when an array processing routine is completed. This is the way that the PECU returns scalar data to the MCU. The MCU has three locations for data returned by the PECU: Return-A, Return-B, and Return-C (see PECU RETURN REGISTERS). Two bits in the call to an array processing routine specify the disposition of common register data when the routine is completed (no return or a return to one of the MCU locations).

A PECU operation loads the values of the corner elements

of an ARU memory plane into the low order 16 bits of the common register (See the subsection on MEMORY PLANES in the chapter ARRAY UNIT). Other PECU operations load the value of the Sum-Or status bit or its complement into a selected bit of the common register (W).

PECU operations can test the value of a selected common register bit (W) and either branch if the value is 0 or branch if the value is 1. The state of common register bit W can determine which P-plane logic operation is performed - this mechanism is used to send scalar data to the ARU, e.g. the P-plane can be set to the all-one state if W equals 1 or cleared to the all-zero state if W equals 0. A PECU operation combines the values in the high order 21 bits of the common register with the ARU control field of the PECU instruction using an inclusive-or function. Since the MCU can initialize the common register with a call parameter, it can directly specify an ARU operation this way.

TOPOLOGY REGISTER

The topology register selects the P-plane topology (See the subsection of PROCESSING PLANES in the chapter ARRAY UNIT). A PECU operation loads the topology register with any of the eight possible topologies. The selected topology remains fixed from routine to routine until the topology register is loaded with a new topology. System software initializes the topology register with topology 0.

PROGRAM COUNTER

The 16-bit program counter addresses the PE Control Memory

for the location of the next PECU instruction - since each instruction is eight bytes long the program counter counts in 8-byte steps. PECU instructions are executed in order until a branch operation, subroutine call operation, or return operation is encountered.

SUBROUTINE STACK

Array processing routines can be called as subroutines by other routines so there is a subroutine stack in the PECU to hold the return address of each subroutine call - calling a subroutine pushes the program counter onto the stack and returning from a subroutine pops the stack into the program counter.

There is no difference between the code for a subroutine and the code for an array processing routine called by the call queue. When a routine exits with a return operation the PECU checks the subroutine stack. If the routine just completed was originally called as a subroutine, the stack will contain the return address of its caller and the PECU will return to the caller. If the routine just completed was originally called by the MCU through the call queue, the subroutine stack will be empty and the PECU jumps to the next routine in the call queue. Thus, any array processing routine can serve dual purposes: as a main routine called by MCU and as a subroutine called by another array processing routine.

INSTRUCTION REGISTER

The instruction register holds the 64-bit PECU instruction

as its operations are performed. A PECU instruction is divided into a number of fields. The fields are grouped as depicted in figure 2

```
-----------------------------------------------------------------
|                      |               |Special |                 |
|        Array         |    Index      | Opera- |                 |
|        Unit          |   Register    | tions  |       K         |
|      Operations      |  Operations   |(8 bits)|                 |
|      (24 bits)       |  (16 bits)    |        |   (16 bits)     |
-----------------------------------------------------------------
```

Figure 2 - PECU Instruction Field Groups

The leftmost group of 24 bits specifies array unit operations. The first 21 bits of this group specify the processing plane operations discussed in the subsection PROCESSING PLANES in the chapter ARRAY UNIT. The last 3 bits of this group select an ARU memory plane address.

The second group of 16 bits specifies index register operations as discussed previously. The third group of 8 bits specifies code-3 index register operations, common register operations, branch operations, a topology register operation, a subroutine call operation, and a return operation.

The last group of 16 bits holds the value of an immediate constant, K. The constant can be used in index register operations, the ARU memory plane address, the position of common register bit W, and in the topology register operation. The value of K is used as a branch address in branch instructions and as the entry point address in the subroutine call operation.

CALL QUEUE

The call queue holds calls to the array processing

routines until they are executed by the PECU.   A call enters the
queue when inserted by the MCU and remains there until the
PECU has executed all previously called routines - then the PECU
jumps to the called routine.   Up to 16 calls can be held in the
queue at one time.

Each   call can contain 208 bits of information.   The entry
point of the called routine is given by a   13-bit   parameter.
Eight 16-bit   parameters   are   Q0 through   Q7   giving   the
initial   states of   the PECU index registers.   Two flag bits
specify the disposition of PECU common register data at the end
of the called routine.   An initialization flag bit   specifies
whether or not the common register should be initialized from the
call - a 64-bit parameter gives the initial state of the common
register if the flag is set.

If   the   call   queue is empty the PECU idles until   the   MCU
enters a new call.   If the MCU attempts to enter a new call when
the call queue is full the MCU will idle   until   the   PECU
removes a call from the queue.   Status flags in MCU registers
show the status of the call queue - empty,   full,   or   partially
full.

INPUT-OUTPUT CONTROL UNIT (IOCU)

The   IOCU   controls   S-plane operations   in   the   ARU.   It
executes a program of IO commands located in   Main   Control
Memory.   Some IO commands cause simple actions such as shifting
the S-plane one or a few columns - others cause complex
actions like moving several planes in or out of the ARU.   Thus,
standard IO programs can be coded with a few high-level commands.

Users requiring non-standard IO actions can use a series of simple commands to control the S-plane at the lowest level.

The IOCU can also control the Staging Memory by transmitting control bytes over the Stager Command Bus (SCB). Normally, when the MCU initiates an IO transfer it invokes system software executing in the front-end computer to set up the staging memory and operate the IOCU. Users can bypass the system software by coding their own IOCU programs but there is a risk that other data in the Staging Memory may be overwritten. Thus, the practice is not recommended unless throughput considerations require it - one should debug the program first with the standard IO instructions before attempting to bypass the system software.

The IOCU has two registers to hold ARU bit-plane addresses. The In Address Register points to the ARU memory plane to receive the next data plane transmitted from the Staging Memory. The Out Address Register points to the ARU memory plane holding the next data plane to be sent to the Staging Memory.

The IOCU has 21 commands divided into four groups: data transfer commands, address register commands, device commands, and miscellaneous commands. Each command has two flag bits. One flag bit issues an interrupt to the PDMU - this is used to signal the end of an IO program or the occurrence of other significant events. The other flag bit indicates the end of a loop of IO commands. Each group is discussed in the subsequent sub-items.

DATA TRANSFER COMMANDS

Nine commands control the transfer of data in the S-plane of the ARU. Four commands shift the S-plane 1 to 255 times: IOSHFT shifts the S-plane with no staging memory column transfers, INCOL shifts the S-plane while transferring data columns from the staging memory to the ARU, OUTCOL shifts the S-plane while transferring data columns from the ARU to the staging memory, and IOCOL shifts the S-plane while transferring data columns both from the ARU to the staging memory and from the staging memory to the ARU.

Two commands combine a transfer of data to or from an ARU memory plane with 0 to 255 column shifts. IOSHFS shifts the S-plane with no staging memory transfers, then moves the S-plane to the ARU plane whose address is in the In Address Register, and then increments the In Address Register by a given amount. IOLSHF loads the S-plane with data from the ARU plane whose address is in the Out Address Register, then increments the Out Address Register by a given amount, and then performs 0 to 255 column shifts on the S-plane.

Three commands transfer a number of planes between the ARU and the staging memory. INPLN moves 1 to 255 planes of data from the staging memory to the ARU while incrementing the In Address Register by a given amount between planes. OUTPLN moves 1 to 255 planes of data from the ARU to the staging memory while incrementing the Out Address Register by a given amount between planes. IOPLN moves 1 to 255 planes of data from the staging memory to the ARU and the same number of planes

from the ARU to the staging memory while incrementing the
In Address Register and the Out Address Register by given
amounts between planes.

ADDRESS REGISTER COMMANDS

Three commands initialize the address registers. IOLIN
loads the In Address Register, IOLOUT loads the Out
Address Register, and IOLIO loads both registers.

DEVICE COMMANDS

Three commands communicate with the staging memory over the
SCB. If other high-speed peripherals are connected to the
MPP in the future the SCB may be extended to communicate with
these devices as well. The PDMU also uses the SCB so the
IOCU must ask for and be granted control of the SCB before these
commands can be executed. IOSDV selects an SCB device.
Subsequent control bytes will be sent to the selected
device. The staging memory uses four of the 256 possible
device addresses. IODBL transmits up to 508 bytes of control
information to the selected device. IODCB sets, clears, or
toggles status bits in the selected device or local status bits.

MISCELLANEOUS COMMANDS

There are six miscellaneous commands. IOLOOP marks the
start of a loop of IO commands to be executed up to 255
times – the last command in the loop is marked by the end loop
flag bit. IOBREAK signals that a loop was exited
prematurely so its loop count should be cleared. IOTBR tests
the state of a local or remote status bit, modifies the state,

and branches conditionally on the original state - one of the local status bits requests control of the SCB and another indicates that control has been granted. IOSTOP stops execution of the IO program - the IOCU idles until restarted by the MCU or by the PDMU. IOTRIG issues special trigger pulses for diagnostic and control purposes. IONOP is a no-operation (unless the interrupt and/or the end loop flags are set).

MAIN CONTROL MEMORY

The main control memory holds IO commands for the IOCU and instructions and scalar data for the MCU. The memory contains 65,536 bytes addressed with 16-bit addresses ranging from 0 to 65535 (the size may be expanded at a later date). A parity bit is added to to the eight data bits of each byte to detect errors.

Both the MCU and the IOCU operate with 16-bit words so all memory references access pairs of bytes (all word addresses are even). The front-end computer loads the main application program into main control memory as a block of 16-bit words through a direct memory access interface (See the CONTROL INTERFACE subsection of THE MASSIVELY PARALLEL PROCESSOR HARDWARE OVERVIEW chapter).

MAIN CONTROL UNIT (MCU)

The main control unit (MCU) executes the main application program of the MPP. All scalar processing is performed within the MCU while the processing of arrays is assigned to the PECU by inserting calls into the call queue and input-output operations are assigned to the IOCU. In many respects MCU looks like a fast 16-bit mini-computer - the basic cycle time in the MCU is 100 nanoseconds.

The MCU reads the instructions of the application program from main control memory - it can also retrieve and store scalar data in the memory. It has fifty 16-bit registers labeled R0 through R49 - these are discussed below.

GENERAL PURPOSE REGISTERS

Registers R0 through R15 are general-purpose registers which can be used as accumulators, index registers, stack pointers, etc.

GROUP DISABLE REGISTERS

Registers R16, R17, and R18 contain bits which disable sections of the ARU planes. As discussed in the ARRAY UNIT chapter each plane in the ARU has 132 columns - 128 columns for normal programming plus 4 spare columns to bypass faulty hardware. These registers specify which columns are enabled and which are bypassed. A validation program checks the ARU hardware and sets these registers to bypass faulty hardware. Normal application programs do not modify these registers. A privilege bit in the privileged operation register (R47) must be set to gain write access to registers R16 through R18.

PECU STATUS REGISTER

Register R19 indicates the status of the PECU. The MCU can not write into this register. Status information reported in this register includes PECU error conditions, call queue full, call queue empty, and pending scalar data returns.

PECU RETURN REGISTERS

Registers R20 through R31 are registers for the return of scalar data from the PECU to the MCU. The registers are divided into three sets with four registers per set - R20 through R23 is the Return-A set, R24 through R27 is the Return-B set, and R28 through R31 is the Return-C set. When the PECU returns scalar data the state of its 64-bit common register is written into the four 16-bit registers of one of the sets. Scalar data is returned at the end of an array processing routine - the choice of the return set is made by a call parameter in the call to the routine. While the call is sitting in the call queue and while the called routine is being executed a status bit in R19 is set to indicate that the return of scalar data is still pending to the return set - the bit is cleared after the scalar data is returned. An attempt to read a return set register while a return is pending to the set will be delayed until the PECU returns the data.

CALL PARAMETER REGISTERS

Registers R32 through R44 are used to transmit PECU calls to the call queue. A call is set up by first loading registers R32 through R43 with the appropriate call parameters. Then register R44 is loaded with the 13-bit entry point of the array processing routine, a bit to indicate whether or not the PECU common register should be initialized with call parameter data, and two bits to indicate the return set for data to be returned (or no return of scalar data). When R44 is loaded the contents of registers R32 through R44 are sent to the call queue.

If the 64-bit common register is to be initialized the initial state is put into registers R32 through R35. Registers R36 through R43 contain the initial values of the PECU index registers, Q0 through Q7, respectively.

IOCU COMMUNICATION REGISTERS

Registers R45 and R46 communicate with the IOCU. Register R45 is loaded with the start address of an IO program (plus unity) to start the IOCU - this is a privileged operation that can only be done if the appropriate bit of the privileged operation register is set.

Register R46 is a read-only register indicating the status of the IOCU. The IOCU status reported includes error conditions and activity.

PRIVILEGED OPERATION REGISTER

Register R47 is the privileged operation register. Certain register modifications are privileged operations - the privileges of an application program are recorded in R47. Privileges are set up by the front-end computer when the application program is loaded and can not be changed by the MCU.

Privileges that can be granted to the program are: the ability to change the ARU memory parity check bit, the ability to reset the PECU, the ability to reset the IOCU, the ability to start the IOCU, and the ability to modify the group disable registers. Each privilege has a corresponding read-only bit in

R47. Other bits in R47 include four flag bits which are affected by most MCU operations: flag bit N is set if the operation result is negative, flag bit Z is set if the operation result is zero, flag bit V is set if signed arithmetic overflow occurred, and flag bit C is set if unsigned arithmetic overflow occurred. Another three bits in R47 can be modified if the program has the necessary privilege: one bit specifies whether or not ARU memory plane parity checking is performed, another bit resets the PECU, and the third bit resets the IOCU.

ROW REGISTERS

Register R48 is the Sum-Or row register. As discussed in the PROCESSING PLANES portion of the ARRAY UNIT chapter, the Sum-Or output of the ARU is a logical inclusive-or of all 16,384 data bits in an ARU plane. R48 contains eight bits where each bit is the logical inclusive-or of 16 rows of the last plane fed to the Sum-Or output - the inclusive-or of the eight R48 bits is the final Sum-Or output.

Register R49 is the parity error row register. If an ARU memory plane parity error occurs, an error status bit in the PECU status register is set and a bit in R49 is set. The bit in R49 indicates which group of 16 rows contains the error - diagnostics can disable column groups to locate which group of columns contain the error to pinpoint the printed-circuit board with the faulty hardware.

MCU INSTRUCTIONS

A move immediate instruction moves constants into one to fifteen registers. A move register to register instruction moves up to fifteen words from one set of registers to another set of registers. Move memory to register and move register to memory instructions move up to fifteen words from the source to the destination.

Single operand instructions modify the contents of single registers. A register can be cleared, complemented, incremented, decremented, negated, and shifted. Some of these operations have conditional modes for coding multiple precision processes. Another single operand instruction replaces the contents of a register by a count of the number of the ones in the register - this is useful to gather statistics from the ARU corner elements.

Double operand instructions combine two source operands into a result operand. One source operand comes from a register and the result is stored back in the register. The other source operand can be a constant, the contents of a register, or the contents of a memory location. The operations include add, subtract, unsigned multiply, signed multiply, and ten logic operations. Some of these operations have conditional modes for coding multiple precision processes. The double-length products in the multiply operations are stored in a pair of registers. Another double operand instruction compares two operands and sets the flag bits appropriately.

Branch instructions transfer control conditionally or unconditionally. The condition for a branch can be the state of any bit of any register, whether or not a register has a zero value, or the result of a compare operation. A decrement and branch instruction is useful for counting through loops.

Miscellaneous instructions in the MCU include no-op, call subroutine, return from subroutine, call PDMU or host, and breakpoint. The last two instructions wake up the PDMU or the host computer (depending on which front end is controlling the MPP) and halt the MCU.

STAGING MEMORY

Kenneth E. Batcher
Digital Technology Department
Goodyear Aerospace Corporation
Akron, Ohio 44315

Introduction -- The staging memory is in the data path
between the array unit and the front-end computer (PDMU or
host). It can buffer arrays of data transmitted over this path
and it can also reformat them. Re-formatting is usually
required because the front-end computer typically operates on an
array of data an item at a time while the array unit
receives and transmits the array a plane at a time. One could
perform this re-formatting in the array unit or in the front-end
computer but at a slow rate - the staging memory performs the
re-formatting as the array enters and leaves the memory so there
is no loss in throughput.

Array dimensions vary over a wide range. A band of a
satellite image is a three dimensional array of data bits with a
number of lines, a number of pixels per line, and a
number of bits per pixel - each of these numbers exhibits a
wide range of values considering all the satellites that have
been and will be launched. Imagery is stored and processed in
different formats; for example, band interleaved or band
sequential. In the array unit one should be able to choose
an optimum layout for an array to minimize processing time; for
example, to correct for scanning anomalies in a thematic
mapper image it is best to put the forward scanning lines in one

sub-array and the backward-scanning lines in a separate sub-array so they can be corrected independently.

The staging memory has a very flexible re-formatting capability so that all these considerations can be taken into account. An MPP system software module (the staging memory manager) can be used to program the re-formatting of a data array as it goes through the staging memory). One gives the staging memory manager a logical description of the data array (number of dimensions and size of each dimension) and the format of the array as it enters and as it leaves the staging memory (bits per item, items per record, number of records, etc.) Then the staging memory manager programs the staging memory.

As delivered to NASA Goddard Space Flight Center the staging memory has a capacity of 2 megabytes and a transfer rate of 20 megabytes per second. Both the capacity and the transfer rate can be increased at a future time. The capacity and the transfer rate are related to the number of main stager banks and the size of each bank. The number of banks can equal 4, 8, 16, or 32. The transfer rate of each bank is 5 megabytes per second. The banks are driven in parallel so the total transfer rate can equal 20, 40, 80, or 160 megabytes per second depending on the number of banks in the configuration.

Initially, each bank holds 65,536 words with eight bytes per word so each bank can hold 524,288 bytes. The capacity of the staging memory can equal 2, 4, 8, or 16 megabytes depending on the number of banks in the configuration. At a future date, the size of each bank can be quadrupled to hold 262,144 words or 2

megabytes   - this change will quadruple the maximum capacity of
the staging memory to 64 megabytes.   At a later date, the size of
each bank can be quadrupled again for a maximum capacity of 256
megabytes.

Figure 1 shows a block diagram of the staging memory.   The
bulk of the memory is in the main stager. Sub-stagers re-
format data files as they enter and leave the main stager.   Both
the input port and the output port of the staging memory are
connected to the ARU and the front-end computer.   The interfaces
to the front-end computer are described in the DATA INTERFACE
portion of THE MASSIVELY PARALLEL PROCESSOR SYSTEM OVERVIEW
chapter.   Note that a data file can be transferred from the
front-end to the ARU, from the ARU to the front-end, from the ARU
back to the ARU, or from the front-end back to the front-end.
Each file transfer can re-format the data while passing
through the staging memory.

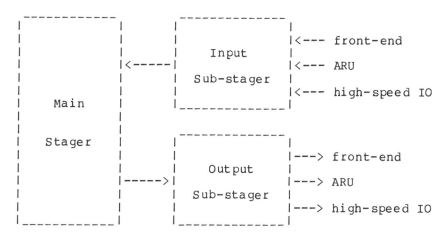

Figure 1 - Block Diagram of Staging Memory

Since neither front-end computer can fully support the 160 megabyte per second transfer rate of the ARU and staging memory, provisions have been made to add high-speed devices to the staging memory ports at a future date.

MAIN STAGER

The main stager contains a number of banks of random-access memory. It is initially delivered with four banks. The number of banks can be expanded to 8, 16, or 32. Each memory bank holds a number of 64-bit words. Initially, each bank contains 65,536 words. When the expected advances in memory technology occur the size of each bank can be incremented to 262,144 words, and later to 1,048,576 words.

The memory banks are accessed in parallel by the sub-stagers. The basic cycle time of a memory bank is 1.6 microseconds. During one cycle each bank can accept a 64-bit word from the input sub-stager and transmit another 64-bit word to the output sub-stager. Thus, each bank has an input transfer rate of 5 megabytes per second and an output transfer rate of 5 megabytes per second. When input and output occur simultaneously the total IO rate of each bank is 10 megabytes per second. A 32-bank main stager fully supports the IO rates of the ARU.

The addresses of main stager words are interleaved. Bank 0 holds words 0, 32, 64, 96, etc., bank 1 holds words 1, 33, 65, 97, etc., etc., and bank 31 holds words 31, 63, 95, 127, etc. If the main stager only has 16 banks they are put into the bank slots with even numbers (banks 0, 2, 4, ..., 30) so only words with even addresses exist.   If the main stager only has 8 banks they are put into bank slots 0, 4, 8, 12, 16, 20, 24, and 28 so only words whose addresses are multiples of four exist.   If the main stager only has four banks they are put   into bank slots 0, 8, 16, and 24 so only words whose addresses are multiples of eight exist.

Each 64-bit memory word has an 8-bit error correction code (ECC) appended to it to correct any single errors and detect any double errors.   The memory of each bank is implemented with 72 MOS random access memory chips (64 for data plus 8   for the ECC).   The main stager cycle time of 1.6 microseconds is sufficiently long to perform a read, a write, and a refresh operation. Initially each chip holds 65,536 bits so the total number of words in each bank is 65,536.   When 262,144- bit memory chips are readily available the main stager can be re-populated with the larger chips to quadruple its capacity. When megabit chips are available the capacity can be quadrupled again.

Word addresses are 25 bits long - the low-order 5 bits of the address contain the number of the bank holding the word and the high-order 20 bits of the address specify the word location within the bank (the high-order four address bits are not used when each bank only contains 65,536 words).

The sub-stagers access all main stager banks in parallel. When a sub-stager accesses the main stager it supplies six address parameters (A, B, C, D, E, and F) to an address tree in the main stager which computes all word addresses for all banks. Each address parameter is also 25 bits long.

Assume there are 32 banks in the main stager so a sub-stager accesses 32 memory words in parallel with parameters A, B, C, D, E, and F. Number the words being accessed from 0 to 31. For I in the range of 0 to 31, the address of word-I is computed as follows. Let I4, I3, I2, I1, and I0 be the binary digits of I so:

$$I = (16 * I4) + (8 * I3) + (4 * I2) + (2 * I1) + I0.$$

The main stager address of word-I will be:

$$(F * I4) + (E * I3) + (D * I2) + (C * I1) + (B * I0) + A.$$

As examples, word-0 has address A, word-1 has address A+B, word-2 has address A+C, and word-31 has address A+B+C+D+E+F. Note that word-I may come from any memory bank.

To guarantee that there are no memory conflicts (each word is in a separate memory bank) constraints are put on address parameters B, C, D, E, and F as follows:

$$B = 1 \quad modulo \quad 2$$
$$C = (2 * B) \quad modulo \quad 32$$
$$D = (4 * B) \quad modulo \quad 32$$
$$E = 8 \quad modulo \quad 16$$
$$F = 16 \quad modulo \quad 32.$$

The statement X = Y modulo Z means that X and Y leave the same remainder when they are divided by Z.

Note that if we set C = 2 * B, D = 4 * B, E = 8 * B, and F = 16 * B then the constraints are satisfied if B is an odd number — in this case the address of word-I will be A + (B * I). If B = 1 then the sub-stager accesses 32 consecutive words in the main stager, if B = 3 then the sub-stager accesses every third word, if B = 5 then the sub-stager accesses every fifth word, etc. This ability to access a set of 32 words spaced apart by an odd amount can be used to do a major re-formatting of a data array.

For example, let element (X,Y) of a 32 X 32 array of data be stored in main stager address (33 * X) + Y. The input sub-stager can store the array into the main stager row-by-row by setting address parameter B to 1 while the output sub-stager can retrieve the array column-by-column by setting address parameter B to 33.

Note that we can access whole main stager words in different ways using different address parameters but we cannot access parts of main stager words. Accessing single bits of a data array requires the sub-stagers to change the format of elements within the main stager words. This is illustrated in the following item.

A RE-FORMATTING EXAMPLE

Suppose we want to transfer an image from the front-end computer to the ARU. The image has 896 lines, 1152 pixels per line, and 8 bits per pixel. In the front-end computer the image is stored and processed pixel by pixel. The front-end will send the image to the staging memory as 896 records with one image line per record. The 1152 consecutive pixels of a line are in 1152 consecutive bytes of the record.

The ARU will receive the image as 63 sub-images with each sub-image containing 128 consecutive pixels of 128 consecutive lines. Each sub-image will be stored in eight consecutive ARU memory planes - one memory plane per bit-plane of the sub-image.

Suppose there were no sub-stagers in the staging memory to

re-format data - the front-end computer and the ARU were directly connected to the main stager. Then the front-end computer would write eight consecutive pixels of an image line in each 64-bit main stager word as shown in figure 2(a). This is incompatible with the way the ARU fetches data. It builds up a bit-plane from 128 columns with 128 bits in each column. A column of data should contain one bit from each of 128 consecutive pixels of one image line. If the ARU reads two main stager words to form a column each main stager word should contain one bit from each of 64 pixels as shown in figure 2(b). This is true regardless of the order that main stager words are written and read.

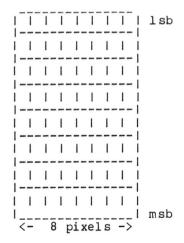

(a) - Written by the front-end

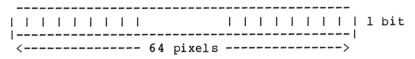

(b) - Required to drive ARU

Figure 2 - Main stager word formats without sub-stagers

To obtain a main stager word format that is compatible between the front-end and the ARU we need to introduce an input sub-stager between the front-end and the main stager. The input sub-stager can accumulate all bits of 64 consecutive pixels from the front-end and then write the data to the main stager as 8 separate words with each word containing 1 bit from each of the 64 pixels. The main stager word format is then like figure 2(b) so the ARU can form a column of data from two words.

Sub-stagers perform minor re-formatting operations on small sub-sets of the data array being transferred so that the input port and the output port can work with the same main stager word format. In general, we need both an input sub-stager and an output sub-stager to treat all the cases that may arise.

The input sub-stager accumulates a sub-set of the array from the source device and writes the sub-set into the main stager as a set of complete 64-bit main stager words. The output sub-stager retrieves a sub-set of the array from the main stager as a set of complete 64-bit main stager words and presents the sub-set to the destination device in the desired format. By using different address parameters in the input and output sub-stagers the shape of the input sub-set can be different from the shape of the output sub-set - this is a major re-formatting operation as described in the MAIN STAGER subsection. Thus, the combination of the two sub-stagers and the main stager can perform a wide variety of re-formatting operations.

Given a logical description of a data array to be

transferred through the staging memory, its format as presented by the input device, and the format required by the output device a programmer can call upon the staging memory manager software module to program the staging memory operations. The manager finds a compatible main stager word format, lays out the data array in the main stager, sets up the address parameters, and programs the minor re-formatting operations in the sub-stagers.

SUB-STAGERS

The sub-stagers are fast, small scale versions of the main stager. Instead of 64-bit words as in the main stager, each sub-stager memory has single-bit words so that single data bits of the data array can be unpacked, re-arranged, and re-packed conveniently.

The main stager has a basic cycle time of 1.6 microseconds - thirty-two 64-bit words can be stored and another set of thirty-two words can be fetched in each cycle. To support the transfer rates of the ARU ports, each sub-stager has a basic cycle time of 100 nanoseconds - 128 single-bit words can be stored and another set of 128 words can be fetched in each cycle.

To reduce the number of wires at the interface between the main stager and each sub-stager; each 64-bit main stager word is split into sixteen 4-bit nibbles and the contents of a word are transferred nibble-by-nibble over four wires with 100 nanoseconds per nibble. Thus, 128 wires between the main stager and a sub-stager allow 32 main stager words to be accessed every 1.6 microseconds by transferring 32 nibbles every 100 nanoseconds.

Each   sub-stager memory has 128 banks with 1024   single-bit
words in each bank. During the 100-nanosecond cycle time of   the
sub-stager   memory 128 words can be stored into the memory and   a
different   set   of   128   words   fetched.   Each single-bit   word
is   given   a   17-bit   address.   It   is convenient to view a sub-
stager   memory   as an 8 X 128 X 128 three-dimensional   array   of
bits.   The high-order three bits of a word address (P) reference
one   of 8 pages,   the next seven   address   bits   (R)   reference
one   of   128   rows,   and   the low-order seven   address   bits   (C)
reference   one   of 128 columns - the intersection of   row-R   and
column-C on page-P holds the single-bit word being addressed.

The   word   at row-R and column-C of   page-P   is   physically
stored   at address (128 * P) + C in memory bank   (R +   C).   The
bank   number   (R   +   C)   is   found   by performing   an   exclusive-
or   operation   between corresponding bits of the row address,   R,
and   the column address,   C.   This storage rule is selected   for
fast   sub-stager   address   generation   -   the   sub-stager   address
generator must generate 128 addresses every 50 nanoseconds   while
the   main stager address tree has   800 nanoseconds to generate 32
addresses.

A   sub-stager   memory   is   accessed   with   three   address
parameters: a   3-bit page address (P),   a 7-bit access mode (M),
and   a 7-bit   local   address   (A).   Each access   will   address
128 sub-stager words that can either be read or written. The page
address (P) selects the page   containing   the   128   locations   to
be   accessed.   The access mode (M) selects the type of   access.
For   example,   if M   =   0 then the 128 bits in one column of page P

will be accessed while if M = 127 then the 128 bits in one row of page P will be accessed. The local address (A) positions the access within page P. If M = 0 then A is the address of the column being accessed while if M = 127 then A is the address of the row being accessed. When M is between 0 and 127, the bits at the intersections of certain rows and certain columns are accessed - some bits of the local address A select the rows while the other address bits select the columns.

Each sub-stager contains a permutation network as well as a memory. When the input sub-stager receives a column of data from the input device, the permutation network scrambles the locations of the data within the column before they are written into the sub-stager memory. When the input substager transfers a set of 128 data bits to the main stager, the permutation network permutes the data bits so each 4-bit nibble is transferred to the appropriate main stager bank. The permutation network in the output sub-stager performs a similar function so the appropriate data bits are transferred to the output device on the correct lines.

STAGING MEMORY CONTROL UNITS

The staging memory has four control units. Control unit 1 handles the transfer of data from the input device to the input sub-stager. Control unit 2 handles the transfer of data from the input sub-stager to the main stager. Control unit 3 handles the transfer of data from the main stager to the output sub-stager. Control unit 4 handles the transfer of data from

the   output sub-stager   to   the   output   device.   Each control
unit   generates the address parameters for the sub-stager   it   is
accessing.   Control   units   2   and   3   also generate the address
parameters for the main stager.

Control   units   1 and 2 are synchronized so that   the   input
sub-stager   memory can be   used   either   as   a   single   buffer,   a
double buffer,   or a quadruple buffer. When the memory is used as
a   single   buffer,   the   control   units   take   turns filling   the
buffer   completely and emptying the buffer completely.   When the
memory   is   used as a double buffer or a   quadruple   buffer,   the
control units can run simultaneously on different buffer areas   -
a   control   unit   only   waits   if   the   other   control   unit   has
not   finished with the next buffer area.   In a similar   manner,
control   units 3 and 4   are   synchronized   to   use   the   output
sub-stager   as a single buffer,   a double buffer,   or a quadruple
buffer.

Each   control   unit has a number of   programmable   counters
that   can be set up to generate a sequence of address   parameters
for the sub-stagers.   Control   units 2   and   3   can also be   set
up   to   generate   a sequence of address parameters for   the   main
stager.   The control units are set up by transferring a   sequence
of   control   bytes   over   the   SCB.   The   SCB can be driven   by
the IOCU or by the front-end computer.

The   staging   memory   manager sets   up   the   staging   memory
through   the   front-end computer.   Normally, control units 1 and
2   are set up simultaneously to move a file from the input device
to the main stager.   Similarly, control units 3 and 4   are set up

simultaneously to move a file from the main stager to the output device. The main stager may contain several different data files and control units 1 and 2 may be transferring one file into the main stager while control units 3 and 4 are transferring another file out. The staging memory manager allocates space in the main stager to the data files.

MPP VLSI MULTIPROCESSOR INTEGRATED CIRCUIT DESIGN

John T. Burkley

Digital Technology Department

Goodyear Aerospace Corporation

Akron, Ohio 44315

INTRODUCTION

A large scale integrated multiprocessor circuit has been developed for use
in the Massively Parallel Processor system (MPP).   The chip, built in an
HCMOS technology, contains eight bit serial procesing elements (PE's) and is
the basic building block for the MPP processing array.

The MPP is a large scale single instruction stream multiple data stream
(SIMD) machine being built by Goodyear Aerospace Corp.   for NASA/GODDARD.
(1,2,3,4) The system block diagram is shown in figure 1.   The array unit
(ARU) processes two dimensional arrays of data.   Array control is generated
by the array control unit (ACU) which executes the user program and performs
any sequential processing and scalar arithmetic necessary to support array
operations.   Array data I/O is through a special Staging Memory which both
stores and permutes array data. The Program and Data Management unit serves
as an external I/O preprocessor.

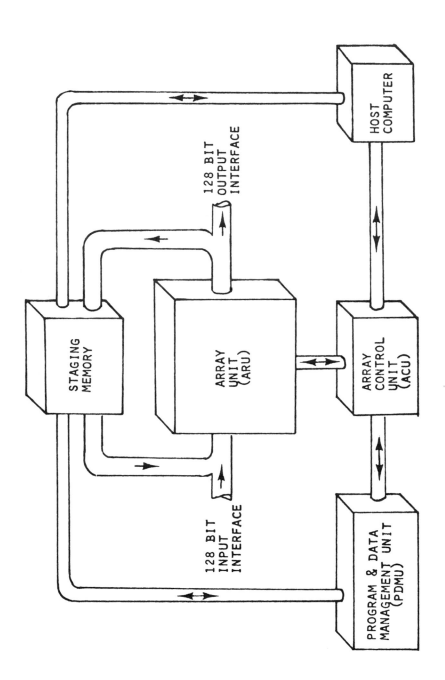

Figure 1 - MPP System

The array unit is what makes this machine special.   The ARU includes 16384
PE's organized   in   a 128 x 128 array and operating at a basic cycle of 100
nsec.   Each PE supports boolean and arithmetic operations, is maskable and
is capable of routing data to its orthogonal neighbors.   The array can
perform 6.5 billion adds or 1.8 billion multiplies per second while
inputting or/and outputting data at 160 megabytes per second.

To build an array of this size and speed required the development of a VLSI
chip.   The chip was partitioned to include eight PE's configured in a 2 x 4
array,   an eight bit bidirectional data port with a parity tree and a SUMOR
tree, and a disable circuit capable of disconnecting the chip from its east-
west neighbors.   This last feature facillitates automatic repair of the
array using redundant processing elements.   This chip replaces some 200 MSI
and SSI circuits.   The chip will execute ten million operations per second
when operating with high speed RAM (45 nsec access).   PE memory was not
included within the chip for several reasons. First, local memory would
have reduced the number of PE's per chip and complicated its design and
development.   Second, the use of external memory allowed the MPP system to
take full advantage of existing memory technology allowing more memory per
PE at a faster access time than is possible in HCMOS. Finally, future
systems could expand PE memory without a major chip redesign. A total of
2112 chips are required to construct an MPP array.   This total includes a
spare column of chips for redundancy.

PE DESIGN

The PE includes six single bit registers (A,B,C,G,P,S), a variable length shift register, a full adder and some combinatorial logic. A PE block diagram is shown in Figure 2. Figure 3 shows the detail PE logic as it is implemented on the chip. The chip is controlled by 16 control lines (L0 - LF). Table 1 shows a decode for various PE operations. The PE may be divided into four subunits; logic and routing, arithmetic, I/O, and masking. These subunits have independent control but share a common clock. The subunits are interconnected by a bidirectional data bus which also connects to external PE memory.

LOGIC & ROUTING SUBUNIT

The logic and routing subunit is formed by the P register together with some supporting combinatorial logic. When L3 is low, P is logically combined with the state of the data bus as dictated by L4-L7 (see Table I) and the result is stored in P. When routing is enabled, L6 and L7 select one of four inputs to the route multiplexor. The multiplexor inputs are the states of the P registers in the north, south, east, and west neighbor PE's. The selected input is latched in P. If L2 is set the logic and routing operations are masked if G is low.

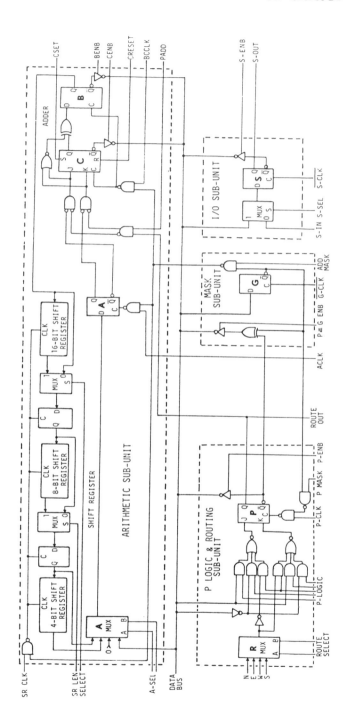

Figure 2 - MPP Processing Element Logic

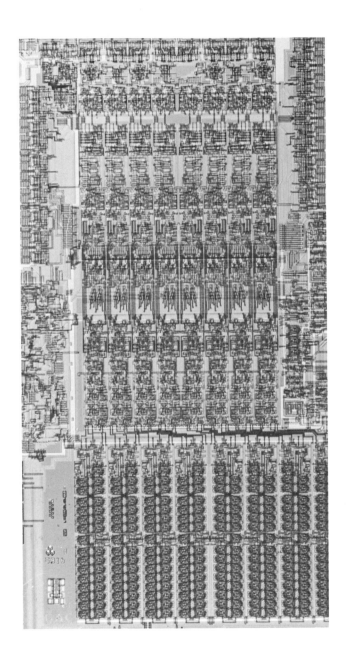

Figure 3 - MPP Processing Element Chip

ARITHMETIC SUBUNIT

The arithmetic subunit consists of a serial by bit adder formed by B and C and a variable length shift register whose output may be stored in A. A may also be loaded from the data bus. The adder receives an input from A and P. When enabled by control (L9-LB), the adder adds the two input bits to a carry bit stored in C and forms a two bit sum. The least significant bit is stored in B and the most significant bit is stored in C so it becomes the carry bit for the next cycle. C may be initialized to either a one or a zero. During a half add operation the P input to the adder is set to zero. If LF is set, arithmetic operations are masked if G is low.

The arithmetic unit also includes a variable length shift register for local storage of partial products. This feature significantly improves multiply and divide operation times. The shift register circulates the output of B back through N stages of delay to the adder input register A. The length of the shift register, N, may be set in steps of 4 from 2 to 30. Since A and B also add two stages of delay, the total shift register length may vary from 4 to 32.

I/O SUBUNIT

The I/O subunit is formed by the S register and a two input multiplexor which selects input from either the data bus or the S register of the PE's west neighbor. S register shifting may go on independent of other PE operations except when data must be stored or loaded from PE memory.

TABLE I   PE CONTROL BUS

Category	Operation	Alt	$\overline{L0L1}$	L2L3	L4L5L6L7	L8	$\overline{L9LALB}$	LCLD	LE	LF
	MEMORY		1 0				1 -			
DATA			1 0				- 1			
	C-REGISTER		0					0 0		
BUS	B-REGISTER		0 0				1			
			0 0					1		
SOURCE	POG		0 1	0						
	S-REGISTER		0 1	1						
	P-REGISTER		1 1							
	NOOP			* 0	0 0 0 0					
	D.D->P	AND		* 0	0 0 0 1					
	$\overline{D}$.P->P			* 0	0 0 1 0					
P	0->P	CLEAR		* 0	0 0 1 1					
	$\overline{D}$+P->P			* 0	0 1 0 0					
REGISTER	$\overline{D}$OP->	XNOR		* 0	0 1 0 1					
	$\overline{D}$->P			* 0	0 1 1 0					
LOGIC	$\overline{D}$.P->P	NOR		* 0	0 1 1 1					
	D+P->P	AND		* 0	1 0 0 0					
	D->P	LOAD		* 0	1 0 0 1					
	DOP->	XOR		* 0	1 0 1 0					
	D.$\overline{P}$->P			* 0	1 0 1 1					
	1->P			* 0	1 1 0 0					
	D+P->P			* 0	1 1 0 1					
	$\overline{D}$+$\overline{P}$->P	NAND		* 0	1 1 1 0					
	P->P	TOGGLE		* 0	1 1 1 1					
P	SOUTH P(NORTH)->P			* 1	0 1 0 0					
REGISTER	WEST P(EAST)->P			* 1	0 1 0 1					
	EAST P(WEST)->P			* 1	0 1 1 0					
ROUTINE	NORTH P(SOUTH)->P			* 1	0 1 1 1					
ADDER	NOOP						1 1 0			*
	FULL ADD						1 0 1			*
(B+C)	P+A+C->(B,C)		0 0				- 0 1			*
	HALF ADD						1 0 0			*
(REGISTERS)	A+C->(C,B)		0 0				- 0 0			*
	CLEAR C						1 1 1			*
	SET C						0 1 0			*
	SHIFT								1	*
		2		0 1	1 0 0 0					
SHIFT REG		6		0 1	1 0 0 1					
	SET	10		0 1	1 0 1 0					
	SR	14		0 1	1 0 1 1					
	LENGTH	18		0 1	1 1 0 0					
	TO	22		0 1	1 1 0 1					
		26		0 1	1 1 1 0					
		30		0 1	1 1 1 1					
	NOOP							0 0		
A-REGISTER	LOAD A FROM S/R							0 1		
	LOAD A FROM D							1 1		
	CLEAR A							1 0		
G-REGISTER	LOAD G					1				
S-REGISTER	LOAD S			0 1	0 0 1					
	OUTPUT SUMOR							0 1 1		
OR	OF DATA BUS		1					0 1		
PARITY	CLEAR PARITY			1 1	0 0 1					

$\overline{L0L1}$ L2LE   L4L5L6L7   L8 $\overline{L9LALB}$ LCLD   LE   LF

* - IF =1 OPERATION IS MASKED CONDITIONALLY BY STATE OF G-REGISTER

MASKING SUBUNIT

The masking subunit is formed by the G register. The mask bit is loaded when L8 is high. Masking is enabled when G is low. Routing and arithmetic operations may be masked separately. In addition the state of P may be outputted to the data bus selectively negated by G. This allows a masked invert of data in PE memory to be executed in two cycles.

MEMORY INTERFACE

The PE subunits are interconnected by a bi-directional data bus. This bus may be used to exchange data between PE registers or to read and write PE memory. The control lines only allow one bus source at a time. The chip includes an eight bit parity tree which generates parity on memory write operations and checks parity on memory read operations. If bad parity is detected a parity error latch is set. Because of the parity tree delay, memory operations with parity will not operate at a 100 nsec cycle. The eight memory buses are also sumored to form a single bit output which is one if any of the data buses is at the one state.

CHIP DISABLE

A chip disable line is provided which logically disconnects the chip from the array by disabling the SUMOR output and enabling a bypass circuit which routes data directly from the west route and S register inputs to the east route and S register outputs. This effectively removes that PE from the array allowing column substitution. Since only a small portion of chip logic must work for the bypass logic to be functional, a failed array could be repaired automatically by substituting a spare column of PE's for a failed column without waiting for a maintenance call.

CHIP FABRICATION

The MPP multiprocessor integrated circuit was fabricated in an HCMOS technology using 5um design rules. The design was implemented using about 8000 transistors and required a chip size of 235 x 131 mil2. The chip requires two power supplies. Internal circuitry operates at 7 volts; the output translators require 5 volts. The chip is packaged in a 52 pin flat pack and dissipates 200mw when operating at 10 megahertz.

The chip design includes a high speed bi-directional data bus. This data bus was implemented as an NMOS type bus using NMOS transistor pull-downs and a current mirror biased pull-up transistor. This bus implementation increased chip power dissipation but greatly improved response time.

All inputs and outputs are TTL compatible. The output translators require a separate power supply of 5 volts. The output drivers are implemented using two stacked N-type drivers rather than the traditional P-type and N-type stack. This resulted in a smaller driver design with no loss in performance.

The chip topology is shown in figure 4. The eight PE's are grouped together in the middle of the chip in long narrow strips. This was done to minimize control line metal runs. The data bus and routing logic is grouped toward the top of the chip. This logic had the most severe timing constraints and was laid out as close to the chip pins as possible to minimize line delays. The shift registers are grouped along the bottom of the chip. The control decode is split and feed in from both sides of the chip.

CONCLUSIONS

The eight PE multiprocessor chip has been developed for use in the MPP. This chip has met all the functional and critical timing specifications first proposed by Batcher (2) in 1979. It served as a building block for the 128x128 MPP processor array and could be used to build arbitrarily large N X N arrays.

$\overline{PAR}$	$\overline{\Sigma OR}$	$\overline{D0}$	$\overline{D1}$	$\overline{D2}$		$\overline{D3}$	$\overline{D4}$	$\overline{D5}$	$\overline{D6}$	$\overline{D7}$

S-OUT 3								S-OUT 4
EAST 3	PE0	PE1	PE2	PE3	PE4	PE5	PE6	PE7	EAST 4
NORTH 3									SOUTH 4
NORTH 2									SOUTH 5
NORTH 1									SOUTH 6
NORTH 0									SOUTH 7
WEST 0									WEST 7

K LOGIC ... K LOGIC

| S/R 0 | S/R 1 | S/R 2 | S/R 3 | S/R 4 | S/R 5 | S/R 6 | S/R 7 |

Figure 4 - MPP Chip Topolog

PART III

SOFTWARE

PROGRAMMING THE MPP

J. L. Potter
Mathematical Sciences Department
Kent State University
Kent, Ohio 44242

Introduction -- SIMD parallel computers such as the
Massively Parallel Processor offer a great increase in computing
power at modest cost. However, their acceptance by the general
computer science community is hindered by the misconception that
they are difficult to program. Since they are single instruction
stream machines as are conventional computers, the basic
operation of these two types of computers are very similar.
Because of the similarity between these two architectures,
programming concepts developed for conventional computers are
directly transferable to SIMD computers.

However, many of todays areas of interest such as artificial
intelligence and data base management are not based on arithmetic
computation alone and therefore can not take full advantage of
the MPP's computing power using this straight forward approach.
In order to effectively apply SIMD processors to these
applications, it is necessary to explore the differences between
SIMD and conventional computers and to question the need for some
of the traditional approaches of conventional sequential
programming. For example, since SIMD processors can search the
entire array memory in parallel sorting data can be eliminated in
many situations.

This chapter will discuss both aspects of programming the MPP. First the traditional approaches will be discussed. The chapter will conclude with a brief introduction to some of the concepts which must be addressed to obtain the full impact of SIMD computing power for non-numerical applications.

CONVENTIONAL PROGRAMMING

One concept is to treat SIMD processors as "hardware loops." In this approach, the elements of a vector (a FORTRAN array) are simply mapped onto the processor array, one vector element per processor. In a conventional computer, adding two vectors of numbers with 1000 elements each would require 1000 iterations of an add loop. In a SIMD computer with 1000 processors, a single add command causes 1000 adds to be performed simultaneously and in parallel - one add per processing element. The advantage of this approach to programming SIMD computers is that they can be applied to problems (i.e. programmed) in the same manner as conventional sequential computers with the provision that 1000 results are being calculated in parallel instead of just one. This approach also allows the straight forward addition of parallel constructs to FORTRAN and PASCAL, enabling a wide range of users access to the SIMD's computational power. However, it must be realized that in SIMD processors the parallelism is in the execution of a single task, not in multi-tasking. Consequently, the parallelism closely models the natural thought process.

LOOPS

Loops are one of the most fundamental constructs in a sequential computer. They are used to make natural parallel thoughts serial. Take for example the parallel thought, "clear array DUMMY to zero." In the MPP, every element of the array DUMMY is cleared simultaneously. In a sequential machine, loop control devices and parameters are required to assure that every element of DUMMY is cleared one location at a time.

The key conceptual relationship between the sequential and parallel implementation of this construct is memory layout. In a sequential environment, the array DUMMY is assigned to a physically contiguous block of memory. In the MPP, each element of DUMMY is assigned to a different processing element (PE). All elements however, have the same memory address. See Figure 1. Thus, the single instruction "clear DUMMY" broadcast from the Array Control Unit to all of the PEs causes all elements of the array DUMMY to be cleared simultaneously and therefore, is equivalent to a loop in a conventional computer.

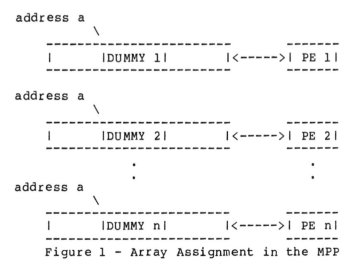

Figure 1 - Array Assignment in the MPP

For notational convenience, the PE memories of Figure 1 will be drawn with the memories adjacent to one another in a one dimensional array and without the PE's as shown below.   In the MPP, the 16,384 PE memories can be configured into a linear array or into a two dimensional 128x128 array.

```
                    DUMMY
           --------------------------
           |    |    |         |
           --------------------------
           |    |  . |         |
           |    |  . |         |
           |    |  . |         |
           --------------------------
           |    |    |         |
           --------------------------
```

Occasionally loops contain statements which are dependent on the loop variable.   In these cases, the MPP may require an auxiliary data array such as I = (1,2,3,---n).   Then, calculations which are a function of the loop index are obtained simply by using the index array.   For example, if K = (5,20,10,7,12,15): then the SIMD statement D($) = K($)*I($) yields D = (5,40,30,28,60,90) and is equivalent to the sequential code:

```
      DO 100 I = 1,6
100   D(I) = I*K(I).
```

The $ notation in D($) indicates that all elements of the array are being processed in parallel.

Frequently, loops have conditional statements in them.   In order to accommodate this situation every processing unit in the MPP array has its own dedicated condition code memory (the Mask or G register).   The G register for each individual PE can be set to true or false as a function of any logical combination of comparisons between constants and variables. During the execution of a conditional statement, the operations are executed normally, except that only those PEs which have a "true" G register participate in the operation. The PEs whose G registers are not true perform no-ops during the conditional operation. As can be seen in Figure 2a and 2b the code for this type of loop is nearly identical for both serial and parallel machines, the loop statements and G register initialization being the only difference.

```
    DO 10 I = 1,5                    G($) = .TRUE.
    B(I) = 2*K(I)                    B($) = 2*K($)
    IF D(I).LE.20                    IF D($).LE.20
       THEN B(I)=D(I)+K(I)              THEN B($)=D($)+K($)
 10 CONTINUE
```

        a. Serial Code   b. Parallel Code

                    Figure 2 - Conditional Execution

FLOW OF CONTROL

    If two identical sequential computers are programmed with an identical algorithm but are presented different data, at any given time they will, in general, be at different program locations as a function of the input data and the decision nodes in the algorithm. In the MPP each processing unit in the array will be processing a different set of data. Therefore, all paths of the algorithm must be traversed by the sequential control unit to assure that every PE executes the portions of the algorithms that the data it was presented requires. A method must be provided to prevent portions of the algorithm from being executed by those PEs whose data does not require them. This can be accomplished quite simply by requiring each PE to perform a no-op when an instruction it should not be executing is presented to it. This is exactly the function the G register performs. The G register mechanism and the requirement that all algorithm paths must be executed are easily dealt with structured programming concepts. (However, blocks of sequential code can be by passed using BRANCH instructions as in a sequential computer if all of the data in the array is to be treated similarly, i.e. if after a search the responses are all true or all false.)

In general, a search of the MPP's array memory can result in any number of matches. The set of words which have responded can be saved by setting a boolean variable as in the following statement:

TRUE($) := FIELD1($) = A AND FIELD2($) = 5.

The responses to a search can be processed sequentially by using the NEXT (get next responder index) and EOR (end of responders) functions and a ^ index variable notation. If there are no responders, i.e. all elements of the variable are false, EOR(TRUE($)) will be true and TRUE($)^ will be undefined. If EOR(TRUE($)) is false, then NEXT(TRUE($)) will assign the internal memory index of the next true word recorded by TRUE($) to TRUE($)^ and sets the value for that word to false. TRUE($)^ can be used as an "index" variable in place of $ in any parallel field reference.

INTRA-ARRAY COMMUNICATIONS

The MPP's inter-processor routing network can be used for intra-array operations. For example, the computation B(I) =

D(I)+D(I+C) where C is a constant, would be performed in the MPP simply by shifting the data C processing units via the inter-processor routine network (i.e. B($) = D($) + SHIFT(D($),C)).

DATA OVERFLOW

In all computers, there is a fundamental relationship between memory size and the amount of data to be processed.   To this point it has been assumed that all of the data would fit into one memory array.   That is, there are more PEs than data elements.   If this is not true, techniques used in conventional serial computer must be used to reconcile the amount of data with the memory capacity available.

Since data is normally broken into records, this discussion will center on the number of records in relation to the number of PEs.   If there are n PEs in a machine, any file with n or fewer records is easily accommodated as discussed above.   If a file has m records where m = 2n+j, then the data can be "folded" and processed as shown in Figure 3. The code shown is the equivalent of a nested loop in a sequential computer where the "inner loop" is performed in parallel.   Thus, it is clear that the solution to the limited memory problem is basically the same whether a sequential computer or the MPP is involved.

NON-NUMERICAL PROGRAMMING

The essence of artificial intelligence and data base management is not large amounts of number crunching but large amounts of searching.   Just as the MPP can perform 1000s of arithmetic operations in parallel, it can perform 1000s of

```
        address I  address I+1
            /        /
    -------------------------------
    |   | D1  | Dn+1 | D2n+1 |      |
    -------------------------------
    |   |  .  |  .   |   .   |      |
    -------------------------------
    |   | Dj  | Dn+j | D2n+j |<- last element
    -------------------------------
    |   |  .  |  .   |   .   |      |
    |   |  .  |  .   |   .   |      |
    -------------------------------
    |   | Dn  | D2n  |       |      |
    -------------------------------


            DO 10 I = 1,[M/N]+1
            D($,I) = computation
         10 CONTINUE
```

Figure 3 - Folded Data

logical search operations in parallel.   Since the MPP can search
an unordered list of 16,384 elements in one operation there is no
need to sort it.   In fact due to the overhead of sorting any
list, it is more efficient for the MPP to search lists which are
several time larger than the processor array than it is sort
them.   The slogan for non-numerical SIMD computation is SEARCH
DON'T SORT.

        The effect of this slogan on conventional programming
practices can be quite dramatic. For example, over one half of
the   COMPUTER ALGORITHMS text by Sara Baase (Addison-Wesley,
Reading, Massachusetts, 1978) concerns sorting algorithms which
are not necessary in a SEARCH DON'T SORT environment.   If this is
any guide, over one half of all programs and programming effort
can be eliminated by using SIMD computers.   It is impossible, of
course, to project the actual effect in such a casual manner, but

the point is that if the complete computational power of SIMD computers are to be exploited for non-numerical applications, it will be necessary to re-examine the pervasive practice of sorting in order to achieve efficient searching. This practice is evident in practically every conventional sequential algorithm program. The effect of eliminating this practice and using searching unordered data instead must be thoroughly analyzed.

The concept of sorted lists even forms the basis of all assembly language programs. That is, the instructions in a program are sorted in the order in which they are to be executed. This assures that the order of application of operators to the data is correct. Since in a SIMD computer, sorting can by enlarge be replaced by searching, it is natural to ask if this affects the fundamentals of computer programming itself?

For example, conventional sequential computers require that a single set of common instructions be used for multiple purposes. Thus control instructions such as conditional and unconditional branches must specify the ORDER in which operators are to be applied. Transformational instructions must describe HOW data are to be manipulated (added, subtracted, moved, etc), and all instructions must identify WHICH data are to be processed (address field). Since every program must accomplish all these tasks with one common set of instructions, the result is a confusing mixture of control (ORDER), address (WHICH) and transformational (HOW) information.

This situation could greatly improved by using the searching power of a SIMD processor to simplify and separate these three functions. In particular, the WHICH function normally performed by memory addressing can be accomplished by using a state field associated with each datum. Consider the simple flow chart in Figure 4a which shows 5 blocks of program code all of which are transformational except for block B which contains a conditional control statement. If a data flow analysis is performed on a datum as it goes through the flow chart, then, as shown in Figure 4b, the initial state of the datum is 1. The state of the datum after transformation A is state 2, etc. Note that while block B does not transform the datum, it does assign it a new state as a function of its values or contents. The new state then determines whether transformation C or D is applied. Both transformations produce a datum with state 5 which is then processed by transformation E producing state 6.

In a SIMD computer the data selection task (WHICH) can be accomplished by searching for tags which reflect the data's state. Those processing elements which contain data in the correct state are left on, the others are turned off. Thus the the instruction only operates on data with the correct tag. Note that consequently, the order of instruction application is immaterial as long as all data are eventually completely processed. Thus the control task is reduced to simply specifying the "next" state of the data. As a result, the instruction set can be tailored to the single task of describing how to OPERATE on data. An assembly language statement would be of the form:

```
OPERATION IS (SF1 SF2 DF) OS
    Where: IS  is the input state
           SF1 is source field 1
           SF2 is source field 2
           DF  is the destination field
           OS  is the output state.
```

For example, ADD 4 (A B C) 5   would cause all data in array A which are in state 4 to be added to the corresponding data of array B.   The sums would be stored in array C and assigned state 5.

Blocks of code would be composed of sequences of statements. Programs would be sets of blocks.   Programs and blocks need not be ordered,   but most frequently would be for ease of generation, reading and efficiency of execution.

As shown above, the concept of tagged data seems well suited to SIMD programming at the assembly language level.   It is important to determine if this same concept can be applied to high level languages also.   If so, a comprehensive approach to programming SIMD computers can be developed.   Thus only one philosophy of programming would have to be learned to become proficient in both assembly and high level languages.   In fact, if the same concept of tagged data is used through out, it should be possible to tailor the level of the language to the problem at hand.

The purpose of this section is to describe some of the concepts which need to be explored to fully understand how to program computers such as the MPP.   The essence of SIMD programming is that every data record has its own individual processor.   Programming is then simply the problem of each processor determining which of the instructions or statements being sent to it should be executed based on the state of the data in the record.   In the tagged data approach, the complex and confusing techniques of time sharing a central processor between

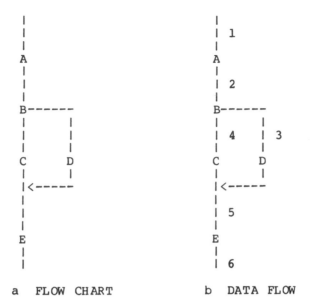

a   FLOW CHART   b   DATA FLOW

Figure 4 - Program Control

all records is eliminated.   An important aspect of this approach
is that it is applicable to existing bit serial SIMD processors.
Programs written with the tag concept can be executed by them
without any hardware modifications.

REFERENCES

Batcher, K. E., "Design of a Massively Parallel Processor," IEEE
    Transactions on Computers, September 1980.

Backus, J., "Can Programming be Liberated from the von Neuman
    Style?," COMMUNICATIONS OF THE ACM, VOL. 21, NO. 8, AUGUST
    1978, PP. 613-641.

Potter, J. L., "The STARAN Architecture and its Application to
    Image Processing and Pattern Recognition Algorithms,"
    Proceedings National Computer Conference, 1978.

Potter, J., "MPP Architecture and Software," NON-CONVENTIONAL
    COMPUTERS FOR IMAGE PROCESSING, L. Uhr and K. Preston (eds.),
    Academic Press, 1982.

PARALLEL PASCAL AND THE MASSIVELY PARALLEL PROCESSOR

Anthony P. Reeves
School of Electrical Engineering
Cornell University
Ithaca, New York 14853

INTRODUCTION

Parallel Pascal is an extended version of the Pascal programming language which is designed for the convenient and efficient programming of parallel computers. Parallel Pascal was designed with the MPP as the initial target architecture. It is the first high level programming language to be implemented on the MPP.

The Parallel Pascal language is outlined in the first section of this chapter; then language restrictions on the current MPP compiler imposed by the MPP architecture are discussed. Finally, algorithm techniques for efficiently programming the MPP are presented.

Conventional serial high-level programming languages are difficult to efficiently implement on parallel computers. Most parallel computers are currently programmed in either assembly language or a machine-dependent special version of Fortran. The main advantages of a general high-level language for parallel computers, such as Parallel Pascal, are portability, better error detection and diagnosis facilities, and efficiency. Efficiency must be a prime consideration since with any parallel system extra hardware is being used to achieve a high speed performance. Portability is perhaps the most difficult goal to achieve while maintaining efficiency since different parallel systems have very dif-

ferent data permutation capabilities. The efficiency of working programs can be enhanced, in some cases, by reprogramming a small number of
critical procedures in assembly code.

There are three fundamental classes of operations on array data
which are frequently implemented as primitives on array computers but
which are not available in conventional programming languages, these
are: data reduction, data permutation and data broadcast. These operations have been included as primitives in Parallel Pascal.

The design of Parallel Pascal was directed towards the MPP; however, it is also suitable for other parallel computers with a similar
interconnection scheme such as Illiac IV and the DAP. Parallel Pascal
is also suitable for parallel computers with a less restrictive interconnection scheme such as is found with many pipeline systems for example. In this case, it may be necessary to implement some additional
data mapping functions in order to take advantage of all the parallel
computers capabilities. A more detailed discussion of the language
design is given in [1]. An in depth description of Parallel Pascal and
other aspects of the MPP is given in [2] and also in [3].

A Parallel Pascal to standard Pascal translator has been developed
to allow initial experimentation with different language features. This
translator is now being used for program development of Parallel Pascal
programs on conventional serial computers.

A compiler has been developed [3,2] which converts a Parallel Pascal program into a parallel p-code form. Interesting features of this
p-code language include: a mechanism for non-primitive data types needed
because of subarrays, an abstract addressing scheme for automatically

allocated variables to permit the code generator to decide the appropriate host for the code, mechanisms for operating on arrays and subarrays, and a symbolic scheme for referencing fields of a record structure. An description of this p-code is given in [4] and also in [2]. A parallel p-code code generator for the MPP has been developed by Computer Sciences Corporation.

PARALLEL EXPRESSIONS

In Parallel Pascal all conventional expressions are extended to array data types. In a parallel expression all operations must have conformable array arguments. A scalar is considered to be conformable to any type compatible array and is conceptually converted to a conformable array with all elements having the scalar value. For example, given the definition

var a, b, c: array [1..10] of integer;

the following statement

a := b + c + 1;

is equivalent to

for i := 1 **to** 10 **do**
        a[i] := b[i] + c[i] + 1;

In many highly parallel computers including the MPP there are at least two different primary memory systems; one in the host and one in the processor array. Parallel Pascal provides the reserved word

parallel to allow programmers to specify the memory in which an array should reside. In standard Pascal an array type is specified with the following syntax

    type newtype = **array** [indextype] **of** eltype;

where indextype specifies the number and ranges of the array dimensions and eltype specifies the type of the array elements. A parallel array type is specified with the syntax

    type newtype = **parallel array** [indextype] **of** eltype;

The parallel specifier exists only to provide information to the the compiler as to the variables usage. In all usage in the language a parallel array is indistinguishable from a conventional array. In some systems there is no distinction between host and processor memories, then the parallel specifier does not have any effect. In any case, a compiler may decline to store the array where requested.

ARRAY SELECTION

Selection of a portion of an array by selecting either a single index value or all index values for each dimension is frequently used in many parallel algorithms; e.g., to select the ith row of a matrix which is a vector. Specification of a single index value is the standard indexing method in standard Pascal. In Parallel Pascal all index values can be specified by eliding the index value for that dimension. For example, given the definition

    var a,b: **array** [1..5,1..10] **of** integer;

in Parallel Pascal the statement

    a[,1] := b[,4];

assigns the fourth column of b to the first column of a. The following
are valid statements in standard Pascal

    a := b;
    a[1] := b[2];

The second statement means assign the second row of b to the first row
of a; in Parallel Pascal this could also be specified by

    a[1,] := b[2,];

SUBRANGE CONSTANTS

It is sometimes necessary to move data between arrays with different dimensions. In Parallel Pascal subarrays consisting of consecutive sets of elements may be specified. If subarrays with other than
consecutive elements are required then they must be packed into the consecutive form with permutation functions. The concept of a constant
subrange is introduced in order to specify a consecutive subset of index
values.

The syntax for the constant subrange is

    const identifier = low..high;

where low and high are either literals or previously defined constant
identifiers.

SUBRANGE INDEXING AND ARRAY PACKING

Subrange constants may be used to index an array in Parallel Pascal. The general syntax for a subrange index is

array-identifier[offset @ subrange-constant]

where offset is an optional conventional scalar index expression. The ordered set of indices specified by a subrange index is the result of adding the value of the offset expression to the values implied by the subrange constant. For example, given the definition

var a, b: **array** [1..10] **of** integer;

the statement

a[@2..6] := b[3 @ 1..5];

is functionally equivalent to

for i := 1 **to** 5 **do**
    a[i + 1] := b[i + 3];

The main reason for introducing subrange indexing was to permit blocks of data to be transferred between arrays having different dimensions. It was not designed to be a tool for algorithm development.

ARRAY CONFORMABILITY

In standard Pascal, data items combined together in an expression must be type compatible. In Parallel Pascal, array data items in a parallel expression must also be conformable, i.e. have the same rank (number of dimensions) and the same range in each dimension. For example, given the definitions

    var a, b: **array** [1..10] **of** integer;

        c: **array** [0..9] **of** integer;

the statement

    a := a + b;

is conformable, while the statement

    a := b + c;

is not conformable since the specified ranges of b and c are different.

While the exact range conformability requirement is in keeping with the strong typing concepts of standard Pascal, there are occasions when the action specified by the above statement is useful. The range requirement can be explicitly circumvented by using subrange indexing. For example, the statements

    a := b + c[@0..9];

    a[@1..10] := b[@1..10] + c;

    a[@1..10] := b[@1..10] + c[@0..9];

are all conformable and have the same effect.

REDUCTION FUNCTIONS

Array reduction operations are achieved with a set of standard functions in Parallel Pascal which are listed in table 1.

Table 1: Reduction Functions

Syntax	Meaning
sum(array, D1, D2, ..., Dn)	reduce array with arithmetic sum
prod(array, D1, D2, ..., Dn)	reduce array with arithmetic product
all(array, D1, D2, ..., Dn)	reduce array with Boolean AND
any(array, D1, D2, ..., Dn)	reduce array with Boolean OR
max(array, D1, D2, ..., Dn)	reduce array with arithmetic maximum
min(array, D1, D2, ..., Dn)	reduce array with arithmetic minimum

The first argument of a reduction function specifies the array to be reduced and the following arguments specify which dimensions are to be reduced. A dimension is specified by a constant expression; the first dimension is dimension 1. The dimension parameters must be constant expressions so that the shape of the result is known at compile time.

For example, given the the definitions

var

      a: **array**[1..10,1..5] **of** integer;

      b: **array**[1..10] **of** integer;

      c: integer;

the following are correct Parallel Pascal statements

```
b := sum(a, 2);      (* sum the rows of a *)

c := sum(a, 1, 2);   (* sum all elements of the array a *)

c := max(b, 1);      (* find the maximum value of b *)
```

Each dimension parameter of a reduction function implies that there will be one less dimension in the result array; a scalar is considered to be an array without any dimensions in this context.

PERMUTATION AND DISTRIBUTION FUNCTIONS

One of the most important features of a parallel programming language is the facility to specify parallel array data permutation and distribution operations. In Parallel Pascal four such operations are available as primitive standard functions; however, for some Parallel Processors it may be necessary to specify more primitive functions for efficiency. The standard Parallel Pascal functions for data permutation and distribution are given in table 2.

Table 2: Permutation and Distribution Functions

Syntax	Meaning
shift(array, S1, S2, ..., Sn)	end-off shift data within array
rotate(array, S1, S2, ..., Sn)	circularly rotate data within array
transpose(array, D1, D2)	transpose two dimensions of array
expand(array, dim, range)	expand array along specified dimension

SHIFT AND ROTATE

The shift and rotate primitives are found in many parallel hardware architectures and also, in many algorithms. The shift function shifts data by the amount specified for each dimension and shifts zeros (null elements) in at the edges of the array. Elements shifted out of the array are discarded. The rotate function is similar to the shift function except that data shifted out of the array is inserted at the opposite edge so that no data is lost. The first argument to the shift and rotate functions is the array to be shifted; then there is an ordered set of parameters, each one specifies the amount of shift in its corresponding dimension. There must be as many shift parameters as there are dimensions in the array; the first shift parameter is associated with the first dimension of the array.

For example, given the definitions

```
var
    a, b: array [1..5,0..9] of integer;
    c, d: array [0..9] of integer;
```

the statement

```
a := shift(b, 0, 3);
```

is functionally equivalent to

```
for i := 1 to 5 do
  begin
    for j := 0 to 6 do
        a[i,j] := b[i,j+3];
    for j := 7 to 9 do
        a[i,j] := 0;
  end;
```

and the statement

```
c := rotate(d, 3);
```

is functionally equivalent to

```
for i := 0 to 9 do
    c[i] := d[(i + 3) mod 10];
```

TRANSPOSE AND EXPAND

While transpose is not a simple function to implement with many parallel architectures, a significant number of matrix algorithms involve this function; therefore, it has been made available as a primitive function in Parallel Pascal. The first parameter to transpose is the array to be transposed and the following two parameters, which are constant expressions, specify which dimensions are to be interchanged. If only one dimension is specified then the array is flipped about that dimension.

The main data distribution function in Parallel Pascal is expand. This function increases the rank of an array by one by repeating the contents of the array along a new dimension. The first parameter of expand specifies the array to be expanded, the second parameter, a constant expression, specifies the number of the new dimension and the last parameter, a subrange or a subrange type, specifies the range of the new dimension.

This function is used to maintain a higher degree of parallelism in a parallel statement; this may result in a clearer expression of the operation and a more direct parallel implementation. In a conventional serial environment such a function would simply waste space.

For example, given the definitions of a, b, and c as specified in section 5.1 the following statement adds a vector to all rows of a matrix

```
a := b + expand(c, 1, 1..5);
```

The above statement is functionally equivalent to the following

```
for i := 1 to 5 do
    a[i,] := b[i,] + c;
```

CONDITIONAL EXECUTION

An important feature of any parallel programming language is the ability to have an operation operate on a subset of the elements of an array. In standard Pascal each array element is processed by a specific sequence of statements and there are a variety of program control structures for the repeated or selective execution of statments. In Parallel Pascal the whole array is processed by a single statement; therefore, an extended program control structure is needed.

The syntax of the Parallel Pascal **where** statement is as follows:

where array-expression **do**
    statement
otherwise
    statement

where array-expression is a Boolean valued array expression and statement is a Parallel Pascal statement. The **otherwise** and the second controlled statement may be omitted.

The execution of a **where** structure is defined as follows. First, the controlling expression is evaluated to obtain a Boolean array (mask array). Next, the first controlled statement is evaluated. Array assignments are masked according to the boolean control array. If there is an otherwise statement it is then evaluated; in this case array assignments are masked with the inverse of the control array.

For example, given the definition

var a, b, c:**array** [1..10] **of** integer;

the following expression

where a < b **do**
    c := b
otherwise
    c := a;

is functionally equivalent to

for i := 1 **to** 10 **do**
  if a[i] < b[i] **then**
    c[i] := b[i]
  else
    c[i] := a[i];

The main semantic difference between the **where-do-otherwise** structure and the **if-then-else** structure is that with the former both controlled statements are evaluated, independent of the value of the control expression, while with the latter only one of the two controlled statements is evaluated.

Where statements may be nested provided that all of the controlling array expressions are type compatible. Other standard Pascal control statements can also be nested within **where** statements. Any array variable which appears on the left hand side of an assignment within a where controlled statement must be type compatible with the controlling array expression. Assignments to other than array variables in a where statement are in no way affected by the where statement. The effect of a where statement is local to the procedure or function in which it occurs; that is, it does not affect the execution of any procedures or functions called from within a where statement or an otherwise statement.

BIT-PLANE INDEXING

A feature of several current highly parallel computers such as the MPP is that arithmetic is conducted at the bit level rather than the word or number level. That is, the computer "word" or bit plane manipulated by these computers is a single bit slice through all elements in the array being processed.

Some algorithms can be made considerably more efficient for these computers if specified at the bit plane level. Bit-plane indexing was added to Parallel Pascal to enable a programmer to conveniently specify most of these special algorithms without resorting to an assembly code subroutine.

A bit-plane index is specified by the last item in an index expression and is separated from other indices by a colon. The result of a bit-plane indexed array has a Boolean element type. For example, given the definition

var a: **array** [1..5,1..10] **of** integer;
var b: **array** [1..5,1..10] **of** Boolean;

then the statement

```
    b := a[:0];
```

is equivalent to

```
    b := odd(a);
```

The next example subtracts one from the selected array element if necessary to make it exactly divisible by 2.

```
    a[3,1:0] := false;
```

The least significant or first bit-plane is always bit-plane 0. Programming with bit-plane indexing requires a knowledge of the internal number representation of the parallel processor and is a highly non portable feature. Furthermore, bit-plane indexing on a processor which does not operate at the bit level is usually very inefficient.

LIBRARY SUBPROGRAMS AND SEPARATE COMPILATION

Standard Pascal has no library facility; all subprograms i.e., procedures and functions, must be present in the source program. A library preprocessor was developed to allow the use of libraries without violating the rules of standard Pascal. The header line of a library subprogram is specified in the source program with an **extern** directive. The library preprocessor replaces the extern directive with the appropriate subprogram body. The type information for the library subprogram is extracted from the declaration statement in the source program. Therefore, library subprograms can be written to work with any user specified array type.

If a library subprogram is to be used for more than one array type in the same block, then a subprogram declaration statement for each unique argument type is necessary. Each unique version of the subprogram is identified by a user specified extension to the subprogram name in both declaration and usage.

For example, consider the ceiling function as defined below:

```
function ceiling(x:xtype) : rtype;
begin
    where x < 0.0 do
        ceiling := trunc(x)
    otherwise
        where x-trunc(x) = 0.0 do
            ceiling := trunc(x)
        otherwise
            ceiling := trunc(x)+1;
end;
```

The following program fragment illustrates how more than one version of this function could be specified for the library preprocessor.

```
    . . .
    type
            ar = array [1..10] of real;
            ai = array [1..10] of integer;
            br = array [1..8, 1..8] of real;
            bi = array [1..8, 1..8] of integer;
```

```
function ceiling.a(x:ar) :ai; extern;

function ceiling.b(x:br) :bi; extern;

var

    ax:ar; ay:ai; bx:br; by:bi;

begin

  . . .

    ay := ceiling.a(ax);

    by := ceiling.b(bx);

  . . .
```

The simple library preprocessor does not solve the separate compilation problem: all requested library subprograms must be recompiled whenever a change is made to the main program. However, it is an expedient solution to the library problem which will work with all Parallel Pascal compilers. External, partially compiled subprograms could be inserted at the p-code level or at the code generator level of a compiler. However, they should be inserted before the optimization stage so that specific parallel computer sensitivities to different array sizes may be considered.

MPP COMPILER RESTRICTIONS

The Parallel Pascal compiler for the MPP currently has several restrictions. The most important of these is that the range of the last two dimensions of a parallel array are constrained to be 128; i.e., to exactly fit the parallel array size of the MPP. It is possible that language support could have been provided to mask the hardware details of the MPP array size from the programmer; however, this would be very

difficult to do and efficient code generation for arbitrary sized arrays
could not be guaranteed. Matrices which are smaller than 128 x 128 can
usually be fit into a 128 x 128 array by the programmer. Frequently,
arrays which are larger than 128 x 128 are required and these are usually fit into arrays which have a conceptual size which is a multiple of
128 x 128.

A large matrix of dimensions (m * 128) x (n * 128) is specified by
a four dimensional array in the MPP version of Parallel Pascal which has
the dimensions m x n x 128 x 128. There are two fundamental methods for
packing the large matrix data into this four dimensional array, this
packing may be directly achieved by the staging memory in both cases.
In the "crinkled" packing scheme a m x n matrix of adjacent large matrix
elements is assigned to each PE; adjacent submatrices are assigned to
adjacent PE's. More formally, element (i,j) of the large matrix is
mapped to location [i mod m, j mod n, i div m, j div n] of the four
dimensional array.

The alternative packing scheme, called "blocked" packing, assigns
adjacent large matrix elements to adjacent PE's in blocks of 128 x 128.
The large matrix is represented by a m x n matrix of adjacent 128 x 128
blocks. More formally, element (i,j) of the large matrix is mapped to
location [i div 128, j div 128, i mod 128, j mod 128] of the four dimensional array.

The best method of large array packing is application dependent
which is one reason that large arrays are not handled automatically by
the compiler.

Programming with large matrices stored as four dimensional arrays is very simple in Parallel Pascal. In general, programs developed for a single 128 x 128 array are easily modified to deal with large packed matrices. Simple arithmetic expressions directly extend to higher dimensioned arrays, reduction functions may require additional dimension specifiers. Shift and rotate operations require special consideration since care must be taken to correctly transfer data between the boundaries of the submatrices. Generic library functions have been written in Parallel Pascal to deal with large matrices. The functions lshift and lrotate will correctly manipulate large matrices stored with the blocked packing scheme and the functions crshift and crrotate will deal with matrices stored with the crinkled packing scheme.

The hardware organization of the MPP currently imposes some further language restrictions. These could be removed with a more advanced version of the code generator. Host programs for the MPP can be run either on the main control unit (MCU) or on the VAX; in the latter case the MCU simply relays commands from the VAX to the PE array. The advantages of running on the VAX is a good programming environment, floating point arithmetic support and large memory (or virtual memory). The advantage of running on the MCU is more direct control of the MPP array.

Compiler directives are used to specify if the generated code should run on the MCU or the VAX. With the current implementation of the code generator, only complete procedures can be assigned to the MCU and only programs on the MCU can manipulate parallel arrays. There are several other language restrictions for programs which are run on the MCU such as no conventional I/O. Therefore, the programmer must isolate sections of code which deal with the PE array in procedures which are directed to the MCU. A better strategy might be to run the majority of the host program code on the VAX with only small sections which deal with PE array on the MCU, then there would be no language restrictions for the programmer but the code generator would be more complex.

LIBRARY PROGRAM DEVELOPMENT

Initial experience with developing algorithms for the MPP indicate that library functions must frequently be developed in three different forms for maximum efficiency. The basic form is a pure Parallel Pascal algorithm which takes the greatest advantage of the parallel features of the language. This form will run directly on the MPP array for arrays with the last two dimensions being 128 x 128.

The second form is for large arrays on the MPP, i.e., arrays with dimensions which are exact multiples of 128 x 128. In many cases, such as the near neighbor operations described in the next section, the transformation to this form from the previous form is very simple. In general, shift and rotate functions are replaced by lshift and lrotate library functions.

The third form is for functions which are to be implemented on the VAX host computer. While parallel algorithms will run correctly on the host computer such algorithms do not take advantage of the direct index-ing capabilities of the VAX and much more efficient serial algorithms may be possible. Furthermore, any algorithms which use the bit-indexing language features can usually be much more efficiently reprogrammed for the VAX since it does not have an efficient bit indexing mechanism.

LIBRARY PACKAGES

The Parallel Pascal language provides basic efficient orthogonal primitives for developing application programs. However, it is expected that for any specific application area application directed primitive library functions will be required. Several application library packages have already been developed for Parallel Pascal. These include: large matrix shift and rotate, near neighbor functions, a general permutation function which is used for matrix rotation and polynomial warping, a parallel random number generator, and pyramid data structure functions.

In the next two sections, programming techniques will be illustrated with examples from the near neighbor package and the permutation package.

THE NEAR NEIGHBOR LIBRARY PACKAGE

The near neighbor package illustrates how Parallel Pascal can provide a convenient environment for specifying application primitives; the need for different forms of the same function is also demonstrated. A near neighbor (nn) operation is one in which each result element of a matrix is computed by a function of only locally adjacent elements in a corresponding input matrix. Near neighbor operations are frequently used in image processing applications. Several high level languages for image processing include such operations as basic primitives.

The basic unit frequently used in near neighbor operations is a small matrix (3 x 3 to 7 x 7) of constant values. The first nn library function, called mx3, is used for specifying 3 x 3 matrices. The use of this function is illustrated in the following example.

```
    type
         mtype = array [1..3, 1..3] of integer;
    function  mx3(v00, v01, v02,
                  v10, v11, v12,
                  v20, v21, v22: integer): mtype; extern;

    var  mc: mtype;

  . . .

    mc := mx3( -1, -1, -1,
               -1,  8, -1,
               -1, -1, -1);
```

The matrix mc is set with all boundary elements to -1 and the center element to 8 as is pictorially shown. A typical filtering operation is to convolve a large image matrix with a small kernel matrix; the generic library function conv is designed for this operation. A possible definition for conv is shown below:

```
    type  . . .
         mx = parallel array [1..128, 1..128] of eltype;
    function conv(matrix:mx; kernel:mtype):mx;
        var i,j: integer;
            sum: mx;
        begin
            sum:=0;
            for i:= 1 to 3 do begin
                for j:= 1 to 3 do begin
```

```
                 if (kernel[i,j] <> 0) then
               sum := sum + kernel[i,j] * shift(matrix,i-2,j-2);
             end;
           end;
           conv := sum
         end;
      var . . .
        ma, mb:mx;
```

the convolution of ma with the kernel mc is specified by

```
    mb := conv(ma, mc);
```

The contents of the kernel may also be expressed in the same statement; e.g.,

```
    mb := conv(ma, mx3(0, 1, 0,
                       0, 0, 1,
                       0, 1, 0);
```

Sparse kernels with only a few 1 elements occur frequently in some applications. In these cases programmers often prefer to specify the kernel in a short-hand form consisting of a list of the cardinal directions of the 1's. The library function mxd converts such a list to the 3 x 3 matrix; using this function the above statement may be rewritten as

```
    mb := conv(ma, mxd([N, E, S]));
```

The large matrix version of conv is simply specified by changing the word shift to lshift of crshift, as is appropriate, and redefining mx to be a four dimensional array. Conv is also reasonably organized for a serial processor. An improvement may be possible in this case by explicitly writing the loops so that the convolution is computed in one pass through the data since better use of a cache memory would result.

THE PERMUTATION LIBRARY PACKAGE

The need for more than one version of a library function for the same operation is illustrated with the permutation function. The matrix permutation function has three arguments: a data matrix to be permuted, a row matrix which indicates in which row from the data matrix the corresponding result element is to be obtained and a column matrix which indicates in which column the result is to be obtained. The function returns the permuted matrix (in fact any data mapping is possible). A serial version of this function is shown below:

```
type
     pa = array [lol..hil, lo2..hi2] of integer;

function perm2s(mx:pa; r:pa; c:pa):pa;
var
    i, j: integer;
begin
    for i := lol to hil do
      for j := lo2 to hi2 do
          perm2s[i,j] := mx[r[i,j],c[i,j]];
```

```
    end;
```

This function is efficiently programmed for a serial computer such as the VAX host and would execute in $O(n^2)$ time for a n x n data matrix. In contrast, this would be a very poor algorithm for a parallel array. A single data transfer would require $O(n)$ time since only near neighbor shifts are possible; therefore, the total algorithm would require $O(n^3)$ time.

We have developed a parallel algorithm for this task which attempts to move all the data together as much as possible. On a parallel processor with $O(n^2)$ PE's this algorithm still has a worst case time complexity of $O(n^2)$ but for many structured permutations such as rotation and warping the complexity will be closer to $O(n)$.

The parallel algorithm will execute much more slowly on a serial processor than the serial algorithm since the serial algorithm makes direct use of the serial processors indexing capability. The parallel algorithm can be easily extended to large matrices which are multiples of 128 x 128 by directly replacing shift operations with lshift operations; however, this will not be optimal with respect to the number of shift operations needed. For example, with the blocked storage scheme a horizontal shift which is a multiple of 128 steps requires no shift operations at all since the data is already in the correct PE. A large matrix version of the algorithm is currently under development which will attempt to minimize the actual number of shift operations executed.

EXTENDED I/O

For many applications the standard I/O facilities of Pascal will be adequate. The staging buffer of the MPP can be very useful for directly performing certain data permutations; these permutations cannot be directly specified in the basic language of Parallel Pascal. A high level language facility for using the staging buffer has not yet been implemented; a proposal for how the staging buffer may be programmed and used is outlined below.

There are three new capabilities, made possible with the staging buffer, which we would like to specify in the language.

1. File reformatting

Raw data files may not be in the correct format for the MPP array. For example we may wish to do large matrix packing or select one band of a multiband file.

2. Sub-array file I/O

In some cases it is useful to assemble a large array from sub arrays (which may be smaller than 128 x 128).

3. Data permutations

The staging buffer is capable of implementing a large range of data permutations. In some cases it is effective to transfer data from the PE array through the staging buffer and back to the array in order to achieve a data permutation.

These new capabilities could be made available by introducing two new procedures to Parallel Pascal and relaxing one of the Pascal I/O constraints as indicated below: FILE REFORMATTING

File reformatting can be achieved by the "reformat" procedure which specifies a reordering of the dimensions of an array structure. For example consider that we have a disk file of a set of 128 x 128 images with 6 bands. The file is declared as follows:

    var f: file of parallel array [1..6, 1..128, 1..128] of 0..255;

This will work correctly if each image is stored on the disk as a sequence of 6 consecutive 128 x 128 matrices. If the data is stored in pixel interleaved format (i.e. as a sequence of 6 element pixels) then the staging buffer must be set to do the format conversion; this can be achieved with the following call to the reformat procedure:

    reformat(f, 2, 3, 1);

This specifies that the ordering of the dimensions for the data on the disk is 2, 3, 1; i.e., the disk file array has the shape 128 x 128 x 6.

SUB-ARRAY I/O

In general, array I/O is done with a file having records of type array; an I/O operation then specifies the transfer of a complete array. Sub-array I/O may be achieved by relaxing the Pascal restriction that complete file data types must be read or written. The range of the dimensions of the subarray must match the last dimensions of the file array. For example, consider the 6 band image file described above and the following array declarations.

    type ar = parallel array[1..128, 1..128] of 0..255;

    var a: ar;

```
      b: array [1..6] of ar;
```

With the conventional Pascal I/O restrictions only whole images can be read; i.e., read(f, b) is a valid statement whereas read(f, a) is not since a is not the same type as the file type.

In the extended I/O scheme, read(f, a) is permitted and reads the bands of an image one at a time. Parallel array files having the last dimensions smaller than 128 x 128 may be declared in which case a variable in an I/O statement such as a must have a subrange index for conformability.

DATA PERMUTATIONS

Data permutations can be achieved with a "link" procedure which links two files. Linked files form a virtual channel through the staging buffer and, in general, do not require any disk space. The data permutation is specified by reformatting the two files.

The syntax for link is:

```
      link(f,g);
```

where f and g are files.

Link also implies a "rewrite" on file f and a "reset" on file g.

For example: a transpose permutation could be specified as follows:

```
type
      at = parallel array [1..128, 1..128] of real;
var
      fa, fb: file of at;
      a, b: at;
```

. . .

```
reformat(fa, 2, 1);

link(fa, fb);

write(fa, a);

read(fb, b);
```

The above set of statements is equivalent to

```
b := transpose(a, 2, 1);
```

CONCLUSION

A version of the Pascal programming language for parallel computers has been developed which required very few new language features. One of the main features of this language is that permutations are achieved with conventional function forms. In this way it is simple to introduce new permutation functions for the efficient programming of a new parallel computer, when necessary, without changing the language.

No attempt was made with the first implementation of the MPP compiler to hide the 128 x 128 dimensions of the PE array. This was considered to be necessary in order to ensure that efficient algorithms are developed and also ensure that the very limited local memory is not squandered. Programming tools have been outlined for programming larger arrays. A future compiler may hide these details from the user as effective programming techniques are better understood.

The only extensions needed for Parallel Pascal to effectively use the MPP hardware are the I/O extensions which consist of two new procedures and the relaxation of a standard Pascal constraint. These enable the staging buffer to be effectively utilized for data permutations and file reformatting.

Parallel Pascal provides convenient orthogonal efficient high level primitives on which to build application programs. It is more difficult to efficiently program a parallel computer than a serial computer; therefore, the establishment of library packages for application oriented primitives is even more important than for the conventional serial case. Some of the programming techniques for Parallel Pascal have been outlined in the context of packages which are currently being developed.

ACKNOWLEDGEMENTS

I gratefully acknowledge the assistance of John Bruner who helped specify the language and wrote the P-code compiler, Mark Poret and Tony Brewer who developed the Parallel Pascal translator, and Steve Elias who developed the library preprocessor. Most of this work was supported with NASA grant NAG 5-3.

REFERENCES

1. A. P. Reeves, "Parallel Pascal: An extended Pascal for Parallel computers," _Journal of Parallel and Distributed Computng_ Vol. **1**(1984).

2. A. P. Reeves and J. D. Bruner, "The Language Parallel Pascal and Other Aspects of the Massively Parallel Processor," Cornell University Technical Report (December 1982).

3. J. D. Bruner, "Efficient Implementation of a High -level Language on a Bit-Serial Parallel Matrix Processor," Ph.D. Thesis, Purdue University (1982).

4. J. D. Bruner and A. P. Reeves, "A Parallel P-Code for Parallel Pascal and Other High Level languages," _1983 International Conference on Parallel Processing_, pp. 240-243 (August 1983).

MPP SYSTEM SOFTWARE

Kenneth E. Batcher
Digital Technology Department
Goodyear Aerospace Corporation
Akron, Ohio 44315

Introduction -- Software in the massively parallel processor supports the features of the hardware elements. As described in another chapter of this book, the array control unit has three independent control units: the Processing Element Control Unit (PECU), the Input-Output Control Unit (IOCU), and the Main Control Unit (MCU). Users can program these control units using the PE Array Language (PRL) for the micro-coded array processing routines executing in the PECU and the Main Control Language (MCL) for the IO programs executing in the IOCU and for the main application program executing in the MCU.

Application programs using standard array processing routines and standard IO operations can be coded completely in the main control unit using MCL. Such programs are developed as follows:

1. MCL source language modules are coded using editors in the front-end computer.

2. The main control assembler, MCL, is called to create object modules from the source modules.

3. The task builder or linker in the front-end is called to link the object modules together into a load module of the application program. A symbol table of the standard library of PECU array processing routines is used as one of the source files to the linker to resolve all entry points to the routines.

4. The MPP control and debug module, CAD, is called to

load the PE control memory with the standard library of array processing routines and to load the main control memory with the load module of the application program. A CAD command can be used to bring a standard IO support task into the front-end computer to support the IO required by the application program. Another CAD command initiates execution. Other CAD commands can be used to stop execution, dump memory, do traces, etc. to debug the application program.

If the application program performs non-standard array operations then new array processing routines are developed as follows:

1. PRL source language modules are created using the editors in the front-end computer.

2. The PECU assembler, PRL, is called to create object modules from the PRL source modules.

3. The front-end task builder or linker is called to link the PECU object modules with any library modules required by the application program to create a load module for the PE control memory. The symbol table of this link is saved and used instead of the standard library symbol table when the main application program is linked.

4. CAD loads the load module created in step 3 into the PE control memory instead of the standard library of array processing routines.

If the application program requires special IO operations then a special IO support task can be coded to run in the front-end. The task can be written in FORTRAN or some other high-order language. A CAD command can bring it into play in place of the standard IO support task. Users can also code special IOCU programs in MCL.

Note that the front-end task builder or linker is used to create load modules for the MPP main control memory and PE control memory. This means that the front-end facilities for creating and maintaining libraries of object modules, etc. can be used for libraries of main control object modules and PE control object modules.

MAIN CONTROL ASSEMBLER (MCL)

The main control assembler (MCL) assembles object modules for the main control memory of the MPP. The object modules may be programs to be executed by the main control unit (MCU), scalar data items to be referenced by the MCU, and IO programs to be executed by the input output control unit (IOCU). The object modules produced by MCL are linked into a main control memory task image by the front-end task builder or linker. A listing file is also produced by MCL. Each object module may be created from one or more source files.

To ease the burden of generating application programs, MCL is a macro-assembler so that a simple one-line statement written by the programmer can create a sequence of MCU instructions. This facility is used extensively in calling array processing routines to be executed by the PECU. For example, the MCL statement:

    ADAA   REALA, REALB, REALC

performs a floating-point add on floating-point arrays REALA and REALB and stores the sum into floating-point array REALC. It calls three array processing routines to be executed in order by the PECU: a routine to compare corresponding entries in REALA and REALB, a routine to align fractions and add them, and a routine to normalize the result. Each call is performed by loading the appropriate call parameters into registers R36 through R44 of the MCU (see item 3.6.5). A macro in the system macro library creates the required MCU instructions from the single line of user code.

As the library of array processing routines is extended, the library of calling macros can also be extended so MCL programmers can call the new routines with simple one-line statements. For example, an array processing routine to read the entries of an angle array and put their sines in a second array may be called by MCL programmers using a simple statement like:

SINEAA   ANGLE,SINE

if the required macro is added to the library.

Variables in MCL may be arrays, bit-planes, or scalars. Arrays and bit-planes are stored in ARU memory planes while scalars are stored in main control memory. Arrays and scalars have four data types: cardinal (non-negative integers), integer (signed), short real, and long real. Cardinals and integers can have arbitrary lengths. A short real is a floating-point number with a single sign bit, a 7-bit base-16 characteristic, and a 24-bit fraction. A long real is a floating-point number with a single sign bit, a 9-bit base-2 characteristic, and a 30-bit fraction.

MCL directives control the listing, allocate memory, define ARU variables, assemble statements conditionally, define macros, output error messages, and indicate the end of assembly. Other statements in MCL are main control instructions, calls to PECU array processing routines, IOCU commands, and IO macros.

PECU ASSEMBLER (PRL)

The PECU assembler (PRL) assembles array processing routines to be executed by the PECU. Object modules created by PRL are linked with other PECU object modules to create a load module for the PE control memory. The assembler also produces a listing file. Each object module is produced from one or more source files.

As discussed in the ARRAY CONTROL UNIT chapter, a PECU instruction is 64 bits wide and may contain several operations which are executed simultaneously. In PRL each operation is written as a separate line and merged together into one instruction using a "+" sign in column 1. For example, the following PRL statements:

```
          FULLADD
+         SHIFT      A
+         LOAD       P,R6
+         DECR       R6,R7
+         BNZ,R7     $
```

will create one PECU instruction with several operations. In the ARU, a full add is performed, the planar shift register is shifted and sent to the A-plane, and the P-plane is loaded from the ARU memory plane whose address is in PECU index register R6. In the PECU, index registers R6 and R7 are decremented (item 3.2.1) and the value in R7 is tested - if R7 is not zero the whole PECU instruction is executed again.

PRL instructions cover all processing plane operations described in PROCESSING PLANES subsection of the ARRAY UNIT chapter and all PECU operations described in the PROCESSING ELEMENT CONTROL UNIT subsection of the ARRAY CONTROL UNIT chapter. PRL directives output error messages, mark the end of assembly, define symbols, declare global symbols, and control the listing.

The entry point to an array processing routine is usually given a unique name and declared to be global so it will appear in the symbol table when the routine is linked with other array processing routines. To call the routine, an MCL programmer declares the unique entry point name as global and references it in an instruction to load MCU register R44. When the MCU program is linked the linker resolves the symbol using the symbol table created when the PECU array processing routines were linked.

CONTROL AND DEBUG MODULE (CAD)

The control and debug module (CAD) lets a user control the MPP. Only one user can use the MPP at a time - other software such as the assemblers can be used by many front-end users at one time. CAD uses the last fifty ARU memory planes (planes 974 through 1023) for special purposes. One plane is set to the all-one state. Another seven planes are in an array (XCOL$) containing the column address of each element - columns are numbered from 0 at the west edge to 127 at the east edge. Another seven planes are in an array (YROW$) containing the row address of each element - rows are numbered from 0 at the north edge to 127 at the south edge. The address arrays, XCOL$ and YROW$, can be read and searched by MPP programs to identify array elements at certain geographic locations. The other 35 memory planes are used as temporary storage of the processing planes when MPP execution is halted and the user is inspecting, dumping, or changing ARU planes. Users should allocate their arrays at the start of ARU memory (plane 0 and up) to avoid conflicts.

CAD accepts commands from a user and calls from a running MPP program.

USER COMMANDS

User commands to CAD include commands to load programs, start execution, halt execution, continue execution, execute programs step by step, set breakpoints, reset control units, trace execution, display status, dump registers and memories, inspect and change registers and memories, save registers and memories, and run the performance monitor. Another command links another front-end task called the IO support task with CAD and invokes it.

PROGRAM CALLS

A running MPP program can call CAD to perform certain functions. An exit call tells CAD that the program is finished. Other calls are used to open files, read and write data, and close files. Scalar data can be transferred to and from main control memory. Array data can be transferred to and from ARU memory planes. IO calls must be supported by an IO support task running in the front-end computer — the support task is linked with CAD and invoked with a user command to CAD.

IO transfers to and from ARU memory planes go through the staging memory and are managed by the staging memory manager (SMM) which runs as an ancillary control processor or

ACP.   These   transfers   must   also   be supported   by   the   IO
support task.

STAGING MEMORY MANAGER (SMM)

The   staging   memory manager (SMM) supports the features   of
the staging memory.   There are two   versions   of   the   SMM: an
off-line version that   can   be   called   by   a   user with an SMM
command and an on-line version that runs as an ancillary   control
processor   with   CAD.   Many   users   can call the off-line version at
one   time   but   the   on-line   version is only   available   to   the
single user using CAD.

Both   versions   accept   a   logical   description   of   the
data   array   to   be transferred,   its   format   in   the   source
device,   and   its   format   in   the destination device.   From
these   descriptions the SMM finds a compatible main   stager   word
format,   allocates   main   stager   storage,   sets   up   the
address   parameters,   and programs the sub-stagers to perform the
required re-formatting operations.

Before   running   an   MPP   program a   user   can   check   the
efficiency   of the staging memory operations using   the   off-line
version   of   SMM.   The   off-line   version computes main   stager
packing   efficiency,   percent of main stager capacity   used,   and
the   transfer   rates.   Users can also check the efficiency with
different staging memory configurations.

The   on-line   version   of   SMM   is   invoked   when   an   MPP
application   program   opens   a virtual   channel   to   transfer   ARU
array data in or out.   The open call contains parameters pointing
to the descriptors of the logical array,   its   input   format,   and

its output format. The descriptors are used to allocate main stager storage and set up the staging memory control units. Several virtual channels may be open simultaneously as long as the main stager has sufficient capacity to hold all the arrays being transferred.

To illustrate the use of the SMM we use the example described in RE-FORMATING EXAMPLE of the STAGING MEMORY chapter. We want to transfer an image from the host computer to the ARU. The image has 896 lines with 1152 pixels per line and 8 bits per pixel. The basic image has three logical dimensions (lines, pixels, and bits) but it is split up into an 7 X 9 array of sub-images with each sub-image containing 128 pixels of 128 lines so the image really has five dimensions (line sets, lines within a set, pixel groups, pixels within a group, and bits). Thus, the logical description of the array has five dimensions which we number as follows:

Dimension 1: The bit dimension with a length of 8 (there are 8 bits per pixel).

Dimension 2: The pixel within a group dimension with a length of 128 (there are 128 pixels within each group or sub-image).

Dimension 3: The pixel group dimension with a length of 9 (there are 9 pixel groups or sub-images across any image line).

Dimension 4: The line within a set dimension with a length of 128 (there are 128 lines within each line set or sub-image).

Dimension 5: The line set dimension with a length of 7 (there are 7 line sets or sub-images down through the image).

The logical description of the array says that there are five dimensions with lengths 8, 128, 9, 128, and 7, respectively. Note that SMM does not know the names of the dimensions (bits, pixels within a group, etc.) - SMM only uses the dimension numbers and each descriptor describes the dimensions in the same order.

The input format descriptor is found as follows. The host computer transfers the image to the staging memory in 896 records with one image line per record. Each record has 1152 bytes with one pixel per byte in the normal order. The input format descriptor contains a multiplier for each dimension. The dimension-1 multiplier is unity because consecutive bits of a pixel are next to each other. The dimension-2 multiplier is 8 because consecutive pixels are 8 bits (one byte) apart. The dimension-3 multiplier is 1024 because consecutive pixel-groups are 1024 bits (128 bytes) apart. The dimension-4 multiplier is 9216 because consecutive lines are 9216 bits (1152 bytes) apart. The dimension-5 multiplier is 1179648 because consecutive line-sets are 128 lines or 128 * 9216 = 1179648 bits apart. The input descriptor multipliers are therefore 1, 8, 1024, 9216, and 1179648, respectively.

The output format descriptor is found as follows. The ARU will receive the image as a set of 63 sub-images with 8 bit-planes per sub-image. A column of 128 data bits sent to the ARU will contain one bit from the 128 pixels in one line of the sub-image - consecutive pixels are adjacent so the dimension-2 multiplier is unity. Adjacent columns contain adjacent lines within a line-set so the dimension-4 multiplier is 128 because adjacent columns are 128 data bits apart on the ARU interface.   Consecutive bits of a pixel are on consecutive bit-planes and consecutive bit-planes are 16384 data bits apart on the ARU interface so the dimension-1 multiplier is 16384. Consecutive pixel-groups are 8 bit-planes apart so the dimension-3 multiplier is 8 * 16384 = 131072.   Consecutive-line-sets are 72 bit-planes apart so the dimension-5 multiplier is 72 * 16384 = 1179648.   The output descriptor multipliers are therefore 16384, 1, 131072, 128, and 1179648, respectively.

From the logical descriptor, the input descriptor, and the output descriptor, the SMM finds a compatible main stager word format.   In this example, it packs one bit from 64 consecutive pixels of one image line in each main stager word (when the input record size is 9216 data bits and the output record size is 16384 data bits).   With a 4-bank main stager, SMM allocates 129024 main stager words for the image for a packing efficiency of 100%.   The transfer rate from the input sub-stager to the main stager is 18 megabytes per second - faster than the DR-780 rate from the host to the input sub-stager of 6 megabytes per second.   The transfer rate from the main stager to the output sub-stager is 20 megabytes per second - the maximum limit of a 4-bank main stager.

IO SUPPORT TASK

Most MPP application programs will require a task in the front-end computer to support the input and output of data. Typically, this IO support task will move each input file from a front-end peripheral such as disk or tape to the MPP data interface and move each output file from the MPP data interface to a front-end peripheral. In some cases, the IO support task might perform computations on the input or output data files - for example, one way to check out an MPP application program is to code an IO support task which generates input files of test data and checks the output files.

The IO support task is invoked by a CAD command. It will receive a message from CAD every time the MPP application ms to diagnose faults in the   PE   control memory and PECU registers and instructions.

The ARU   section has groups of programs to diagnose faults in the processing planes, the Sum-Or circuit, and ARU   memory planes.

The l   channel   number which is passed to the IO support task so it knows which file to open, read, write, etc.

The IO support task can either be custom-tailored   for a   particular MPP application program or it can be generalized to support the IO of several application   programs. When coding the support task for a   particular application program one knows the order in which the program will ask for input data and present the output data so one can have the support task read the input data items in advance so they are immediately available when the program needs them and   have the task supply output buffers immediately. Buffer   sizes in a custom-tailored support task can be chosen to maximize throughput.

A standard IO support task is supplied in the package of MPP system   software. It will support the IO requirements of some application programs and since it is written in FORTRAN it can be used as a model for custom-tailored support tasks. When invoked by CAD, the standard support task prompts the user to supply a command line specifying the names of input and output files. Each file corresponds to a particular virtual channel number in the application program.

HARDWARE DIAGNOSTICS

A set of hardware diagnostic programs is supplied to minimize the burden of locating and replacing faulty hardware modules. A validation program is also supplied which performs a quick check of the MPP hardware and configures the ARU to bypass faulty columns in the planes.

VALIDATION PROGRAM

The validation program is designed to be run periodically between application programs to perform a quick check of the hardware. The program checks the array control unit, the array unit, the staging memory, and the interfaces to the front-end computer.

As discussed in the introduction to ARRAY UNIT all planes in the ARU contain 132 columns of which 128 are used by application programs and four are spare. The columns are grouped into 33 groups with four columns per group. The group disable registers in the main control unit select the group to be bypassed. Normal application programs do not modify these registers.

When the validation program checks the ARU it checks all 33

groups.   If   it   discovers   a   fault   in a group it   tries   to
correct the fault by bypassing the faulty group.   The validation
program   displays   a   message   on   the   console   indicating   the
status of the MPP hardware.   The status can be:

VALID.   All MPP hardware elements are functional including
all 33 groups of the ARU.   The validation program disables a
fixed   group   in   the   group   disable   registers.   Application
programs use the remaining 32 groups (128 columns).

CONDITIONALLY VALID.   All   MPP   hardware   elements   are
functional except for a fault in a group in the ARU.   The fault
is corrected by disabling the faulty group in the group disable
registers.   Application   programs   use   the remaining 32 groups
(128 columns).

NOT VALID.   A critical element in the MPP is faulty and the
fault can not be bypassed.   Other   hardware diagnostic programs
are run to locate the fault.

The validation program also logs the hardware status   on   a
front-end   system disk file so maintenance   personnel   have a
history.

One   can   run   the validation program before and after   an
application   program.   The first run tells the user which   column
group of the ARU is bypassed.   The second   run tells the   user
if any new faults have been discovered - unless the new fault was
in the bypassed column group,   the   results   of   the   application
program can not be trusted.

OTHER DIAGNOSTIC PROGRAMS

A number of other diagnostic programs are available to help locate faulty MPP hardware elements.   There are four sections of diagnostic programs: the MCU section,   the PECU   section, the   ARU   section,   and the IOCU section.   Each section has   a number of groups of programs.   Maintenance   personnel   can   run single   diagnostic   programs,   all   programs   in   a   group,   all programs in a section, or all programs in the set.

The   MCU section has groups of programs to diagnose   faults in   the   front-end control   interface,   main   control   memory, and   main   control   registers and instructions.   The PECU section has   groups   of programs to diagnose faults in the   PE   control memory and PECU registers and instructions.

The   ARU   section   has groups of programs to diagnose faults in   the   processing planes,   the Sum-Or circuit,   and ARU   memory planes.

The   IOCU   section   has groups of   programs   to   diagnose faults   in   the   IOCU,   S-plane   data   transfers,   the   staging memory, and the front-end data interface.

MPP PROGRAM DEVELOPMENT AND SIMULATION[a]

E. J. Gallopoulos
Scott D. McEwan
Daniel L. Slotnick
Andrew J. Spry
Department of Computer Science
University of Illinois
Urbana, Ill. 61801

and

Daniel J. Kopetzky
Compion Incorporated
Urbana, Ill. 61801.

Introduction -- A software environment simulating the Massively Parallel Processor (MPP) will be described. The environment consists of packages each corresponding to some MPP hardware or software component. These packages are a Parallel Pascal package, an Assembler package, a Library Maintenance package and an Array Simulator Generator (ASG) package. They all run under the Berkeley Unix Operating System for maximal portability within University environments. A VMS version is also available. The system has been used for training programmers to use the MPP system, for developing basic applications software, and for developing and testing parallel algorithms for various applications. It can also be used for experimenting with architectural variants. The system, moreover, played a significant role in the MPP design.

BACKGROUND

At about the same time the design of the MPP had started, NASA funded research at the University of Illinois in the application and design of the MPP. Algorithms were

[a]Research supported in part by NASA under contract NAS5-26405

being investigated and written for the future machine for the types of applications it was originally conceived, namely Image Processing.

Two important factors contributed to the complexity of the above task. The first is the Single-Instruction Multiple-Data (SIMD) architecture together with the small memory available per Processing Element (PE). The second is the bit-serial arithmetic and logical operation of the array. Although the importance of the first issue should not be underestimated, it is the latter which complicates the programming task a great deal. Merging of instructions and careful use of the shift-register can make a difference of orders of magnitude on the performance of most algorithms. The parallel vs. serial algorithm design issue has been discussed in the literature and many parallel algorithms have been written in various application areas. Our experience shows that although one can frequently be confident about the efficiency and correctness of a code designed on paper using some high-level language exploiting the machine parallelism, the same cannot be said for the latter complexity issue arising from the bit-serial nature of the array hardware.

Traditional simulators are designed to provide preliminary information to the computer designer in order to help select the best parameters determining the architecture. The system we will describe, apart from allowing the preparation of large amounts of MPP software has also helped in improving the initial design decisions.

The aforementioned issues provided enough justification for designing a simulator system for the MPP. The environment that will be described is based on the simulator system and will be seen to differ from most efforts in the area of computer system simulation where either a gross functional simulation of the entire system or a detailed simulation of some critical subsystem is made. An important difference with other computer system simulators is that this system is being used extensively even now that the real machine is available. For a unique resource like the MPP the users will be competing for access. Hence it is much more cost-effective to provide them with an environment in which they will be able i) to gain experience in MPP programming and ii) to test and debug their codes without wasting valuable machine time. A large amount of application codes have been developed in the environment we are discussing and only a small number of changes were needed to port the code to the MPP.

GENERAL DISCUSSION

The portable MPP simulation and programming environment is derived from the MPP's support software and the Array Simulator Generator (ASG) [1]. The environment has been designed to allow the production of MPP programs on any VAX computer running the VMS or UNIX operating systems. This environment will replace the current PDP-11/UNIX and VAX/VMS environments based on ASG [2, 3] and the current VAX/VMS environment using the MPP, with one environment that can use both the simulator or the MPP. Although the environment had not been completed at the time of this writing, the description presented here deals only with the functional specification and component organization of the environment which have already been finalized.

The portable MPP simulation and programming environment duplicates the MPP software development cycle existing on the MPP's host computer. The software development cycles for Parallel Pascal and the MPP's assembly languages are given in figures 1 and 2. The dashed sections of the figures show the avenues available for accessing the MPP's host system from the remote program development system. Since both software cycles exactly parallel the development cycles for MPP software on the MPP's host, these avenues provide the means of transferring from one system to another at various stages in the software development cycle. The primary difference between the development of MPP programs on the simulator based system and on the MPP's host itself is that the simulator replaces the MPP. The simulator provides a virtual MPP with debugging capabilities superior to the MPP host's control and debug (CAD) software. The support software for the two environments is identical, with the exception of the library maintenance programs described later.

The design of the portable MPP programming environment was constrained by the following goals. The software development cycles had to parallel the software development cycles of the MPP's host system. The programming environment had to be available for both the VMS and UNIX operating systems. The environment had to be able to produce executable code for both the ASG and the MPP. The software components of the system had to be easy and inexpensive to maintain. The components of the system had to follow the usual conventions of, and have the command syntax of the particular operating system they were on. The corresponding components of the environment on the various operating systems had to be functionally equivalent.

To meet these goals a number of components of the MPP host's programming environment were ported to the UNIX operating system. These programs were extended to handle inputs from the differing support software and to produce multiple output formats where needed. The resulting package was integrated with a new

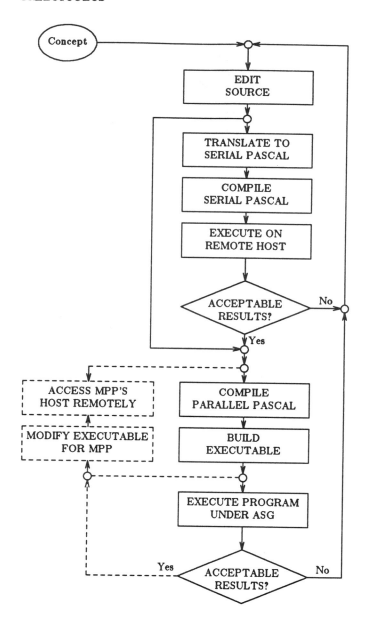

Fig. 1: MPP VAX-UNIX Parallel Pascal Software Cycle.

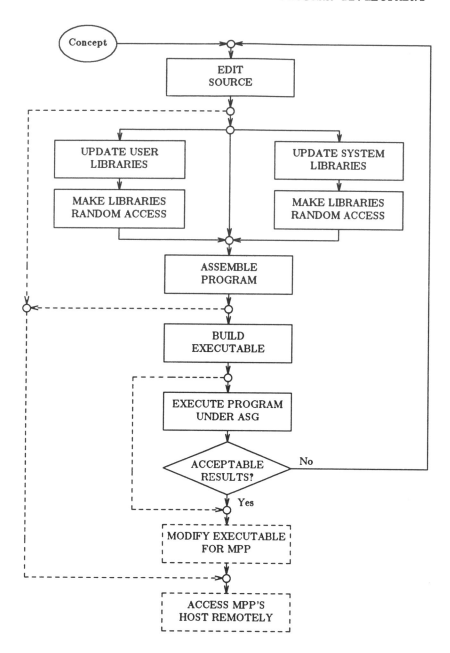

Fig 2: MPP VAX-UNIX Assembly Language Software Cycle.

portable version of the ASG to create the portable MPP programming environment. The final environment consists of four packages: the Parallel Pascal package, the MPP Assembler package, the Library Maintenance package, and the Array Simulator Generator package. All packages of the environment are available for the UNIX and VMS operating systems on VAX computers. Some packages are available for a larger group of systems. The exact requirements of each package and its portability are described later.

THE PARALLEL PASCAL PACKAGE. The Parallel Pascal package consists of a translator and a compiler. The package was developed by Professor A. P. Reeves and Dr. J. D. Bruner. The translator converts programs written in Parallel Pascal to regular Pascal which can then be compiled by the local system's Pascal compiler. The compiler converts programs written in Parallel Pascal into MCL assembly language programs. These programs can then be assembled and run either on the ASG or the MPP. The Parallel Pascal package provides the portable programming environment with a high level language suitable for expressing parallel algorithms. The language is discussed in length in part III of this book.

THE ASSEMBLER PACKAGE. The MPP Assembler package consists of an assembler for the MPP's Main Control Language (MCL), an assembler for the MPP's Processing Element Array Language (PEARL), and a macro processor. The MCL and PEARL assemblers accept the languages specified   with a number of extensions to enhance the capabilities of the MPP's CAD software. The macro processor provides the repeat and conditional assembly capabilities, as well as the macro definition and expansion capabilities for both assemblers. It is designed to interface with the different library formats on the UNIX and VMS systems. A major feature of the assembler package is its ability to produce object files in the format of the object code editor of the system it is on in addition to the format of the MPP's host linker. Thus, the outputs of these programs can be handled like any object file generated by a compiler or assembler native the the particular system. Like the Parallel Pascal package, the components of the MPP Assembler package are identical on the UNIX and VMS systems. In addition the components of this package were written so that extension to additional operating systems could be easily accomplished. Currently this package is available for only the UNIX and VMS operating systems. In addition to generating machine code for the MPP or ASG from the Parallel Pascal compiler output, the assembler package provides the means of writing efficient code for the MPP where efficiency is an important consideration.

THE LIBRARY MAINTENANCE PACKAGE. The Library Maintenance package is different for the UNIX and VMS operating systems, although a single librarian for both systems may be produced in the future. The library package of the UNIX environment is based on the UNIX utility AR, which can be used to create archives of UNIX files. Macro library archives are then converted to the random access format needed for the Macro Processor by the program MACLIB. Object file libraries are handled in the same fashion as regular UNIX object file libraries. The library package of the VMS system is the MPP host's LIBRARIAN program. The LIBRARIAN is used interactively to create and maintain libraries of both macro definitions and object files. In addition the Library Maintenance package contains programs for converting libraries from UNIX to VMS and from VMS to UNIX formats. Reguardless of the format or the program used to maintain them, there are three types of libraries used by the MPP programming environment: the system macro library, user macro libraries, and object code libraries. The system macro library provides the definitions of over half of the MCL language's standard instruction set and is always loaded by the assemblers. The user macro libraries can be used to redefine language instructions, or to develop packages of applications macros. The object code libraries are used by the systems object code editor to construct executable code. They can either be random collections of object files, or the object files of a set of applications routines such as ISODATA. The library maintenance package provides the organizational capabilities of the programming environment.

THE ARRAY SIMULATOR GENERATOR PACKAGE. The Array Simulator Generator (ASG) is a software system for testing and debugging programs for bit-serial array computers. ASG has been used to create simulators for the ICL Distributed Array Processor (DAP) and the University College CLIP, as well as the MPP, although only the MPP simulator is currently supported. An ASG simulator consists of a user interface (the ASG debugger), a full functional emulation of the target machine, and routines to link the modules and simulate parallel operation of the various functional units of the simulated machine. The ASG package was developed as part of one of the authors' Ph. D. thesis. It is completely described in [1].

The ASG debugger is a powerful programmable debugger which acts as the overall controller for the simulation. Through the debugger, the user has complete control over all components of the simulated MPP. All memory and machine registers can be viewed or changed, individual emulated hardware units can be started, halted or single-stepped; even hardware parameters can be changed (e.g., array dimensions, memory depth, clock speed.) Accurate estimates of program running times can be gotten by reading the simulated system clock, and the number of MCU and PCU instructions executed are recorded.

The debugger also acts as an interface to the host machine's file system. The emulated machine's memory can be loaded from a file and results can be saved by the debugger, substituting for the elementary IO operations that are not yet implemented in the MPP emulator. The input and output to and from the debugger itself can also be redirected to a file.

The MPP emulator is a full functional simulation of the MCU, PCU and ARU. These functional units behave exactly the same as the corresponding units of the MPP. The only major difference from the actual MPP is that the simulated array must consist of fewer PE's depending on the memory that the host has available. In any case the dimensions may be changed dynamically.

The ASG system provides tools to quickly and easily write emulators for different machines (the DAP and CLIP emulators were written in one man-week each.) The machine emulation is totally independent of the ASG debugger; the debugger uses the symbol table from the emulator to access and modify the emulator's data. The independence of the modules making up an ASG simulator means that the writer of an emulator does not need to be concerned with the details of how the emulated hardware is accessed; similarly, the debugger does not have to be modified when working with different emulators - the necessary information is provided as data at runtime. Similarly, the simulator for an existing machine can be altered to compare variations in architecture. Simple changes can be done dynamically from the debugger, more complicated changes only require modifying the code that emulates the functional unit being altered. For example, to simulate a variant on the MPP architecture with power-of-two inter-connections in the ARU, only the routine that performs array shifts would need to be rewritten.

COMMENTS ON PORTABILITY

The portability of the individual packages of the MPP programming environment is determined by the hardware and software requirements of the program components of those packages. The Parallel Pascal package has no hardware dependencies. The package is written in Pascal and the translator component produces an output that is a Pascal program. These programs have shown little portability problems between VMS and UNIX, and should be fairly portable to any system with a comparable Pascal compiler. The MPP Assembler package is also hardware independent. It is written in C and was designed for portability between the UNIX and VMS operating systems. The package is potentially portable to any system with a C compiler and the standard C library although only UNIX and VMS versions currently exist. The portability was a primary consideration because only one master version (on the VMS operating system) will be maintained. All updates to the UNIX version will be achieved by porting the master version. The extension to additional operating systems can be achieved by replacing the UNIX version of the few operating system dependent modules. Once this has been done updates to version on the new operating system can be done by porting the VMS master version. The Library maintenance package is currently not portable. However, the Macro Processor component of the MPP Assembler package can be modified to accept a new library format by changing the library input module. The Array Simulator Generator package is the least portable of the programming environments packages due to some hardware dependencies. Although it is written in C, and potentially portable, it is also written to take advantage of the VAX architecture. The ASG, originally written for a PDP-11 and ported to the VAX, could be ported to a new machine although such a port would not be trivial. In summary, the Parallel Pascal package is the most portable package in the environment. The MPP Assembler package's portability is limited to systems that support the C language. Since, the primary targets of the environment were the UNIX and VMS operating systems on VAX computers the assembler package is portable enough. The portability aspects of the Library Maintenance package have been sidesteped by providing a functionally equivalent package for the two target systems. The Array Simulator Generator package, although the least portable of the packages, is still portable across the two target operating systems as long as they are on a VAX computer.

SIMULATOR SOFTWARE QUALITY CHARACTERISTICS

The portable MPP simulation and programming environment is by its nature a complicated software system. In order to understand and evaluate its performance and characteristics we will discuss its important attributes. In the same time we will show why many of these attributes are desirable in any such environment. We will try to use terms which have been used in software engineering.

The first such characteristic is accountability. The system must provide facilities for measuring the number of virtual machine cycles spent during the execution of the code which is being tested. As we have discussed, counters are provided to measure the number of PCU and MCU cycles spent by a particular code. There are two factors which may degrade the validity of these measurements and which the user must take into account. The first is that for any simulation to finish in an acceptable amount of time, the virtual ARU size will be at most 32 $\times$ 32 for a VAX and 16 $\times$ 16 for a PDP-11 based environment. Timing estimates depending on the size of the array (e.g. in case array spreads are involved) must thus be modified. The second factor contributing to the degradation of the accountability attribute is the IO activity in and out the ARU. The system offers no simulation and measurement facilities for such IO activity and instructions to the IOCU are translated to no-ops.

The run-time ratio, i.e. the ratio of the time needed to execute a program on the realization of the virtual machine to the time needed to execute the program on the simulator, is sometimes referred to in discussions of computer system simulators. For the VAX/VMS based simulator system it has been estimated that one cycle of 32 $\times$ 32 ARU simulated ARU processing is completed in the same time that 50,000 cycles of 128 $\times$ 128 real MPP processing are completed.

The next characteristic is accuracy. Given a program for the virtual machine and a set of inputs, the system simulation will be called accurate if the outputs to the program are the same as if it were run on the realization of the virtual machine. The discussed environment fulfills this requirement except where scale considerations are involved.

The next two quality characteristics are defined as system portability and code portability. System portability refers to the ability to port the system from one site to another with no significant amount of code changes. As has already been discussed the overall system has been designed to fulfill this requirement. Choosing C for implementing the system environment and Pascal for implementing the Parallel Pascal package simplified matters. Hence any researcher at a site running Unix or VMS on a PDP-11 or a VAX can use the system. It is only fair to say that a large user community thus able to prepare programs for a unique machine as the MPP. A simulator environment offers code portability if the user can take his code developed to run on the virtual machine and with only minor changes run it on the realization of the virtual machine. The environment under consideration satisfies this characteristic. The minor changes needed refer only to the scale changes needed due to the different ARU sizes and to the additional IO facilities.

The system possesses the characteristic of augmentability because it can easily be expanded to simulate architectural variants. This has already been discussed (dynamically altering the PE memory, implementing a different PE interconnection network etc.)

We must also consider the expenses, in terms of programming effort for code development and maintenance and memory requirements for the entire system. As an indication of some memory requirements for some of the packages, the ASG package takes about 100 Kbytes and the Parallel Pascal Translator about 34 Kbytes. Most of the ASG package was designed as part of a Ph.D. thesis by one of the authors [1].

APPLICATIONS

The MPP had been delivered at NASA Goddard in Spring 1983. At the time of its delivery, a substantial amount of subroutine libraries and application codes were ready to run on it. All of that code (which now runs on the MPP,) had been developed, tested and debugged on the PDP-11/UNIX and VAX/VMS based early versions of the system we have described. One of the application codes is reported in chapter 4 of this book. The other application was the Image Processing package, fully documented in [4]. The effort needed in porting these packages to the real MPP and the accuracy of the simulator based predictions for their performance were in agreement with the discussion in the previous section.

CONCLUSIONS

The portable MPP simulation and programming environment was discussed. It was shown to be an excellent tool for experimenting with new algorithms, getting used to the real MPP environment and as a significant tool design. With such a system, a large user community can now gain experience with this new architecture and many more ideas can be tested.

REFERENCES

[1]. D. J. Kopetzky, AN ARRAY SIMULATOR GENERATOR, Department of Computer Science, University of Illinois at Urbana-Champaign, Report UIUCDCS-R-80-1031, September, 1980.

[2]. E. Gallopoulos, Scott D. McEwan, and Dianna Visek, MPP SIMULATOR MANUAL, Department of Computer Science, University of Illinois at Urbana-Champaign, Report UIUCDCS-R-82-1075, April, 1982.

[3]. D. Lynch, P. Jones, J. Reese and C. Weger, THE MASSIVELY PARALLEL PROCESSOR SYSTEM, Computer Sciences Corporation, Report CSC/TM-82/6034, February, 1982.

[4]. Neil B. Coletti, IMAGE PROCESSING ON MPP-LIKE ARRAYS, Department of Computer Science, University of Illinois at Urbana-Champaign, Report UIUCDCS-R-83-1132, May, 1983.

EPILOGUE - November 1, 1984

James R. Fischer
MPP Group Leader
Goddard Space Flight Center
Greenbelt, Maryland 20771

The MPP has been at Goddard for eighteen months. This article describes some of the Goddard experiences using the MPP over this period of time, followed by a description of the development work that is now taking place, and concludes with a discussion of the system's reliability, limitations and future augmentations.

On the day that the MPP was delivered, two debugged demonstration programs were at Goddard waiting to be implemented immediately. Both programs, ISODATA - an unsupervised clustering algorithm and the shallow water model - a two-dimensional partial differential equation evaluator (see chapter 6), were developed in MPP assembly language at the University of Illinois using the MPP Simulator. ISODATA, demonstrated on the MPP 34 days after delivery, finds sixteen spectral signature clusters in a 512 by 512 four-band image. For the cropland dataset chosen, one hundred ten iterations of the algorithm were required and MPP completed the job in 18 seconds. This was 360 times faster than the same algorithm run on a VAX-11/780 with an AP180V array processor and written in VAX Fortran. The shallow water model, demonstrated on the 81st day after delivery, ran three times faster on MPP than on a CDC CYBER-205 with two pipeline processors.

Further demonstrations on the MPP awaited implementation of

necessary language features in the Parallel Pascal compiler (See chapter 14). The first Parallel Pascal program demonstrated was the Maximum Likelihood Classifier, run in October 1983.

In February 1984, a task was started to implement the processing of Synthetic Aperture Radar (SAR) raw signal data into images. This task is very computationally expensive (6 million input pixels must be processed for each output pixel). The heart of this task, the Fast Fourier Transform for one dimensional arrays consisting of 4096 elements, was demonstrated in October 1984. It is written in Parallel Pascal and has been the main driver determining the order in which Parallel Pascal language features have been implemented.

Goodyear developed and integrated the MPP hardware and system software using a PDP-11/34 mini-computer with 128K of memory, a 67 Mbyte removable disk drive, a dual 8-inch floppy disk drive and two terminals. Hardware interfaces were designed into MPP to connect a VAX-11/780 to it as a host.

At delivery in May 1983, the PDP11 was augmented with a third terminal and an International Imaging System (IIS) color image analysis display, and at that point its Unibus was fully loaded. Using this limited system, the first two demonstrations were run on MPP: the ISODATA clustering algorithm, and the shallow water model.

When the VAX was installed as the host computer, the Goodyear operating system (CAD) was transferred from the PDP intact to the VAX where there were several dozen terminals, increased disk space, the Parallel Pascal compiler (under development), and the users. This conversion work required writing a device driver and converting an ancillary control process into a subroutine library for the VAX in addition to porting twelve thousand lines of RATFOR and PDP-11 assembler code. This step was completed in February 1984, and initiated a follow-on effort to redesign CAD to support Parallel Pascal and to take advantage of the newly available VAX capabilities. This new CAD became usable in August 1984.

ONGOING DEVELOPMENT

Several additional applications programs have been written and are awaiting more complete implementations of Parallel Pascal before they are demonstrated. These include an unsupervised clustering classifier, a contextual classifier, a region growing texture classifier, an Ising model for simulating magnetic field changes in materials during temperature changes, and a region labeling algorithm. In addition to the above work, an applications library is being developed for the MPP. Cornell University is programming a convolution algorithm as well as a general image warping algorithm. The University of Illinois is developing matrix manipulation programs including matrix inversion and matrix multiplication. Additional work being done at Goddard includes large number factoring and numerical problems that emphasize the computational power of the MPP in areas other than image processing.

The MPP applications program is being built on Parallel Pascal as the primary language. Currently the compiler system can handle most of the instructions in the Parallel Pascal definition except those which move data to and from the Array through the Staging Memory. A compiler option exists which targets all executable code to run on the VAX. This allows Parallel Pascal programs to be developed and debugged on a VAX under VMS without use of an MPP, but array sizes must often be made smaller than 128 by 128 for processing times to become manageable.

An MPP Simulator exists which is a handy tool for debugging assembly language subroutines written in either PEARL or Main Control Language. It simulates the Main Control Unit, the PE Control Unit, and the Array Unit (but for an array of only 16 by 16 processing elements).

RELIABILITY, LIMITATIONS AND FUTURE AUGMENTATIONS OF THE HARDWARE

The custom HCMOS PE chip was expected to give reliability problems so 500 spares were bought, enough to replace a quarter of the machine. Fortunately, the PE chip has been very reliable, and at most twenty PE chips have been replaced since delivery. The problems that have occurred are typical of other systems, mainly intermittents caused by cracked plated through holes in printed circuit boards.

The work done to date has verified the following two major limitations of the Goddard MPP system. The most severe is the amount of memory in the Array. Of the 1024 bits available in each processor, on average 10% are required by the debugger and for temporary workspace during execution of array instructions. This leaves space for around 28 32-bit floating point numbers or 115 8-bit integers. This limitation has required programmers to be extremely conservative of the number of variables that they use and the complexity of the expressions that they write. Another current limitation is the absence of a high speed disk system connecting directly to the Staging Memory. Because all mass storage devices are on the VAX, all data must pass through the VAX memory to get to or from MPP.

The MPP Staging Memory currently contains two megabytes of storage capacity giving a 20 megabyte per second data transfer rate between the Staging Memory and the Array. This capacity will be increased to sixteen megabytes in late 1985, upping the transfer rate to 40 megabytes per second.

ACKNOWLEDGMENTS

For the MPP Project at Goddard, I would like to acknowledge the contributions of all the individuals who have dedicated so much time and energy in seeing to it that the MPP got its chance to be built and used. I also want to thank Dave Schaefer and Dr. Jim Strong who assisted in the preparation of this Epilogue.

Batcher, K. E., "MPP - A Massively Parallel Processor," 1979 INTERNATIONAL CONFERENCE ON PARALLEL PROCESSING, August 1979.

Batcher, K. E., "The Massively Parallel Processor System," PROCEEDINGS OF THE 2nd AIAA COMPUTERS IN AEROSPACE CONFERENCE, October 1979, pp. 93-97.

Batcher, K. E., "Design of a Massively Parallel Processor," IEEE TRANSACTIONS ON COMPUTING, Volume C-29, Number 9, September 1980, pp. 836-840.

Batcher, K. E., "MPP: a Super System for Satellite Image Processing," NATIONAL COMPUTER CONFERENCE, Volume 51, 1982, pp. 185-191.

Bruner, J. D. and A. P. Reeves, "A Parallel P-Code for Parallel Pascal and Other High Level Languages," PROCEEDINGS OF THE 1983 INTERNATIONAL CONFERENCE ON PARALLEL PROCESSING, August 1983.

Burkley, J. T. "MPP VLSI Multi-Processor Integrated Circuit Design," PROCEEDINGS OF THE 1982 INTERNATIONAL CONFERENCE ON PARALLEL PROCESSING, August, 1982.

Burkley, J. T. and C. T. Mickelson, "MPP: A Case Study of a Highly Parallel System," PROCEEDINGS OF THE AIAA CONFERENCE ON COMPUTERS IN AEROSPACE #4, Oct 1983.

Coletti, N. B., "Image Processing on MPP-Like Arrays," Department of Computer Science, University of Illinois at Urbana-Champaign, Report No. UIUCDCS-R-83-1132, May 1983.

Fountain, T. J., "A Survey of Bit-Serial Array Processor Circuits," COMPUTING STRUCTURES FOR IMAGE PROCESSING, M.J.B. Duff, ed. Academic Press, London, 1983, pp. 1-14.

Fung, L. W., "A Massively Parallel Processing Computer," HIGH SPEED COMPUTER AND ALGORITHM ORGANIZATION, D. J. Kuck et. al. eds., Academic Press, New York, 1977, pp. 203-204.

Gallopoulos, E. J. and S. D. McEwan, "Numerical Experiments with the Massively Parallel Processor," PROCEEDINGS OF THE 1983 INTERNATIONAL CONFERENCE ON PARALLEL PROCESSING, August 1983, pp. 29-35.

Gerritsen, F. A., "A Comparison of the CLIP4, DAP and MPP Processor-Array Implementations," COMPUTING STRUCTURES FOR IMAGE PROCESSING, M.J.B. Duff, ED. Academic Press, London, 1983, pp. 15-30.

Gilmore, P. A., "The Computer MPP," INTERNATIONAL SOCIETY OF PHOTOGRAMMETRY AND REMOTE SENSING COMMISSION II SYMPOSIUM, September 1982, Ottawa, Canada.

298   BIBLIOGRAPHY

Hockney, R. W. and C. R. Jesshope, PARALLEL COMPUTERS, Adam Hilger Ltd., Bristol, England, 1981, pp. 22,393.

Illiffe, J. K., ADVANCED COMPUTER DESIGN, Prentice Hall International, London, 1982, p. 282.

Kolata, G. "Factoring Gets Easier," SCIENCE, Volume 2, December 1983, pp. 999-1001.

Kopetzky, D. J., "An Array Simulator Generator," Department of Computer Science, University of Illinois at Urbana-Champaign, Report No. UIUCDCS-R-80-1031, September 1980.

Kozdrowicki, E. W., "Supercomputers for the Eighties," DIGITAL DESIGN, May, 1983, pp. 94-103.

Kushner, T., A. Y. Wu, and A. Rosenfeld, "Image Processing on MPP," TR-1007, AFSOR-77-3271, Computer Vision Laboratory, University of Maryland at College Park, February 1980.

Love, H. H., "The Highly-Parallel Supercomputers: Definitions, Applications and Predictions," PROCEEDINGS OF THE 1980 NATIONAL COMPUTER CONFERENCE, pp. 181-190.

Mancl, D. M., "Programming Languages for Bit-Serial Array Machines," Department of Computer Science, University of Illinois at Urbana-Champaign, Report No. UIUCDCS-R-81-1071, August, 1981.

Potter, J. L., "Continuous Image Processing on the MPP," PROCEEDINGS OF THE 1981 WORKSHOP ON COMPUTER ARCHITECTURES FOR PATTERN ANALYSIS AND IMAGE DATABASE MANAGEMENT, November 1981, pp. 51-56.

Potter, J. L. ,"MPP Architecture and Programming, " MULTICOMPUTERS AND IMAGE PROCESSING, K. Preston, Jr. and L. Uhr, eds., Academic Press, New York, 1982, pp. 275-289.

Potter, J. L., "Image Processing on the Massively Parallel Processor," IEEE COMPUTER, January 1983, pp. 62-67.

Ramapriyan, H. K. and JH. P. Strong, "Applications of Array Processors in the Analysis of Remote Sensing Images," PROCEEDINGS OF THE 17th INTERNATIONAL SYMPOSIUM ON REMOTE SENSING OF THE ENVIRONMENT, Ann Arbor, MI, May 1983.

Reeves, A. P. and A. Rostampour, "Computational Cost of Image Registration with a Parallel Binary Array Processor," IEEE TRANSACTIONS ON PATTERN ANALYSIS AND MACHINE INTELLIGENCE, Volume PAMI-4, No. 4, July, 1982, pp. 449-455.

Reeves, A. P., "The Local Median and Other Window Operations on SIMD Computers," COMPUTER GRAPHICS AND IMAGE PROCESSING, Volume 19, 1982, pp. 165-178.

Reeves, A. P., "Parallel Algorithms for Real-Time Image
   Processing," MULTICOMPUTERS FOR IMAGE PROCESSING: ALGORITHMS
   AND PROGRAMS, K. Preston and L. Uhr, eds., Academic Press,
   1982.

Reeves, A. P., "Parallel Computer Architectures for Image
   Processing,   " COMPUTER   VISION,   GRAPHICS AND   IMAGE
   PROCESSING, Volume 25, 1984, pp. 68-88.

Schaefer, D. H. and J. R. Fischer, "Beyond the Supercomputer,"
   IEEE SPECTRUM, March 1982, pp. 32-37.

Schaefer, D. H., "Massively Parallel Processing Systems for Space
   Applications," PROCEEDINGS OF THE 2ND AIAA COMPUTERS IN
   AEROSPACE CONFERENCE, October 1979, pp. 284-286.

Schaefer, D. H., J. R. Fischer, K. R. Wallgren, "The Massively
   Parallel Processor, "JOURNAL OF GUIDANCE, CONTROL AND
   DYNAMICS, Volume 5, Number 3, May-June 1982, pp. 313-315.

Schaefer, D. H., "Spatially Parallel Architectures: An
   Overview," COMPUTER DESIGN , August, 1982, pp. 117-124.

Schaefer, D. H., A. M. Veronia, J. C. Salland, "Spatially
   Parallel Architectures for Industrial Robot Vision,"
   PROCEEDINGS OF THE 1983 CONFERENCE ON COMPUTER VISION AND
   PATTERN RECOGNITION, pp. 542-545.

Slotnick, D. L., "The Conception and Development of Parallel
   Processors," ANNALS OF THE HISTORY OF COMPUTING,. January,
   1982, pp. 20-30.

Smit, J. H., "Architecture Descriptions for the Massively
   Parallel Processor (MPP) and the Airborne Associative
   Processor (ASPRO)," PROCEEDINGS OF THE VERY HIGH SPEED
   COMPUTING SYMPOSIUM, Georgia Institute of Technology,
   Atlanta, GA., September 9-10, 1980.

Strong, J. P., D. H. Schaefer, J. R. Fischer, K. R. Wallgren, and
   P. A. Bracken, "The Massively Parallel Processor and Its
   Applications," 13th INTERNATIONAL SYMPOSIUM ON REMOTE
   SENSING OF THE ENVIRONMENT, April 1979.

Strong, J. P., "Basic Image Processing Algorithms on the
   Massively Parallel Processor," MULTICOMPUTERS AND IMAGE
   PROCESSING, K. Preston, Jr. and L. Uhr, eds., Academic
   Press, New York, 1982, pp. 47-85.

Strong, J. P. and P. D. Argentiero, "A Geophysical Application of
   the Massively Parallel Processor," NASA/GSFC X-934-82-25,
   October, 1982.

Tilton, J. C., "Contextual Classification of Multispectral Image
   Data Using Compound Decision Theory," DIGEST OF THE 1983
   IEEE INTERNATIONAL GEOSCIENCE AND REMOTE SENSING SYMPOSIUM,

San Francisco, CA., August 31-September 2, 1983.

Tilton, J. C. and S. C. Cox, "Segmentation of Remotely Sensed Data Using Parallel Region Growing," DIGEST OF THE 1983 IEEE INTERNATIONAL GEOSCIENCE AND REMOTE SENSING SYMPOSIUM, San Francisco, CA., August 31-September 2, 1983.

Tsoras, J., "The Massively Parallel Processor (MPP) Innovation in High Speed Processors," AIAA COMPUTERS IN AEROSPACE CONFERENCE III, October 1981.

Uhr, L., "Pyramid Multi-Computer Structures, and Augmented Pyramids," COMPUTING STRUCTURES FOR IMAGE PROCESSING, M.J.B. Duff, ED. Academic Press, London, 1983, pp. 95ff.

Index